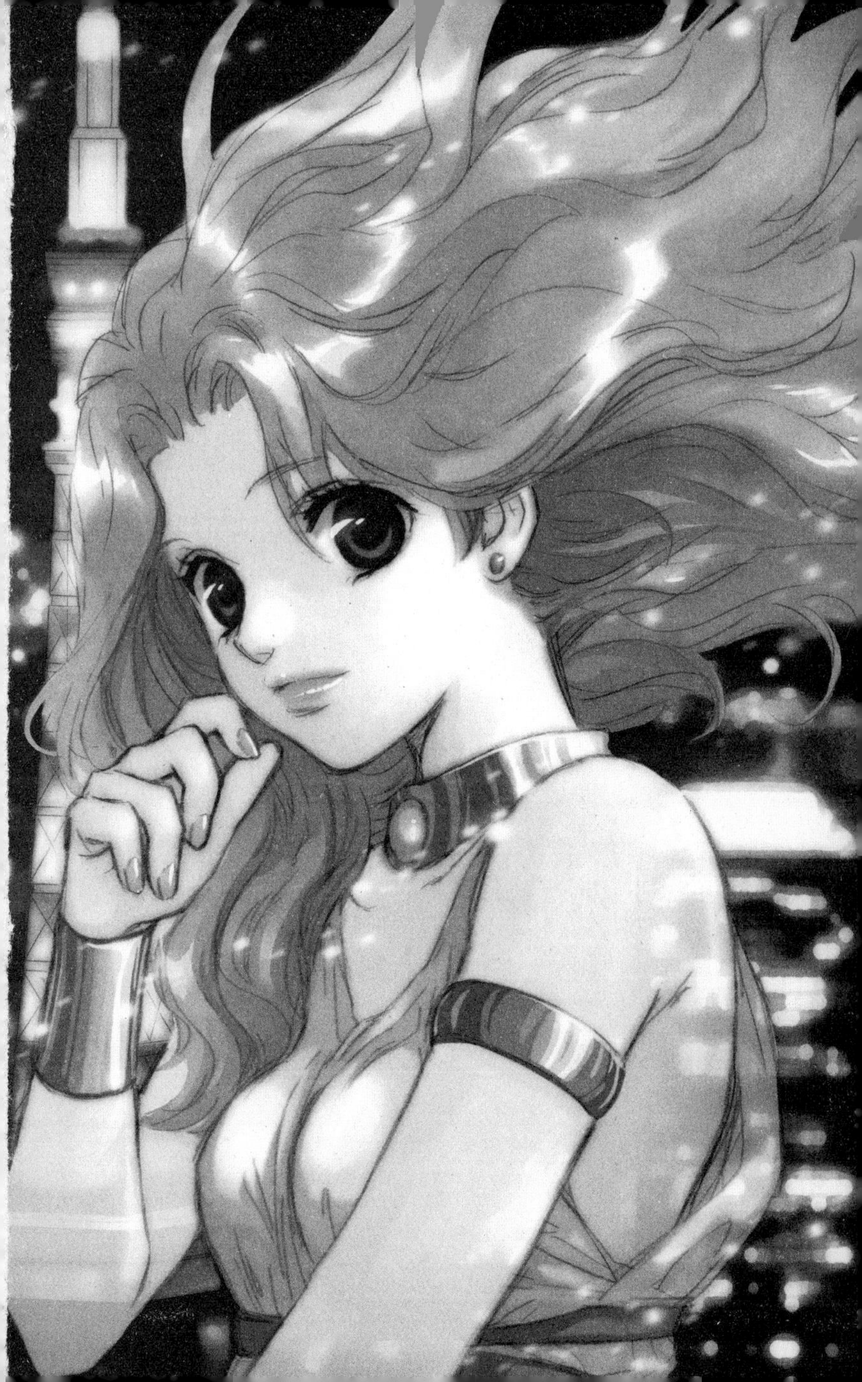

The Spy Goddess novels
by Michael P. Spradlin

Spy Goddess, Book One:
Live and Let Shop

Spy Goddess, Book Two:
To Hawaii, with Love

SPY GODDESS

Volume One
The Chase for the Chalice

Created by
Michael P. Spradlin

Script by
Rachel Manija Brown

Illustrated by
Rainbow Buddy

TOKYOPOP®

HAMBURG // LONDON // LOS ANGELES // TOKYO

HarperCollins*Publishers*

Spy Goddess Vol. 1: The Chase for the Chalice

Created by Michael P. Spradlin
Script by Rachel Manija Brown
Illustrated by Rainbow Buddy

Lettering - Lucas Rivera and Fawn Lau
Cover Illustration - Rainbow Buddy
Cover Design - Jose Macasocol, Jr.

Editor - Luis Reyes
Digital Imaging Manager - Chris Buford
Pre-Production Supervisor - Erika Terriquez
Production Manager - Elisabeth Brizzi
Managing Editor - Vy Nguyen
Creative Director - Anne Marie Horne
Editor-in-Chief - Rob Tokar
Publisher - Mike Kiley
President and C.O.O. - John Parker
C.E.O. and Chief Creative Officer - Stuart Levy

A TOKYOPOP Manga

TOKYOPOP and are trademarks or registered trademarks of TOKYOPOP Inc.

TOKYOPOP Inc.
5900 Wilshire Blvd. Suite 2000
Los Angeles, CA 90036

E-mail: info@TOKYOPOP.com
Come visit us online at www.TOKYOPOP.com

For information address HarperCollins Children's Books, a division of HarperCollins Publishers, 1350 Avenue of the Americas, New York, NY 10019.
www.harperteen.com

Library of Congress catalog card number: 2007942250
ISBN 978-0-06-136299-6

❖

First Edition

CONTENTS

Chapter One..............................6

Chapter Two............................33

Chapter Three.........................57

Chapter Four...........................81

Chapter Five..........................106

Chapter Six...........................132

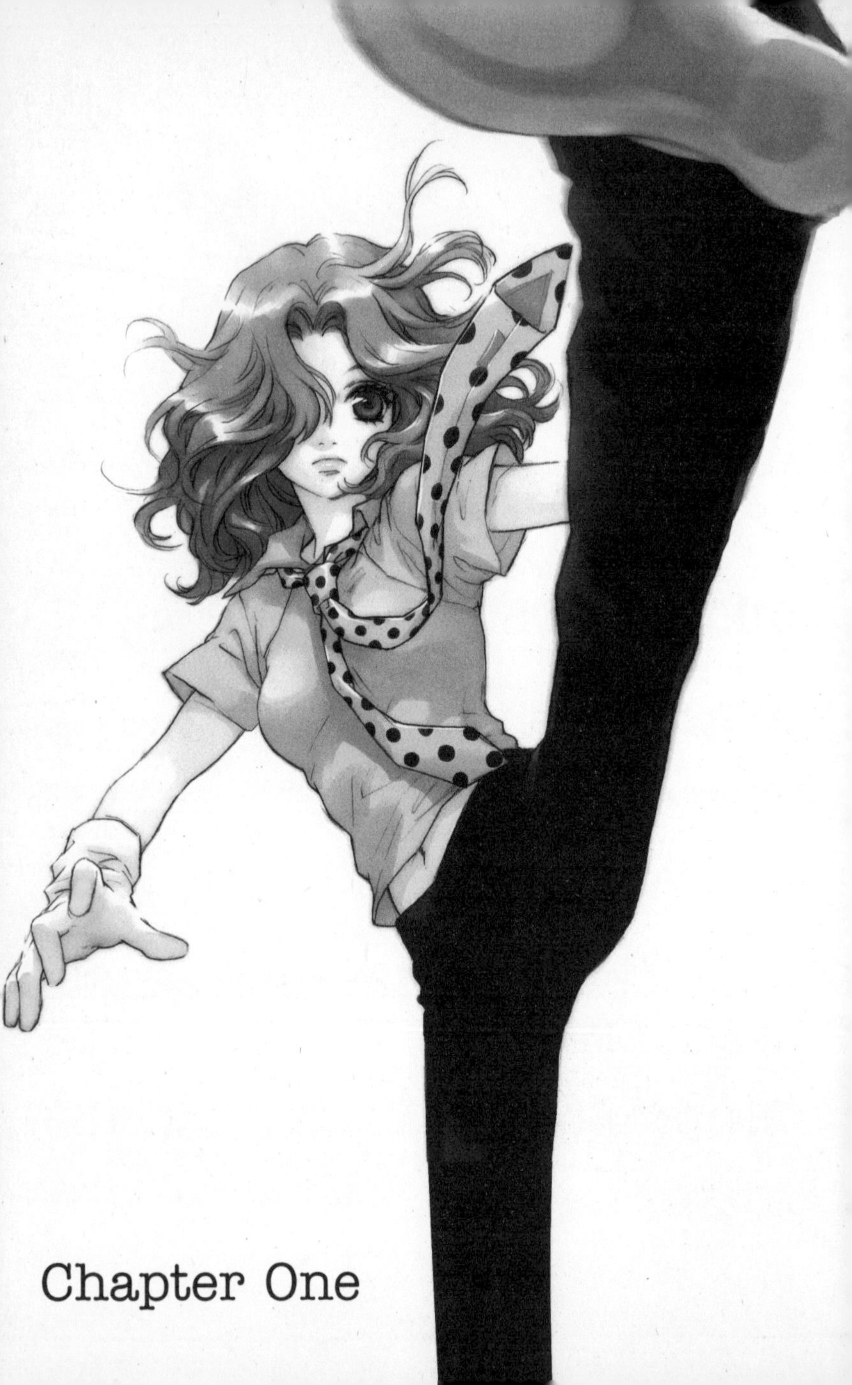

Chapter One

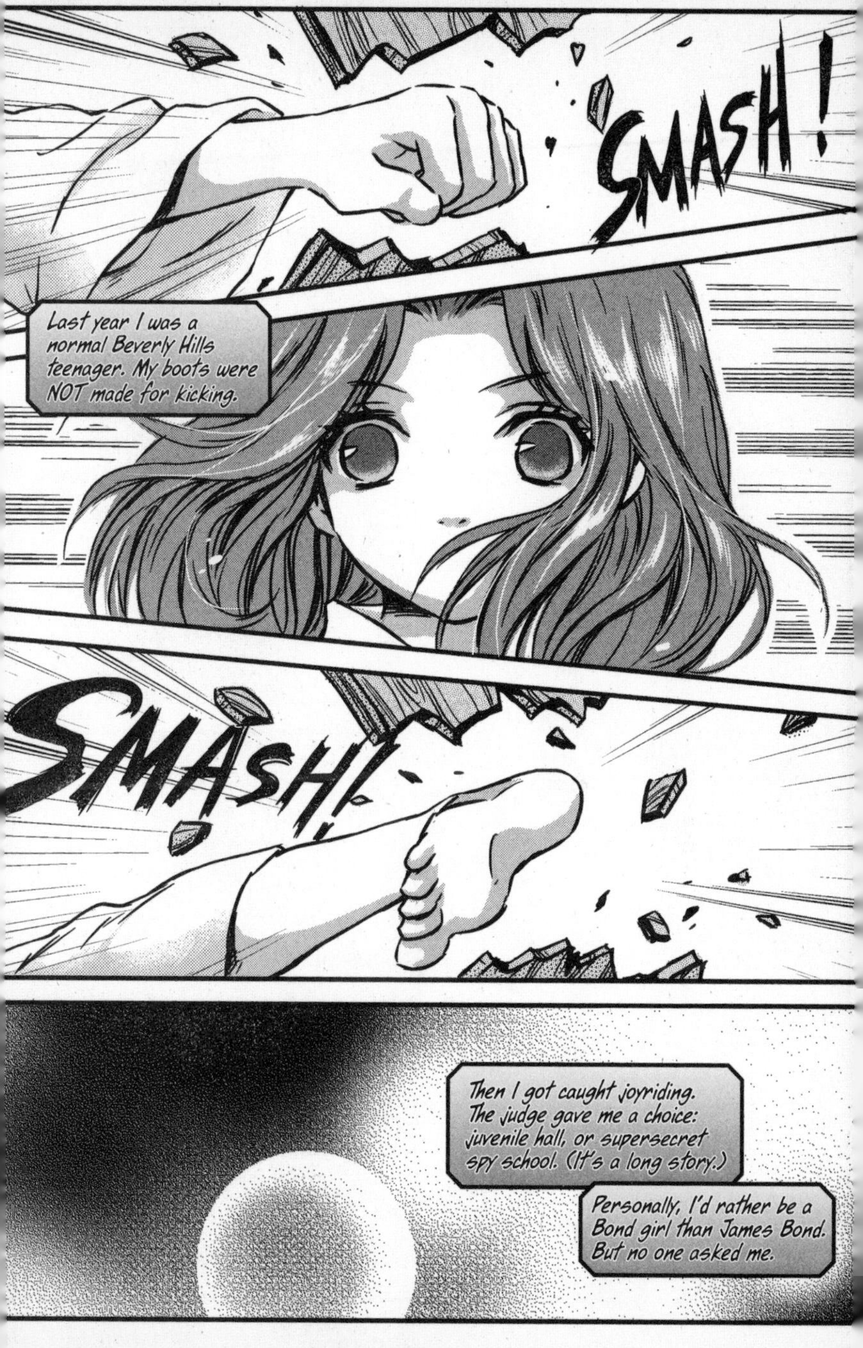
SMASH!
Last year I was a normal Beverly Hills teenager. My boots were NOT made for kicking.
SMASH!
Then I got caught joyriding. The judge gave me a choice: juvenile hall, or supersecret spy school. (It's a long story.)
Personally, I'd rather be a Bond girl than James Bond. But no one asked me.

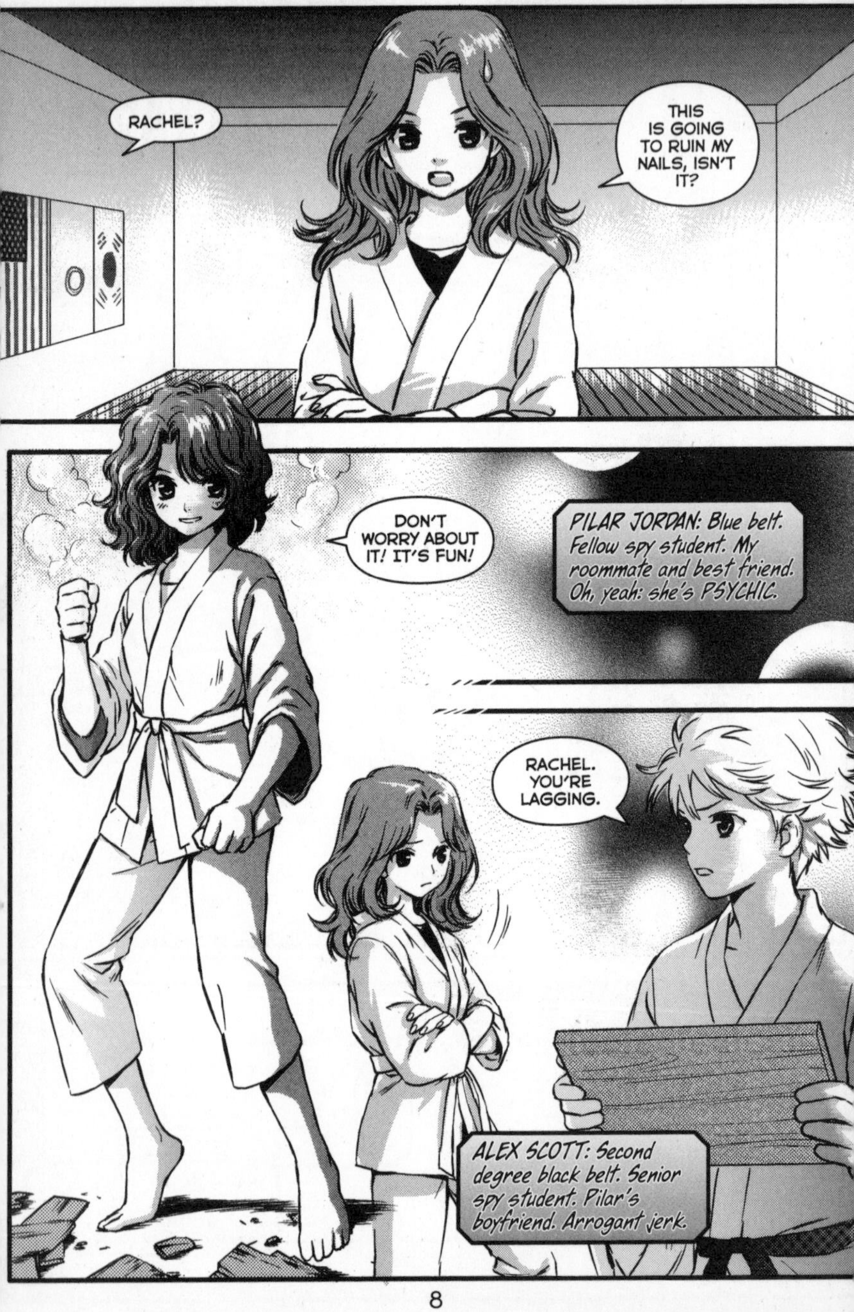
RACHEL?
THIS IS GOING TO RUIN MY NAILS, ISN'T IT?
DON'T WORRY ABOUT IT! IT'S FUN!
PILAR JORDAN: Blue belt. Fellow spy student. My roommate and best friend. Oh, yeah: she's PSYCHIC.
RACHEL. YOU'RE LAGGING.
ALEX SCOTT: Second degree black belt. Senior spy student. Pilar's boyfriend. Arrogant jerk.

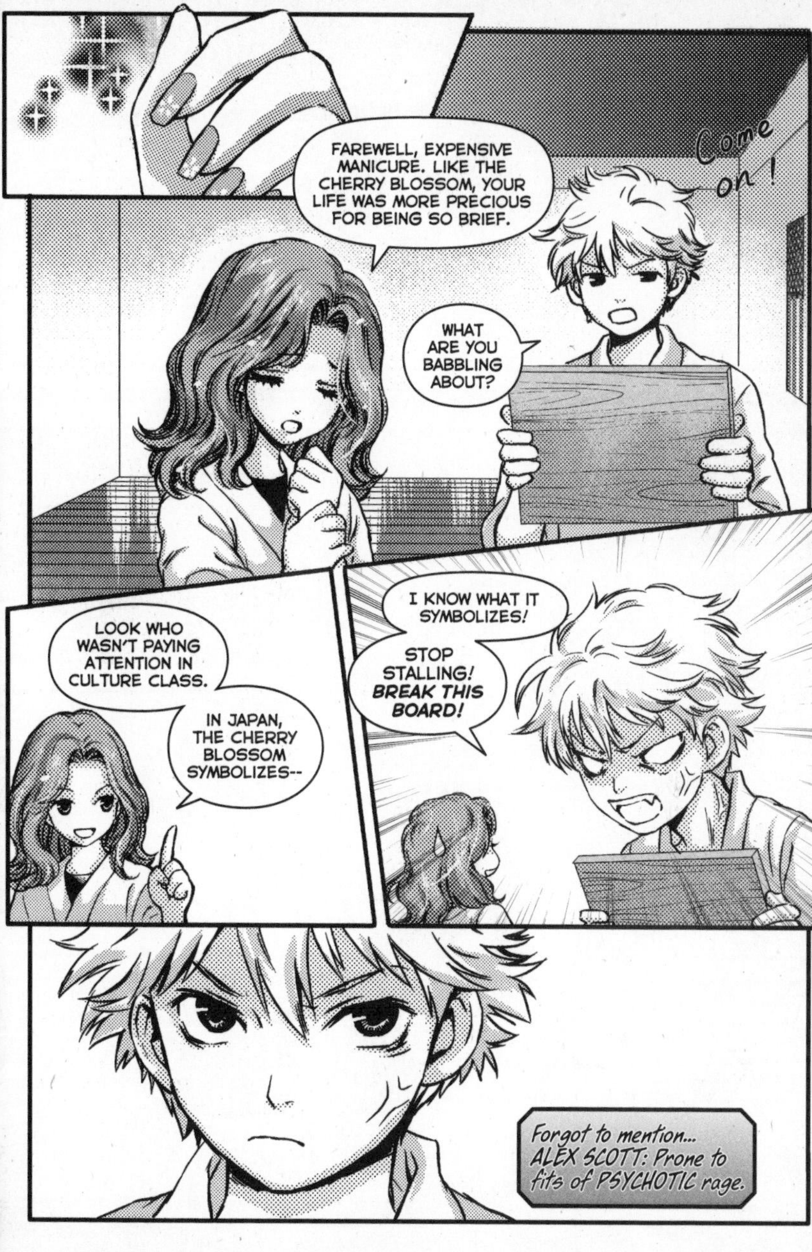
FAREWELL, EXPENSIVE MANICURE. LIKE THE CHERRY BLOSSOM, YOUR LIFE WAS MORE PRECIOUS FOR BEING SO BRIEF.
Come on!
WHAT ARE YOU BABBLING ABOUT?
LOOK WHO WASN'T PAYING ATTENTION IN CULTURE CLASS.
IN JAPAN, THE CHERRY BLOSSOM SYMBOLIZES--
I KNOW WHAT IT SYMBOLIZES!
STOP STALLING! BREAK THIS BOARD!
Forgot to mention... ALEX SCOTT: Prone to fits of PSYCHOTIC rage.

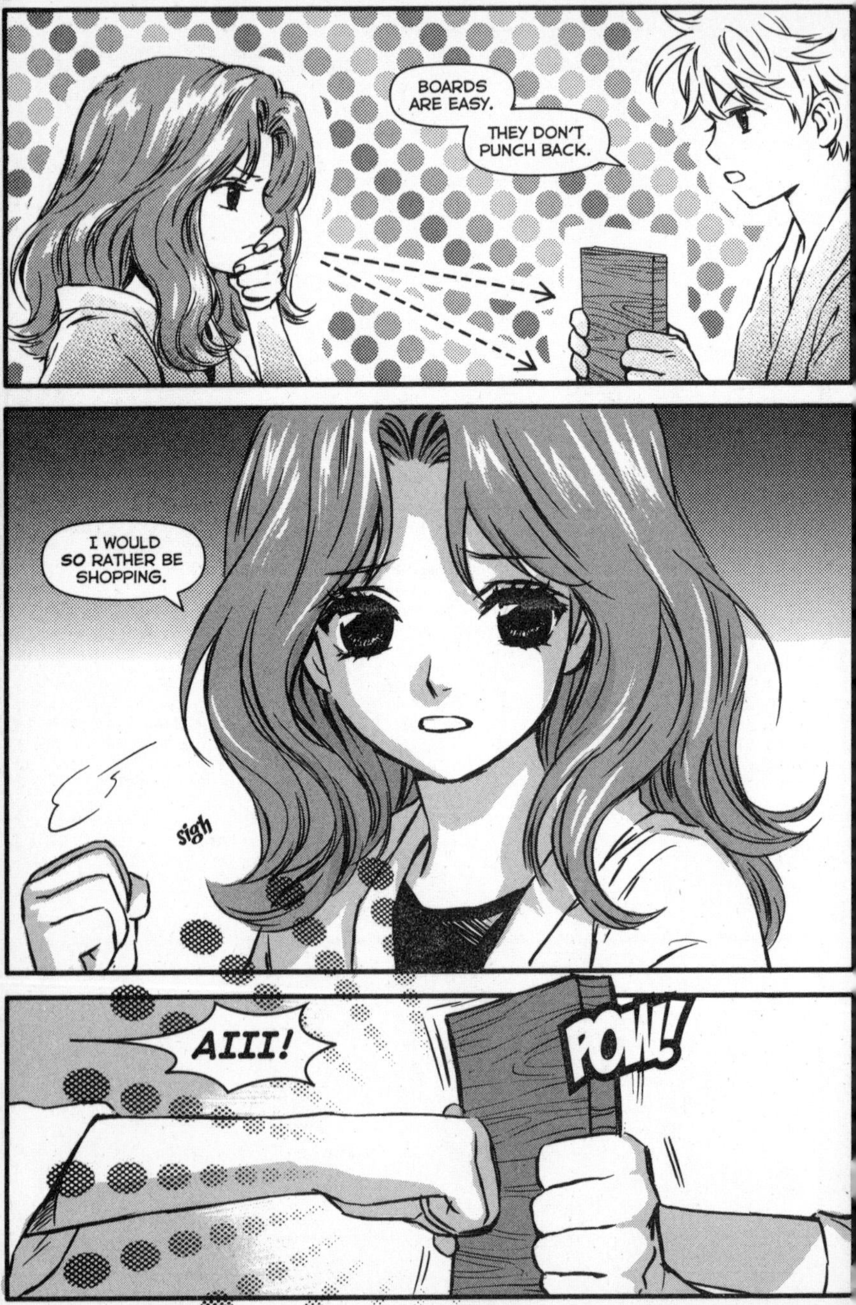
BOARDS ARE EASY.
THEY DON'T PUNCH BACK.
I WOULD SO RATHER BE SHOPPING.
sigh
AIII!
POW!

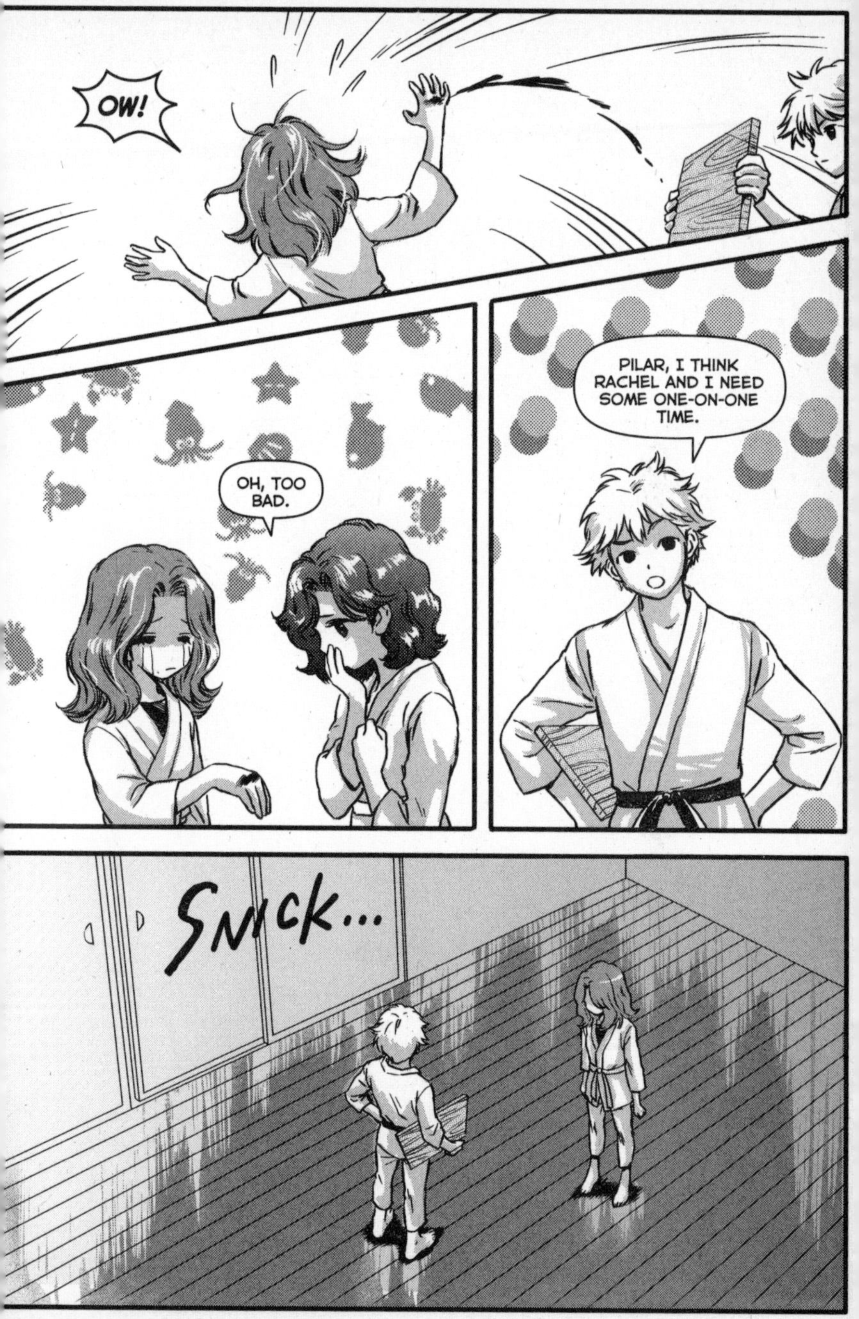
OW!
OH, TOO BAD.
PILAR, I THINK RACHEL AND I NEED SOME ONE-ON-ONE TIME.
SNICK...

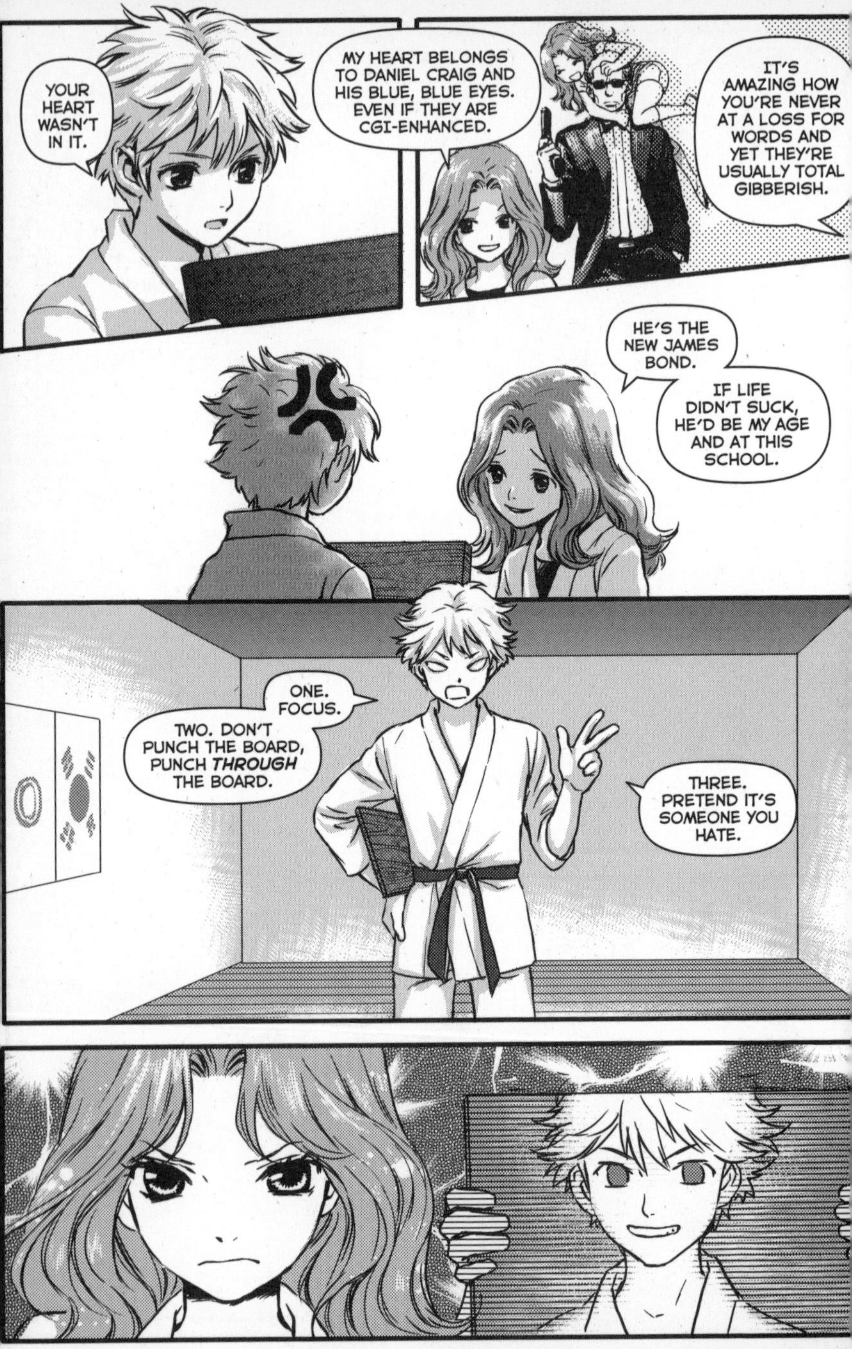
YOUR HEART WASN'T IN IT.
MY HEART BELONGS TO DANIEL CRAIG AND HIS BLUE, BLUE EYES. EVEN IF THEY ARE CGI-ENHANCED.
IT'S AMAZING HOW YOU'RE NEVER AT A LOSS FOR WORDS AND YET THEY'RE USUALLY TOTAL GIBBERISH.
HE'S THE NEW JAMES BOND.
IF LIFE DIDN'T SUCK, HE'D BE MY AGE AND AT THIS SCHOOL.
ONE. FOCUS.
TWO. DON'T PUNCH THE BOARD, PUNCH ***THROUGH*** THE BOARD.
THREE. PRETEND IT'S SOMEONE YOU HATE.

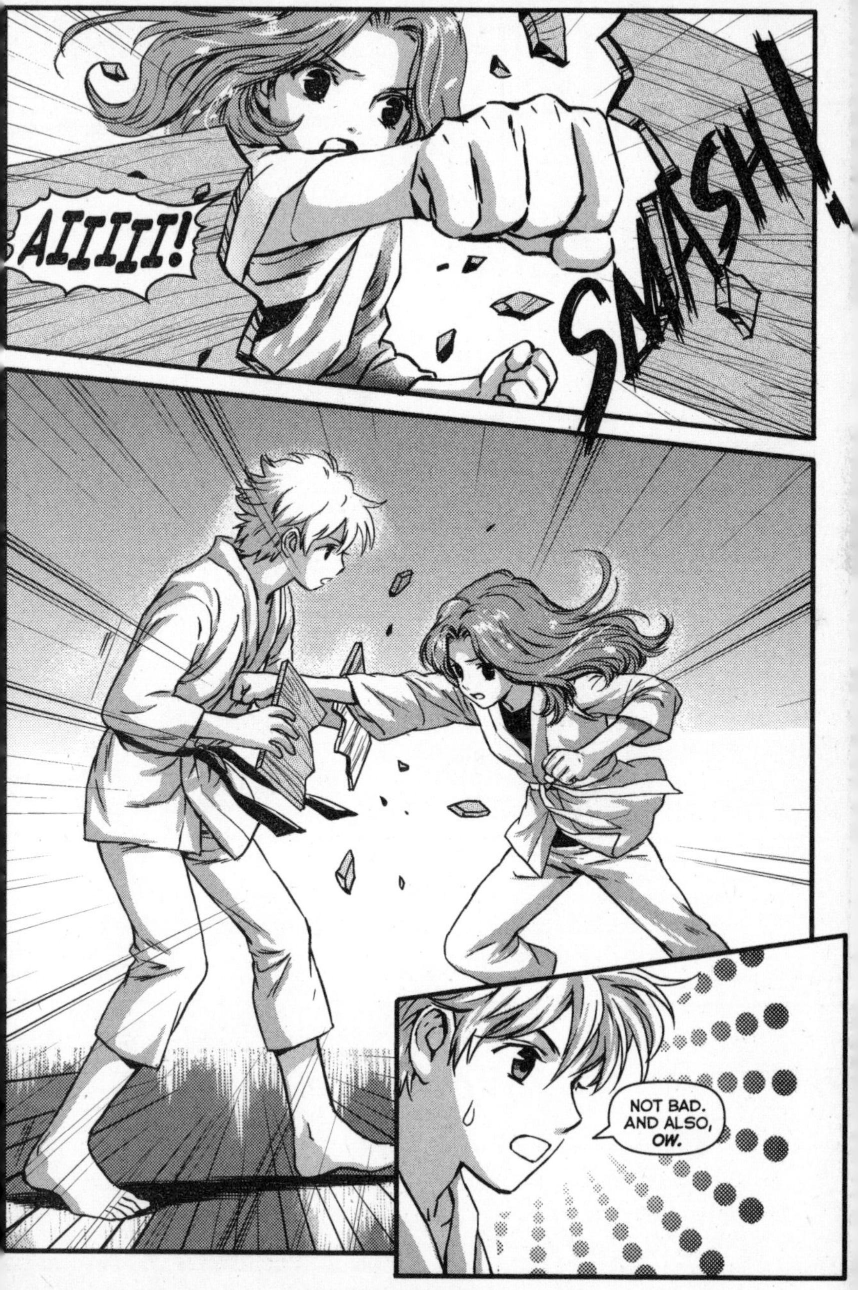
AIIIII!
SMASH!
NOT BAD. AND ALSO, OW.

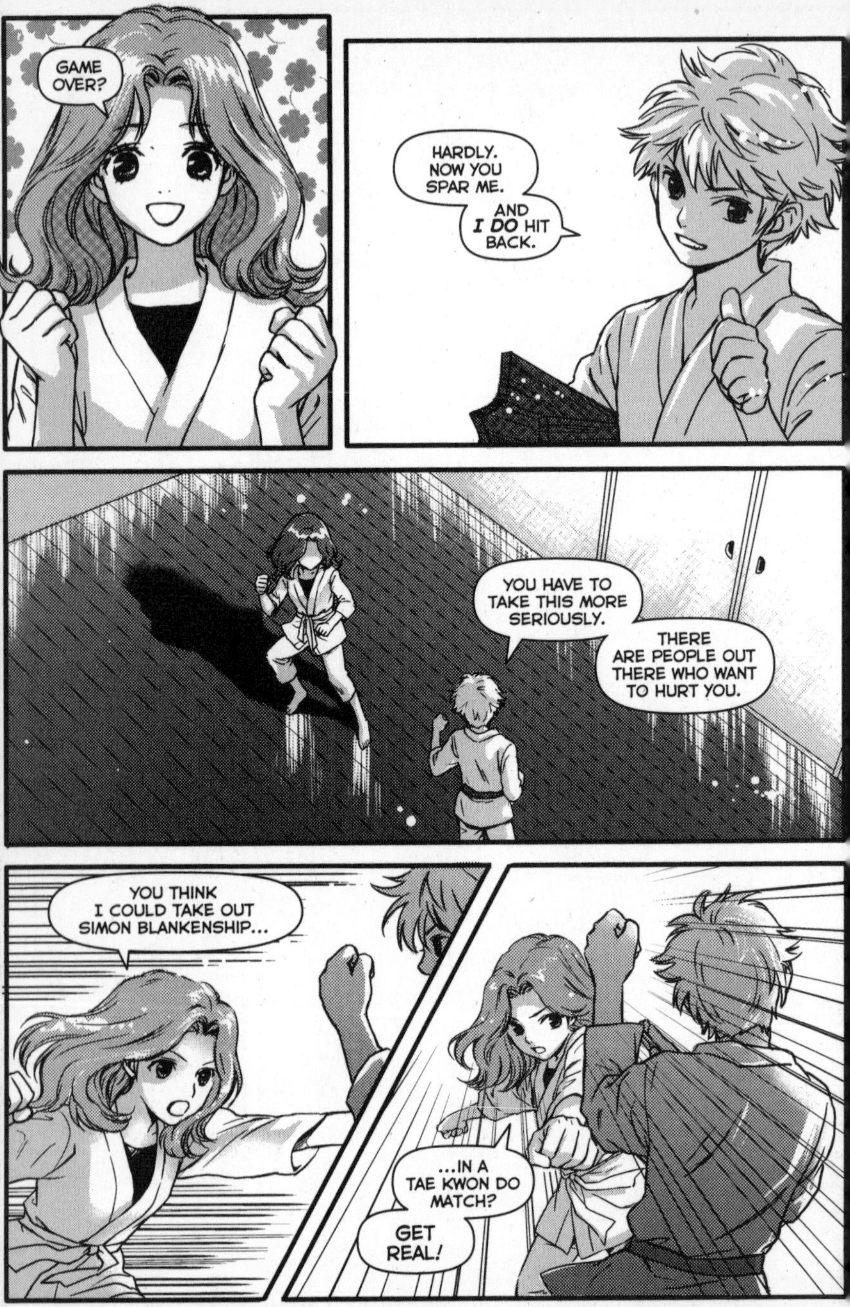
GAME OVER?
HARDLY. NOW YOU SPAR ME.
AND I DO HIT BACK.
YOU HAVE TO TAKE THIS MORE SERIOUSLY.
THERE ARE PEOPLE OUT THERE WHO WANT TO HURT YOU.
YOU THINK I COULD TAKE OUT SIMON BLANKENSHIP...
...IN A TAE KWON DO MATCH?
GET REAL!

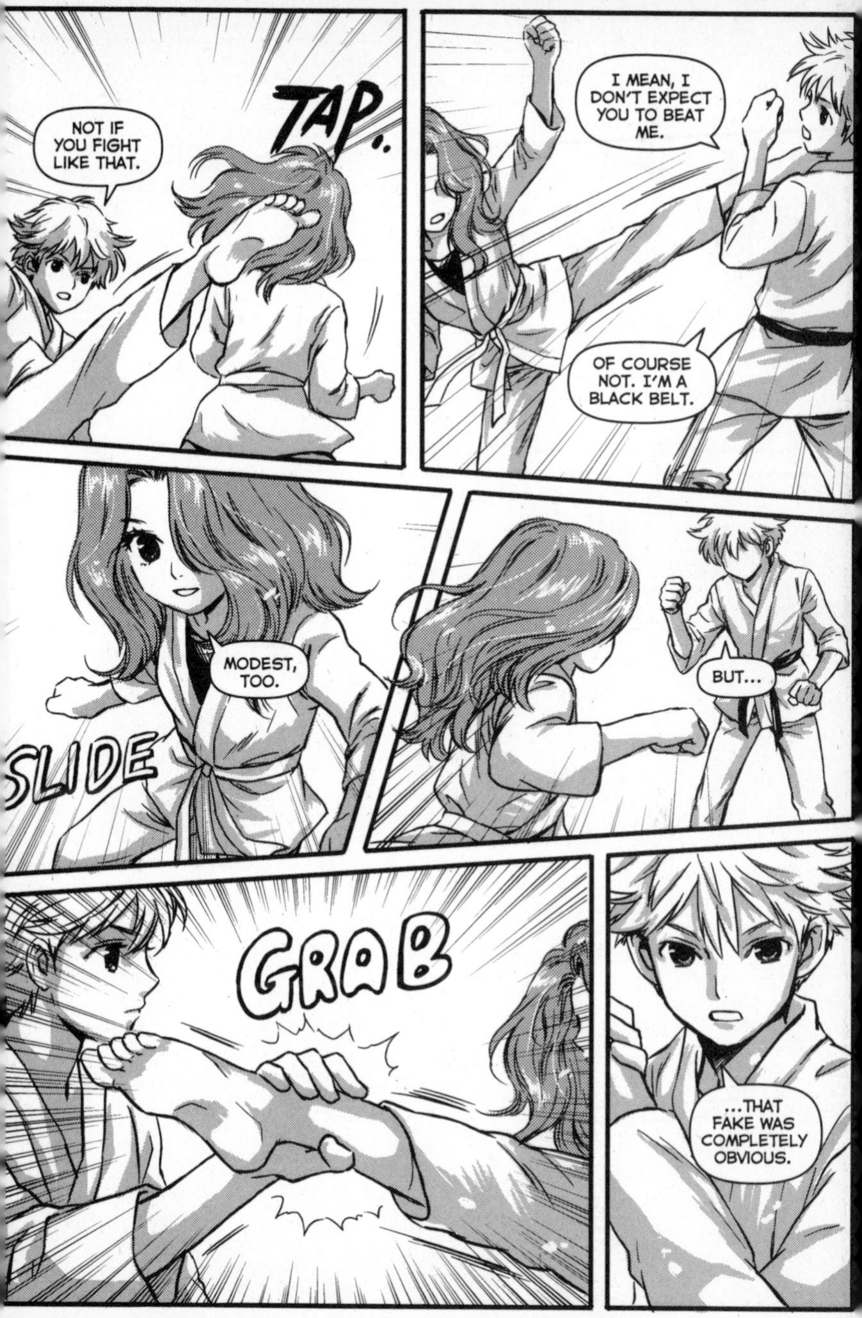
NOT IF YOU FIGHT LIKE THAT.
TAP
I MEAN, I DON'T EXPECT YOU TO BEAT ME.
OF COURSE NOT. I'M A BLACK BELT.
MODEST, TOO.
SLIDE
BUT...
GRAB
...THAT FAKE WAS COMPLETELY OBVIOUS.

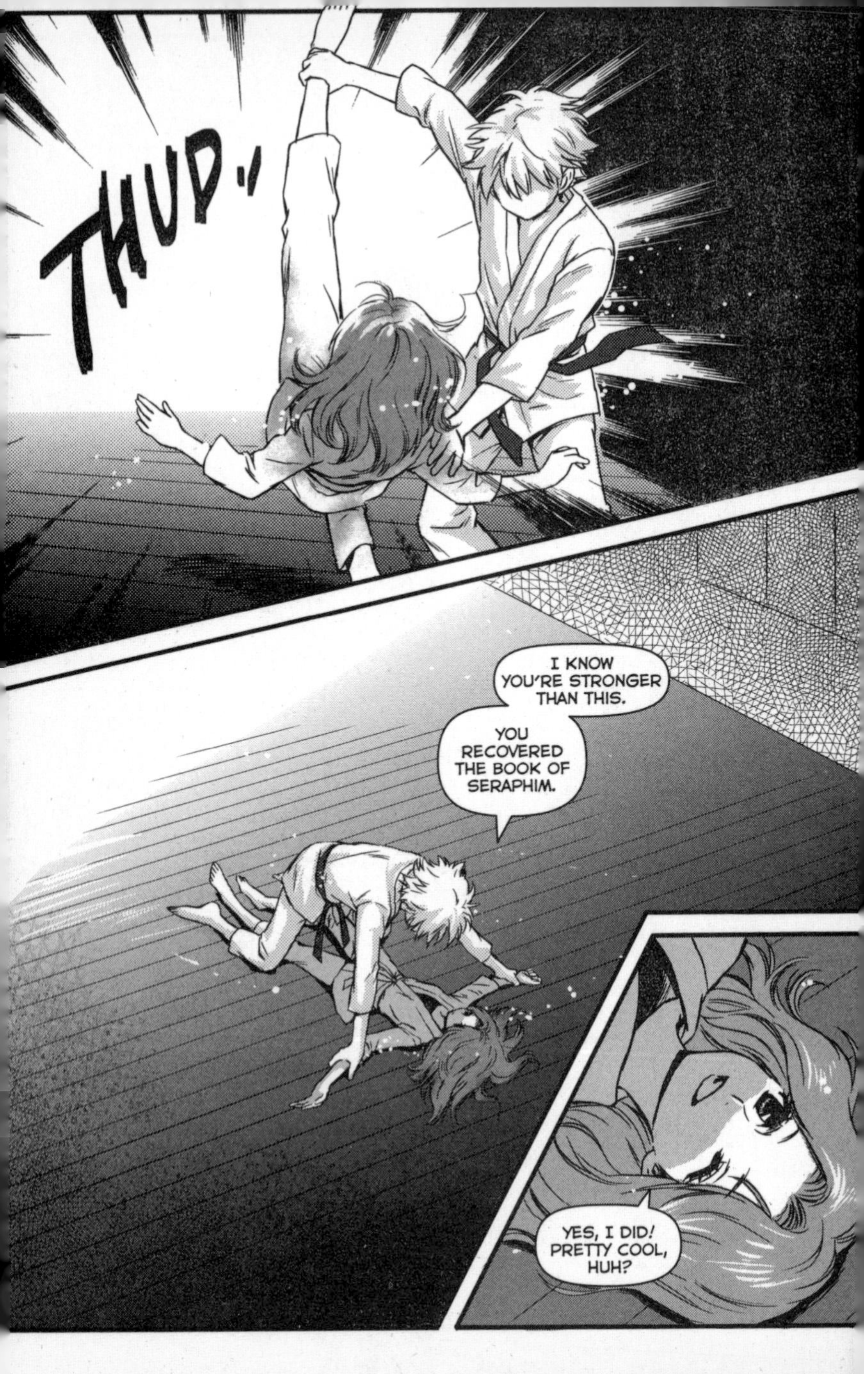
THUD!!
I KNOW YOU'RE STRONGER THAN THIS.
YOU RECOVERED THE BOOK OF SERAPHIM.
YES, I DID! PRETTY COOL, HUH?

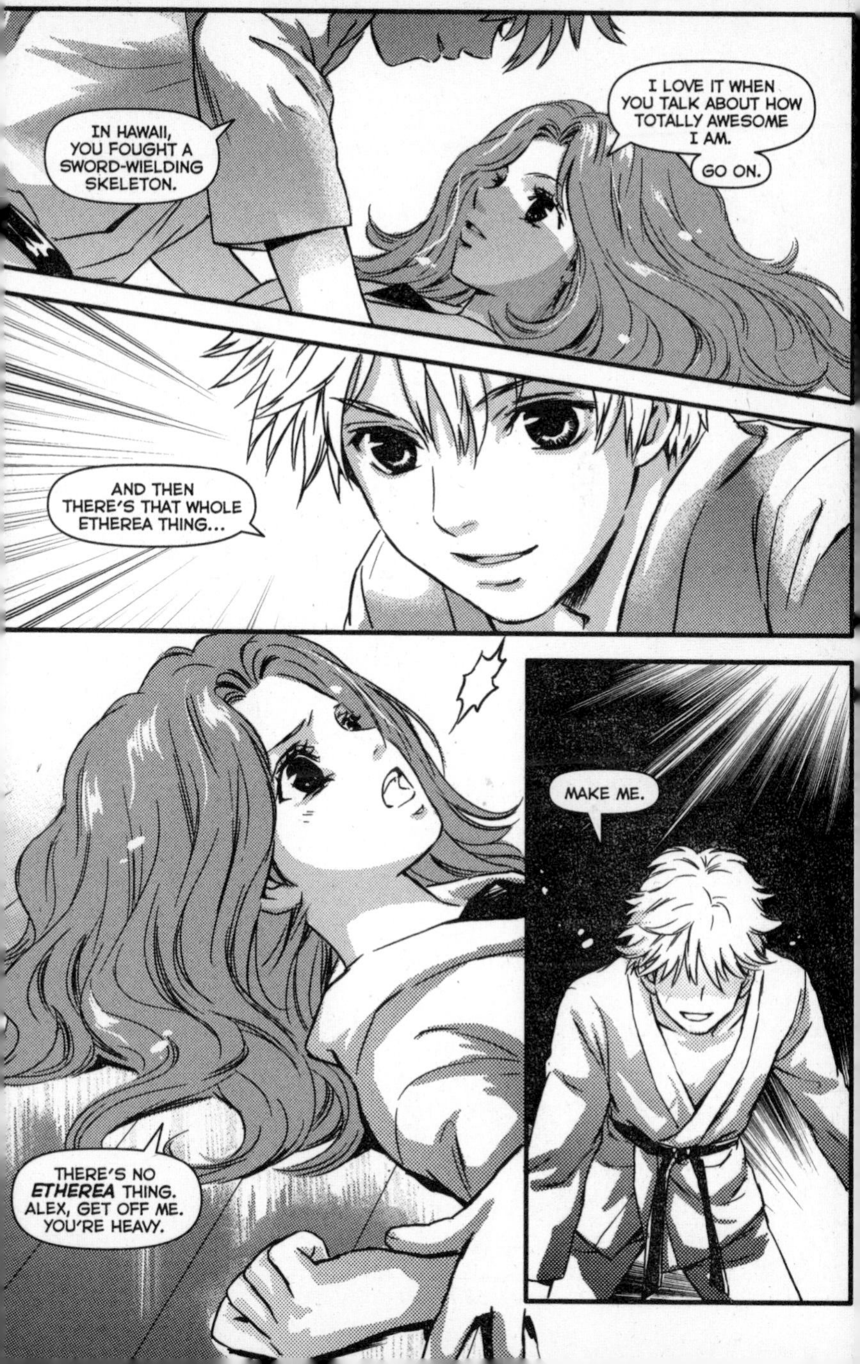
IN HAWAII, YOU FOUGHT A SWORD-WIELDING SKELETON.
I LOVE IT WHEN YOU TALK ABOUT HOW TOTALLY AWESOME I AM.
GO ON.
AND THEN THERE'S THAT WHOLE ETHEREA THING...
THERE'S NO *ETHEREA* THING. ALEX, GET OFF ME. YOU'RE HEAVY.
MAKE ME.

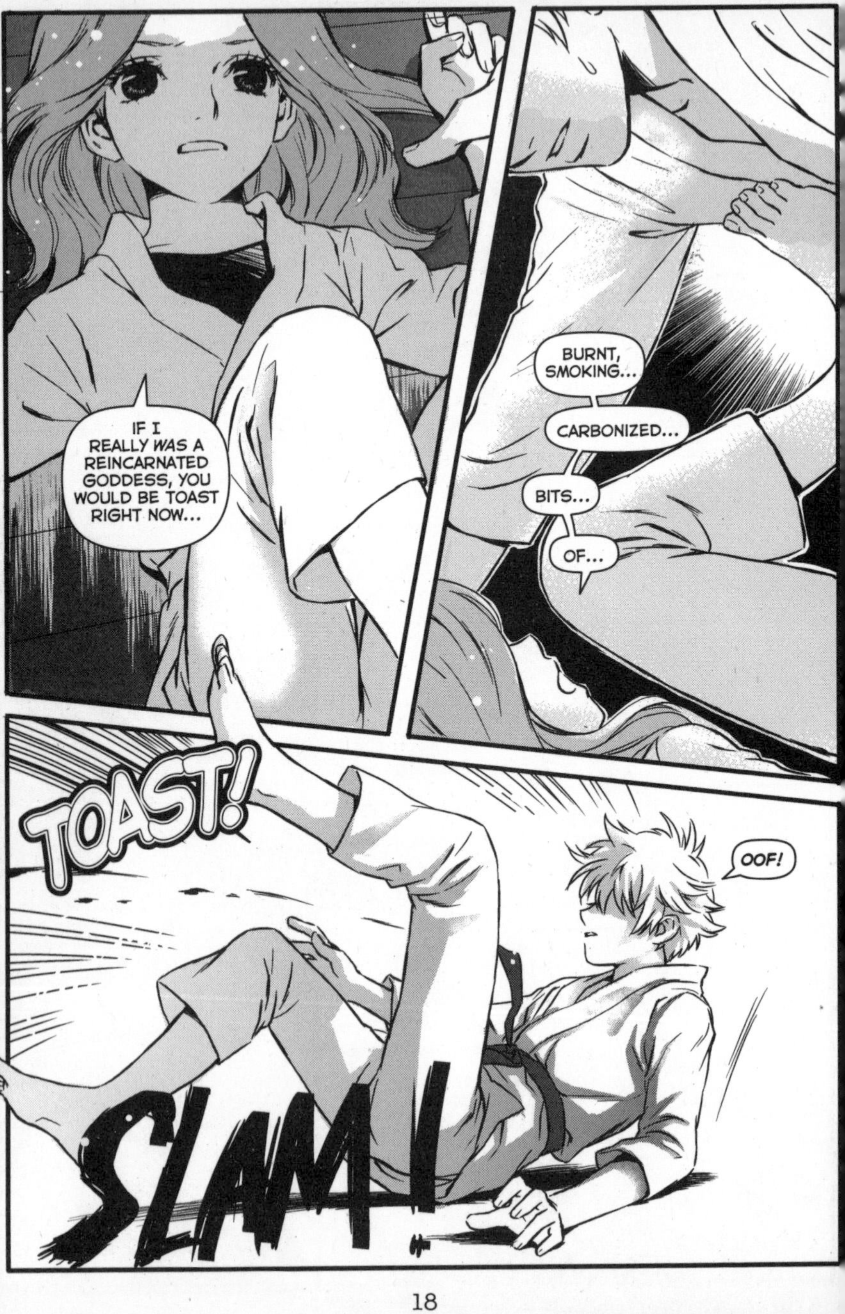
IF I REALLY *WAS* A REINCARNATED GODDESS, YOU WOULD BE TOAST RIGHT NOW...
BURNT, SMOKING...
CARBONIZED...
BITS...
OF...
TOAST!
OOF!
SLAM!!

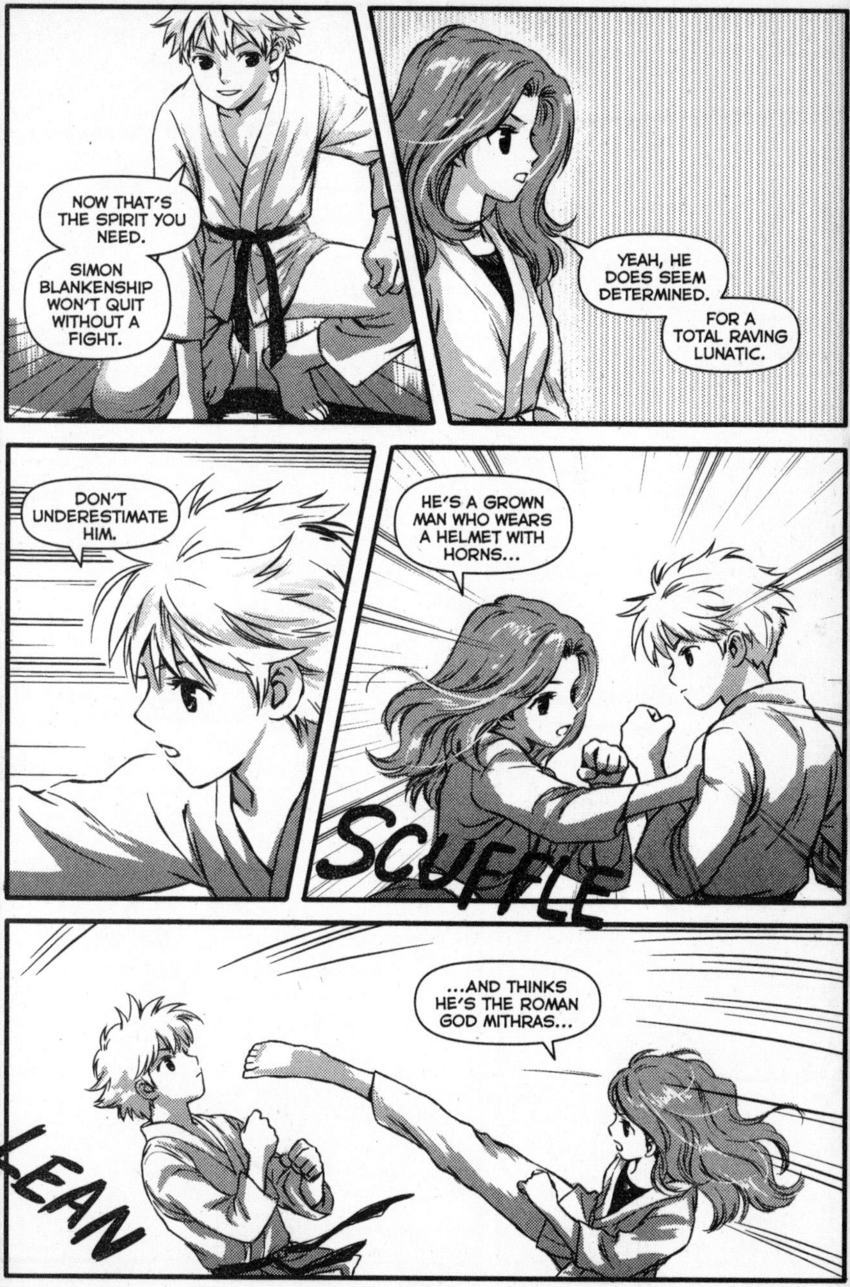
NOW THAT'S THE SPIRIT YOU NEED.
SIMON BLANKENSHIP WON'T QUIT WITHOUT A FIGHT.
YEAH, HE DOES SEEM DETERMINED.
FOR A TOTAL RAVING LUNATIC.
DON'T UNDERESTIMATE HIM.
HE'S A GROWN MAN WHO WEARS A HELMET WITH HORNS...
SCUFFLE
...AND THINKS HE'S THE ROMAN GOD MITHRAS...
LEAN

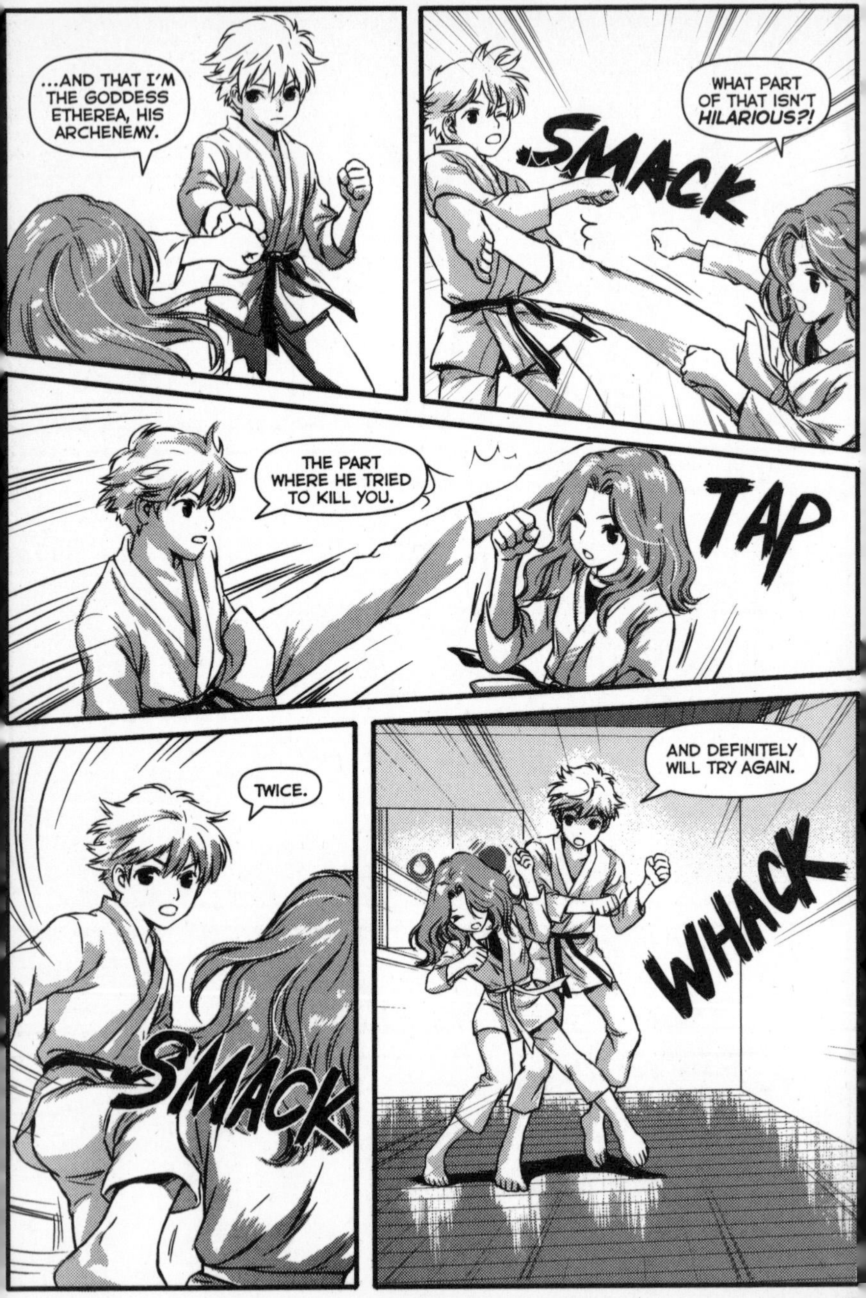
...AND THAT I'M THE GODDESS ETHEREA, HIS ARCHENEMY.
WHAT PART OF THAT ISN'T *HILARIOUS?!*
SMACK
THE PART WHERE HE TRIED TO KILL YOU.
TAP
TWICE.
SMACK
AND DEFINITELY WILL TRY AGAIN.
WHACK

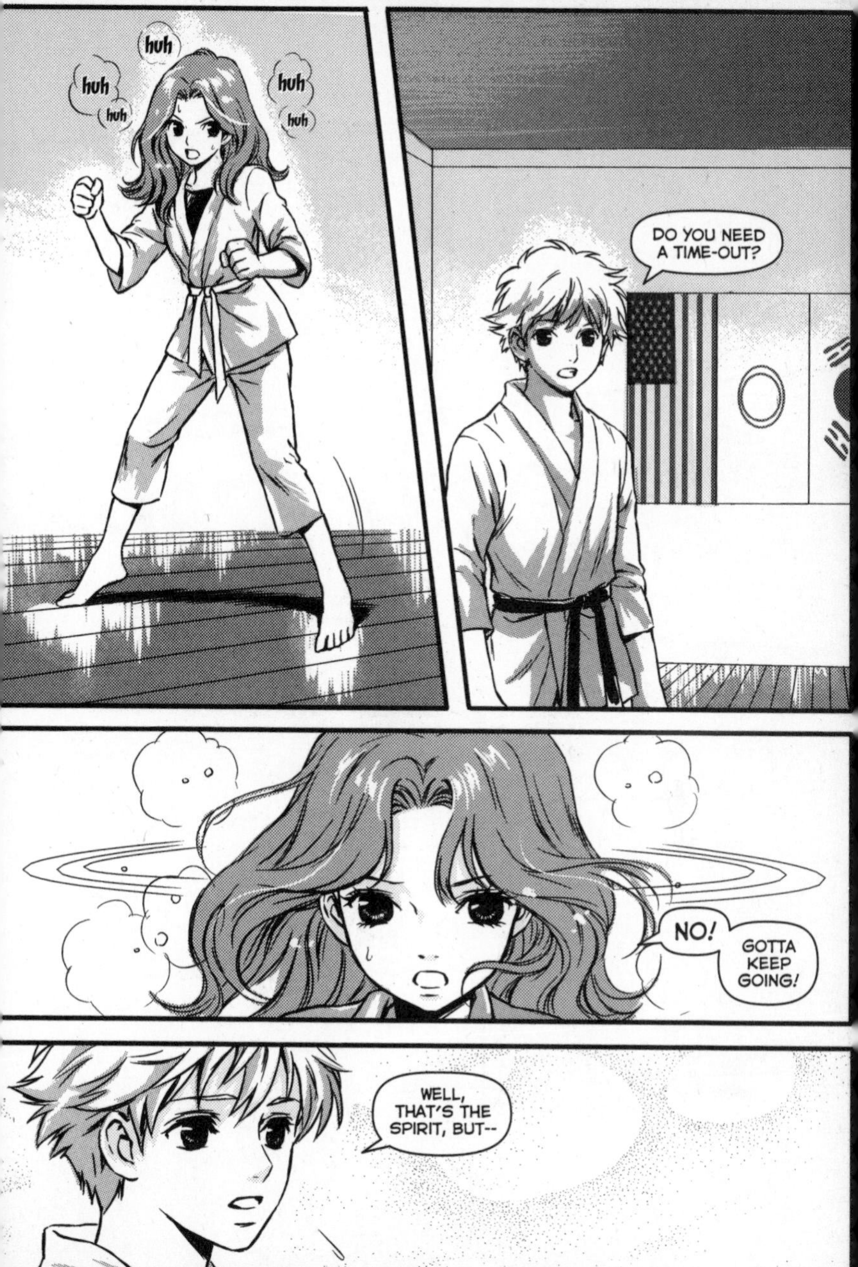
huh
huh
huh
huh
huh
DO YOU NEED A TIME-OUT?
NO!
GOTTA KEEP GOING!
WELL, THAT'S THE SPIRIT, BUT--

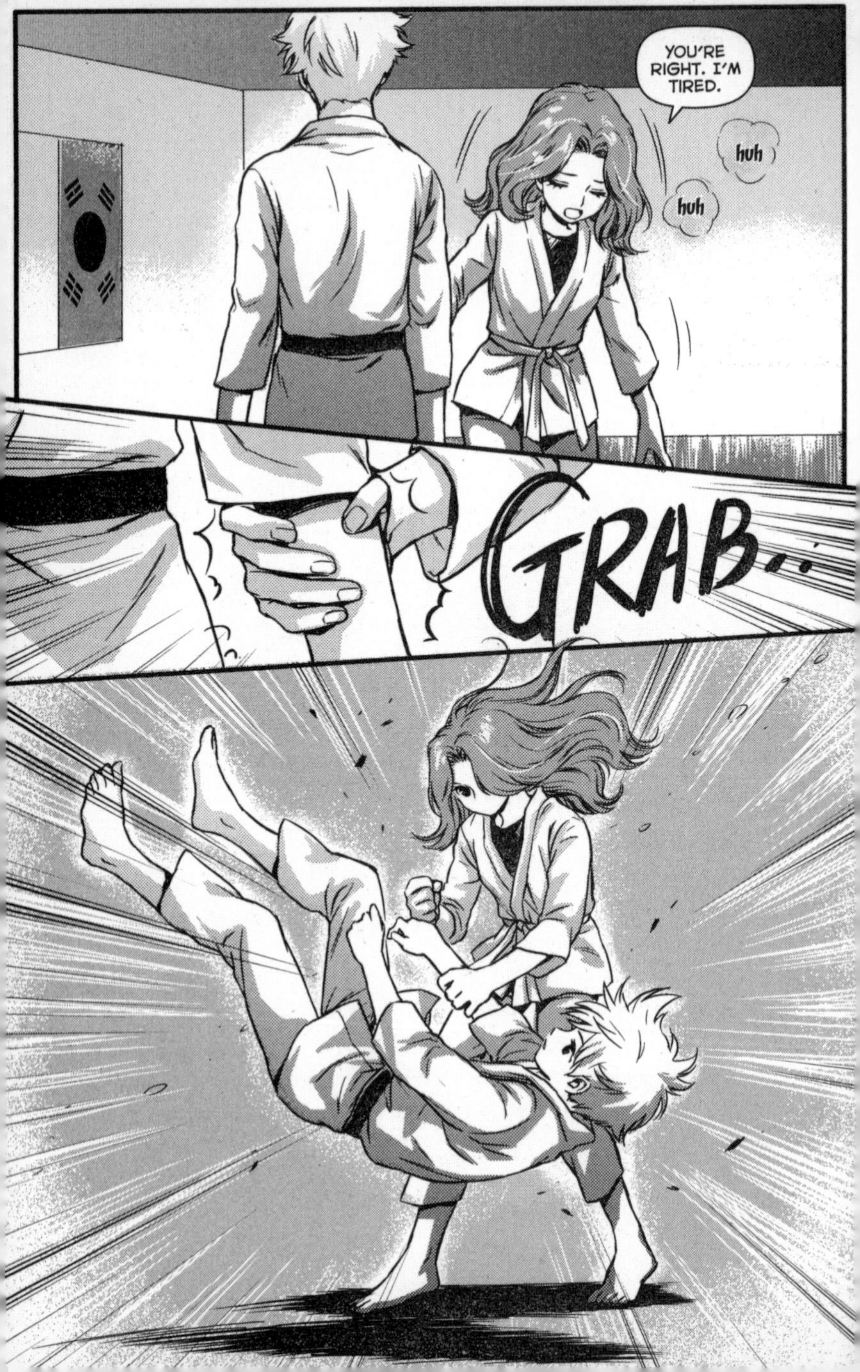
YOU'RE RIGHT. I'M TIRED.
huh
huh
GRAB..

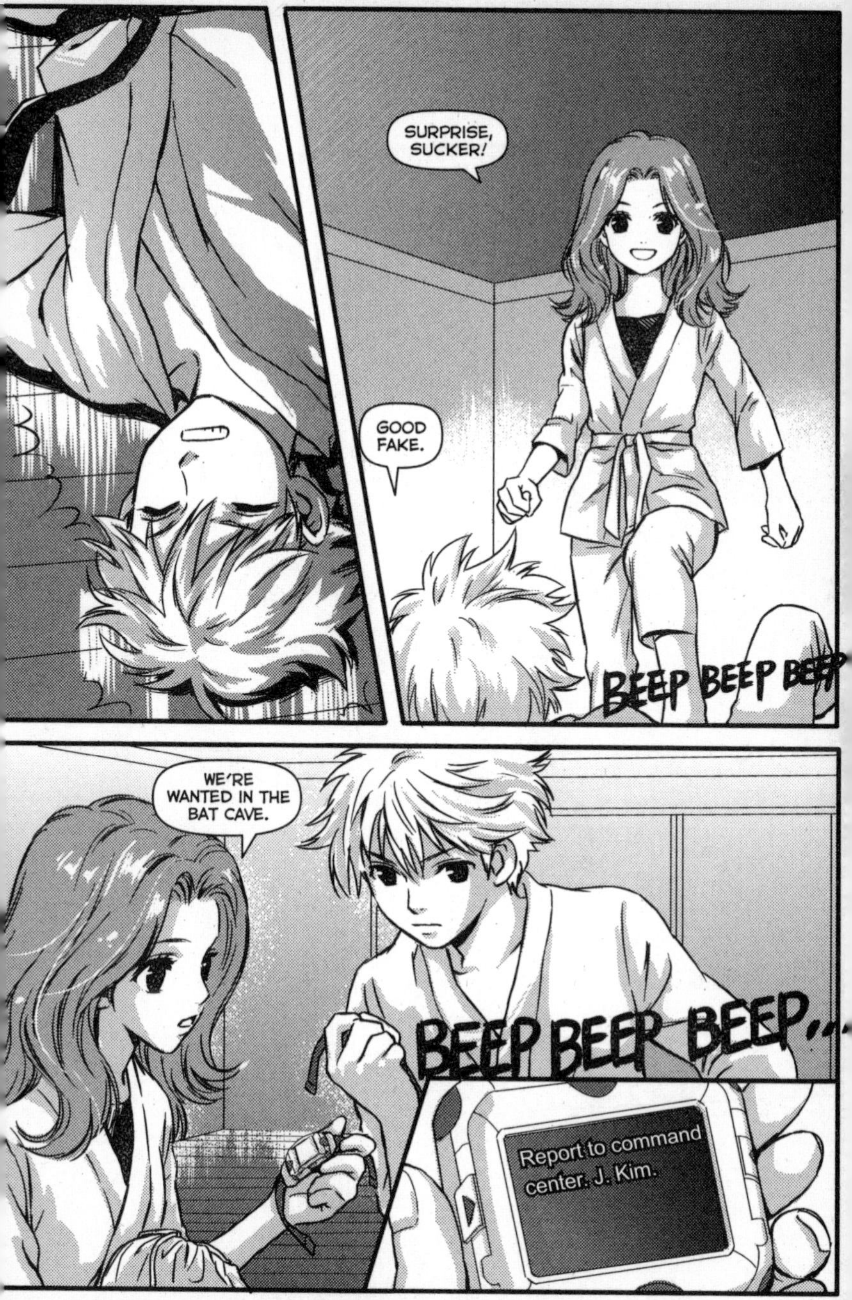
SURPRISE, SUCKER!
GOOD FAKE.
BEEP BEEP BEEP
WE'RE WANTED IN THE BAT CAVE.
BEEP BEEP BEEP...
Report to command center. J. Kim.

Mr. Kim's office.

I LOVE THIS PART.

SWING"

ONWARD TO THE BAT CAVE!

MR. KIM WOULD ONLY SUMMON US TO THE COMMAND CENTER FOR A VERY SERIOUS MATTER.

YOUR POINT BEING...?

DON'T CALL IT THE BAT CAVE.

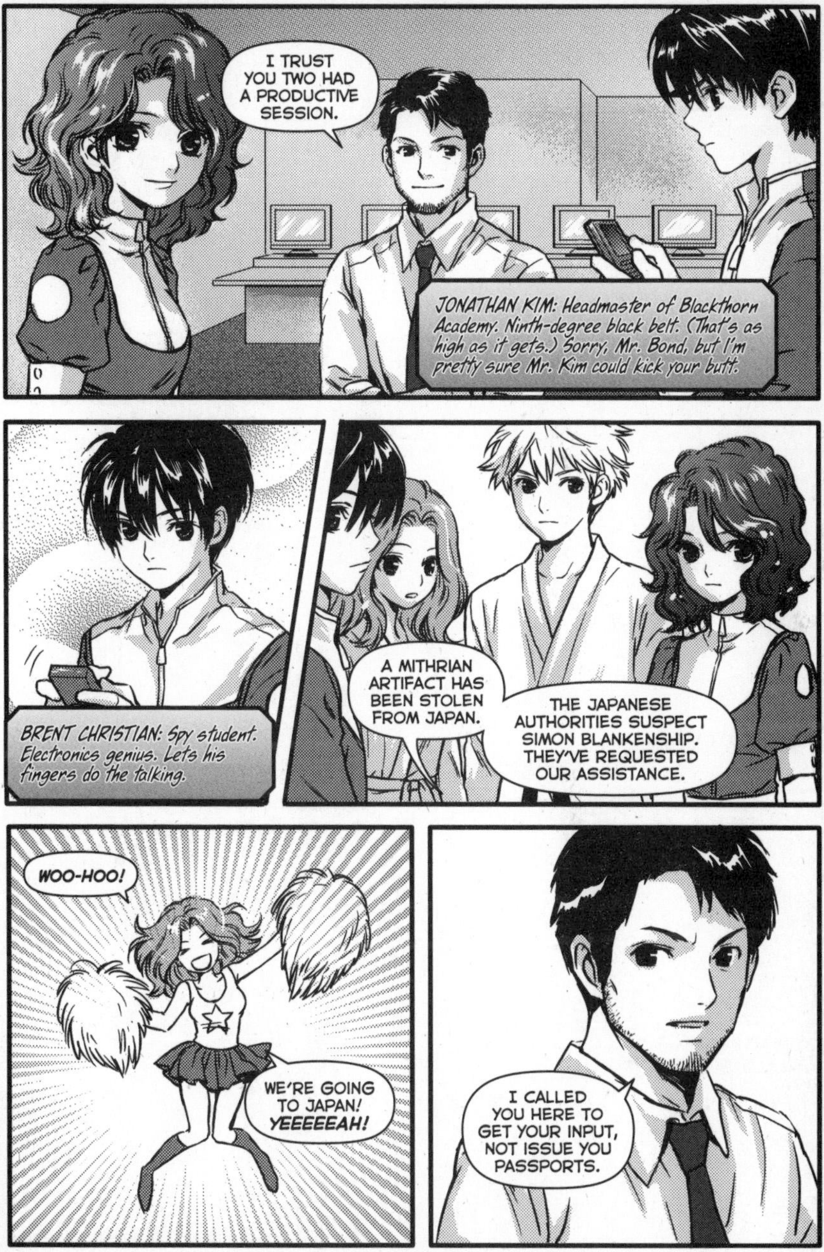
I TRUST YOU TWO HAD A PRODUCTIVE SESSION.
JONATHAN KIM: Headmaster of Blackthorn Academy. Ninth-degree black belt. (That's as high as it gets.) Sorry, Mr. Bond, but I'm pretty sure Mr. Kim could kick your butt.
BRENT CHRISTIAN: Spy student. Electronics genius. Lets his fingers do the talking.
A MITHRIAN ARTIFACT HAS BEEN STOLEN FROM JAPAN.
THE JAPANESE AUTHORITIES SUSPECT SIMON BLANKENSHIP. THEY'VE REQUESTED OUR ASSISTANCE.
WOO-HOO!
WE'RE GOING TO JAPAN! YEEEEEAH!
I CALLED YOU HERE TO GET YOUR INPUT, NOT ISSUE YOU PASSPORTS.

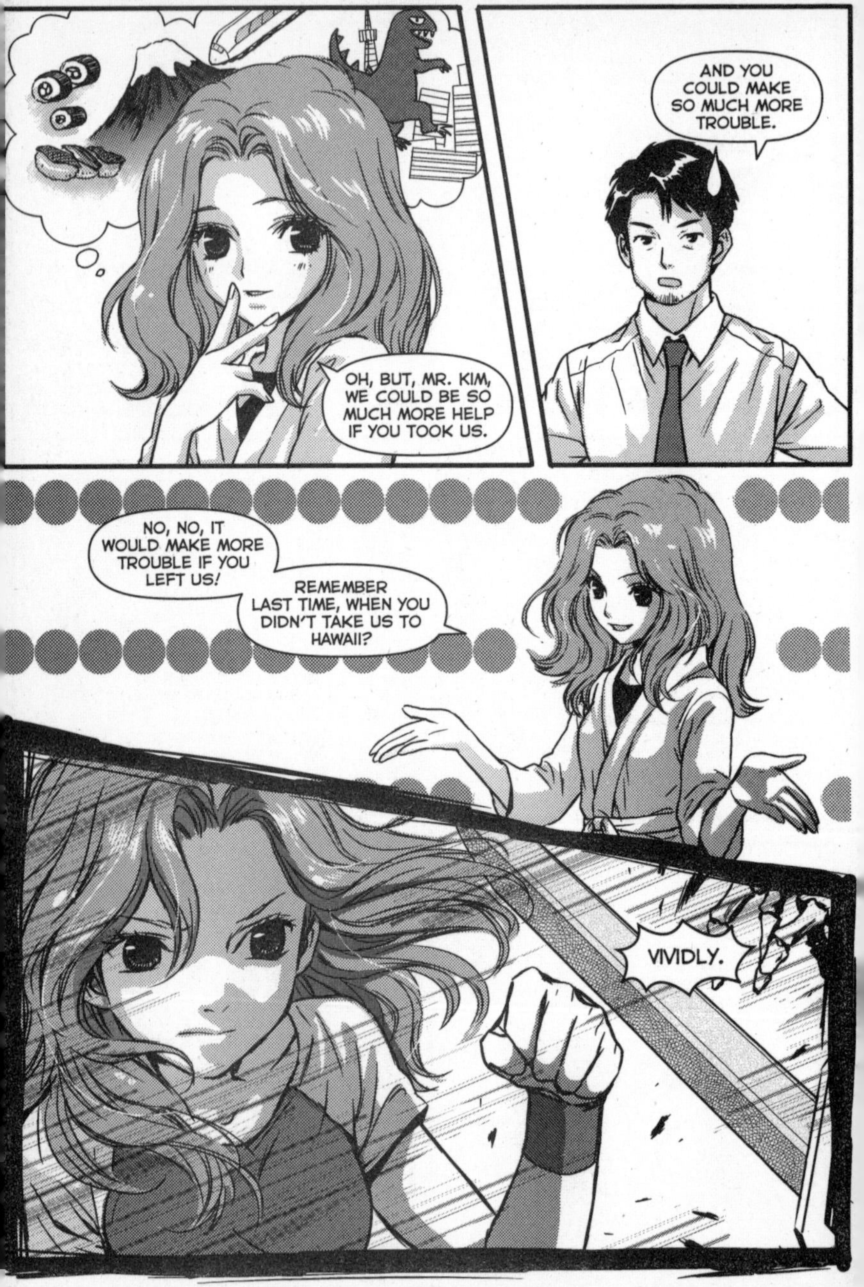
OH, BUT, MR. KIM, WE COULD BE SO MUCH MORE HELP IF YOU TOOK US.
AND YOU COULD MAKE SO MUCH MORE TROUBLE.
NO, NO, IT WOULD MAKE MORE TROUBLE IF YOU LEFT US!
REMEMBER LAST TIME, WHEN YOU DIDN'T TAKE US TO HAWAII?
VIVIDLY.

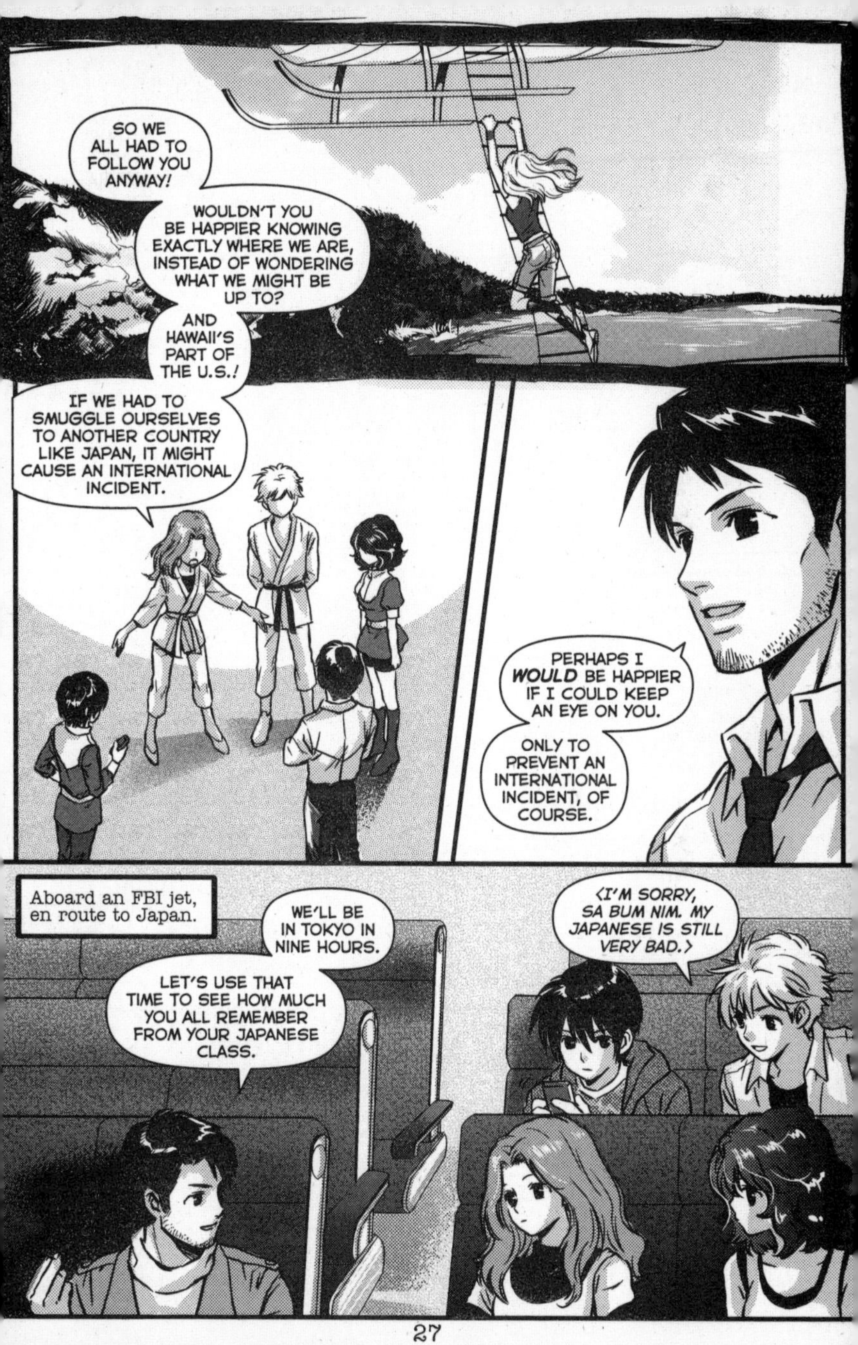
SO WE ALL HAD TO FOLLOW YOU ANYWAY!
WOULDN'T YOU BE HAPPIER KNOWING EXACTLY WHERE WE ARE, INSTEAD OF WONDERING WHAT WE MIGHT BE UP TO?
AND HAWAII'S PART OF THE U.S.!
IF WE HAD TO SMUGGLE OURSELVES TO ANOTHER COUNTRY LIKE JAPAN, IT MIGHT CAUSE AN INTERNATIONAL INCIDENT.
PERHAPS I ***WOULD*** BE HAPPIER IF I COULD KEEP AN EYE ON YOU.
ONLY TO PREVENT AN INTERNATIONAL INCIDENT, OF COURSE.
Aboard an FBI jet, en route to Japan.
WE'LL BE IN TOKYO IN NINE HOURS.
LET'S USE THAT TIME TO SEE HOW MUCH YOU ALL REMEMBER FROM YOUR JAPANESE CLASS.
<I'M SORRY, SA BUM NIM. MY JAPANESE IS STILL VERY BAD.>

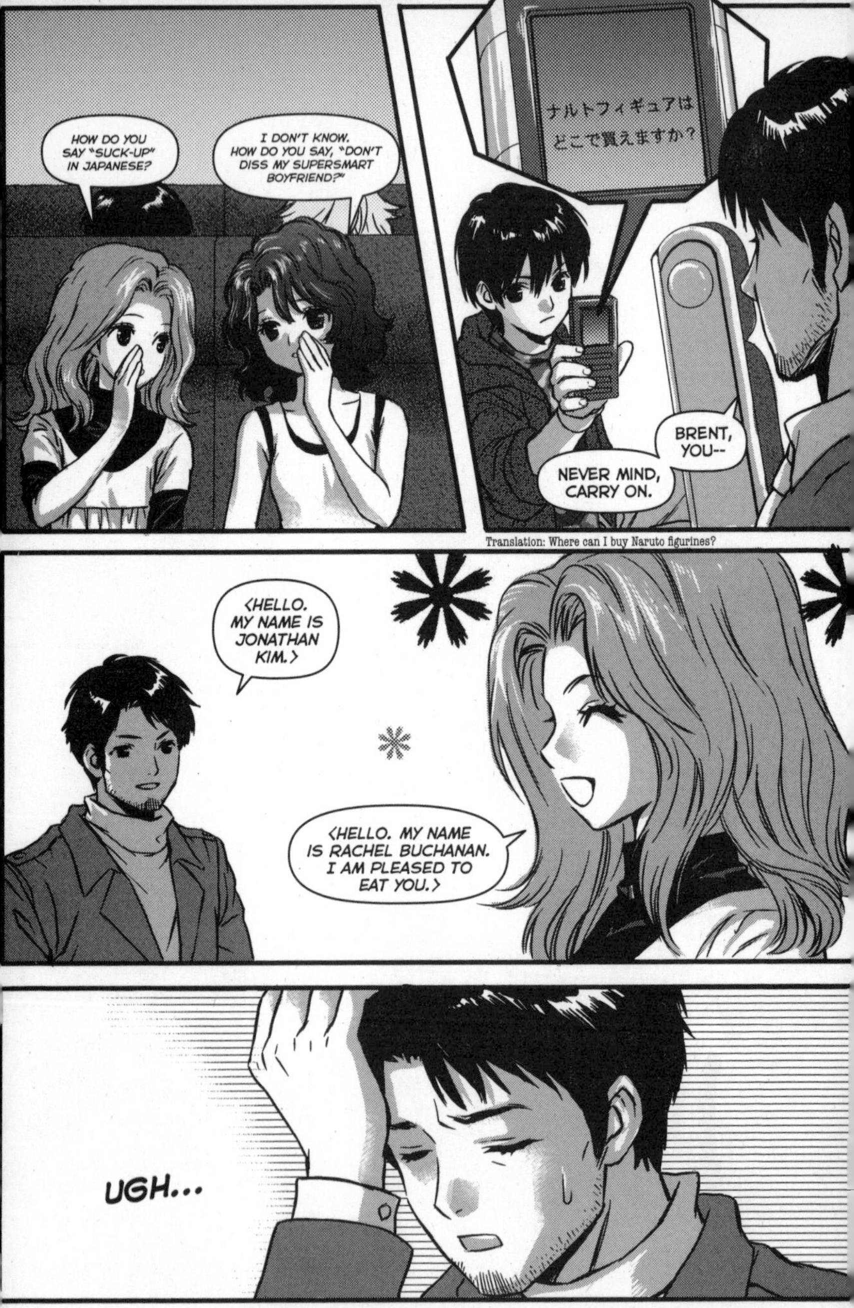
HOW DO YOU SAY "SUCK-UP" IN JAPANESE?
I DON'T KNOW. HOW DO YOU SAY, "DON'T DISS MY SUPERSMART BOYFRIEND?"
ナルトフィギュアはどこで買えますか？
BRENT, YOU--
NEVER MIND, CARRY ON.
Translation: Where can I buy Naruto figurines?
<HELLO. MY NAME IS JONATHAN KIM.>
<HELLO. MY NAME IS RACHEL BUCHANAN. I AM PLEASED TO EAT YOU.>
UGH...

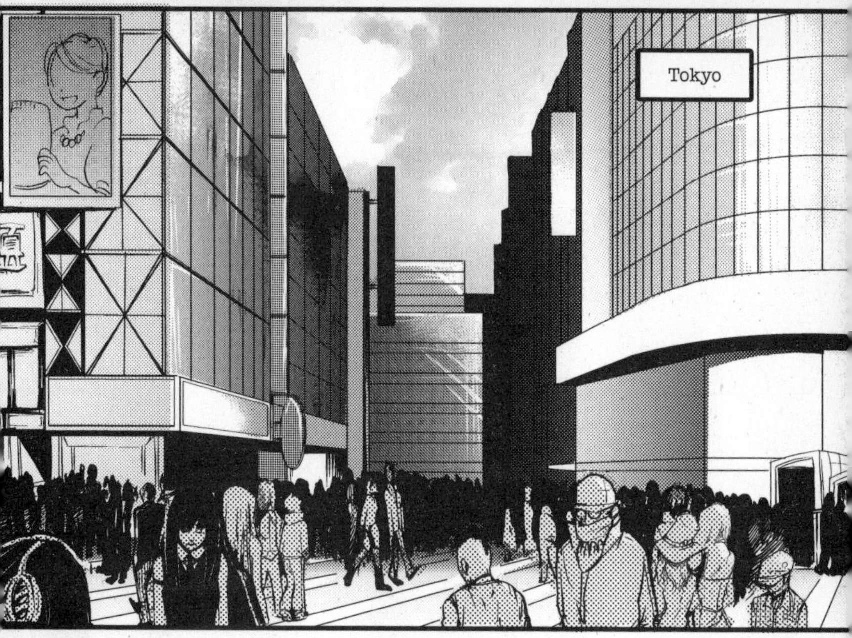
Tokyo
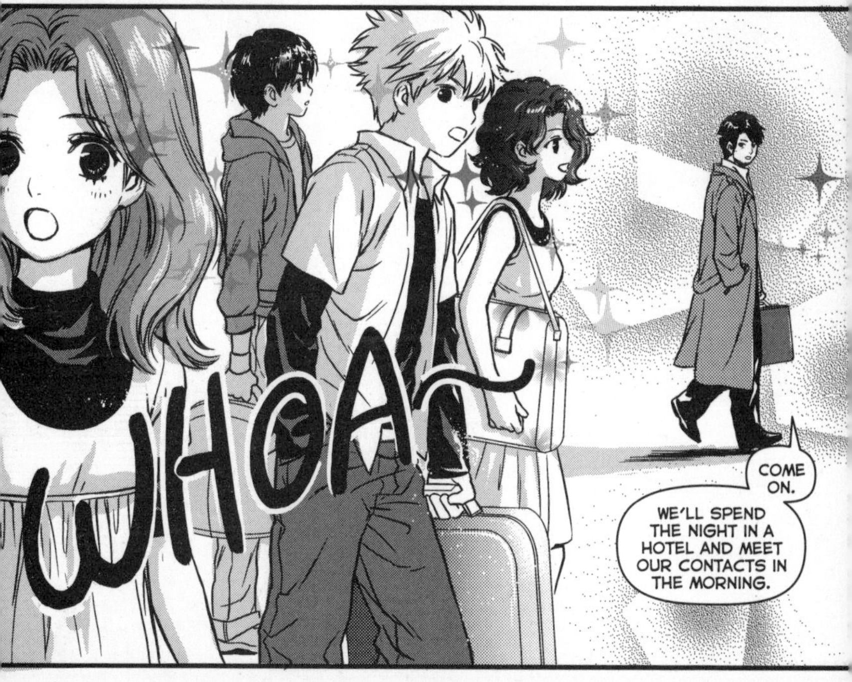
WHOA
COME ON.
WE'LL SPEND THE NIGHT IN A HOTEL AND MEET OUR CONTACTS IN THE MORNING.

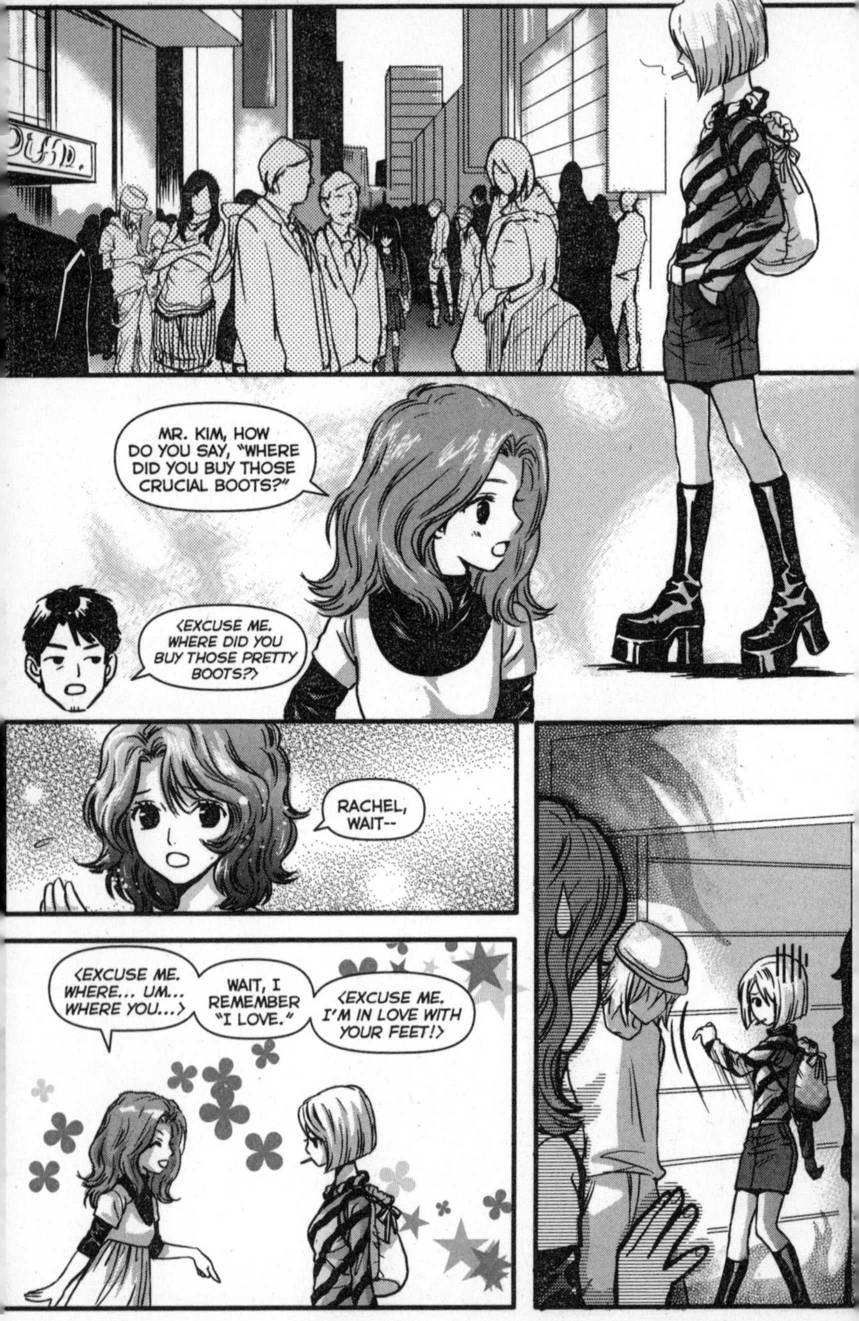
MR. KIM, HOW DO YOU SAY, "WHERE DID YOU BUY THOSE CRUCIAL BOOTS?"
<EXCUSE ME. WHERE DID YOU BUY THOSE PRETTY BOOTS?>
RACHEL, WAIT--
<EXCUSE ME. WHERE... UM... WHERE YOU...>
WAIT, I REMEMBER "I LOVE."
<EXCUSE ME. I'M IN LOVE WITH YOUR FEET!>

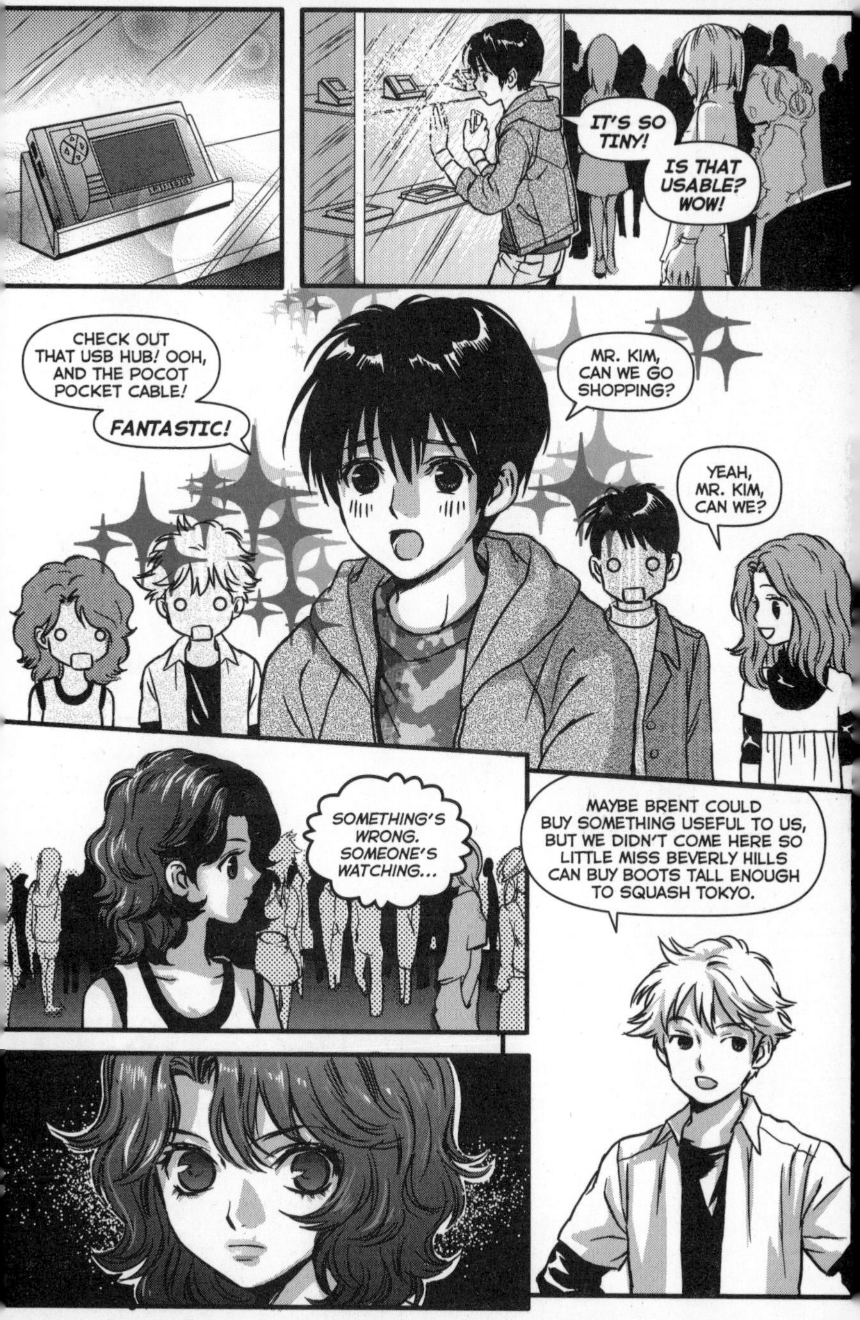
IT'S SO TINY!
IS THAT USABLE? WOW!
CHECK OUT THAT USB HUB! OOH, AND THE POCOT POCKET CABLE!
FANTASTIC!
MR. KIM, CAN WE GO SHOPPING?
YEAH, MR. KIM, CAN WE?
SOMETHING'S WRONG. SOMEONE'S WATCHING...
MAYBE BRENT COULD BUY SOMETHING USEFUL TO US, BUT WE DIDN'T COME HERE SO LITTLE MISS BEVERLY HILLS CAN BUY BOOTS TALL ENOUGH TO SQUASH TOKYO.

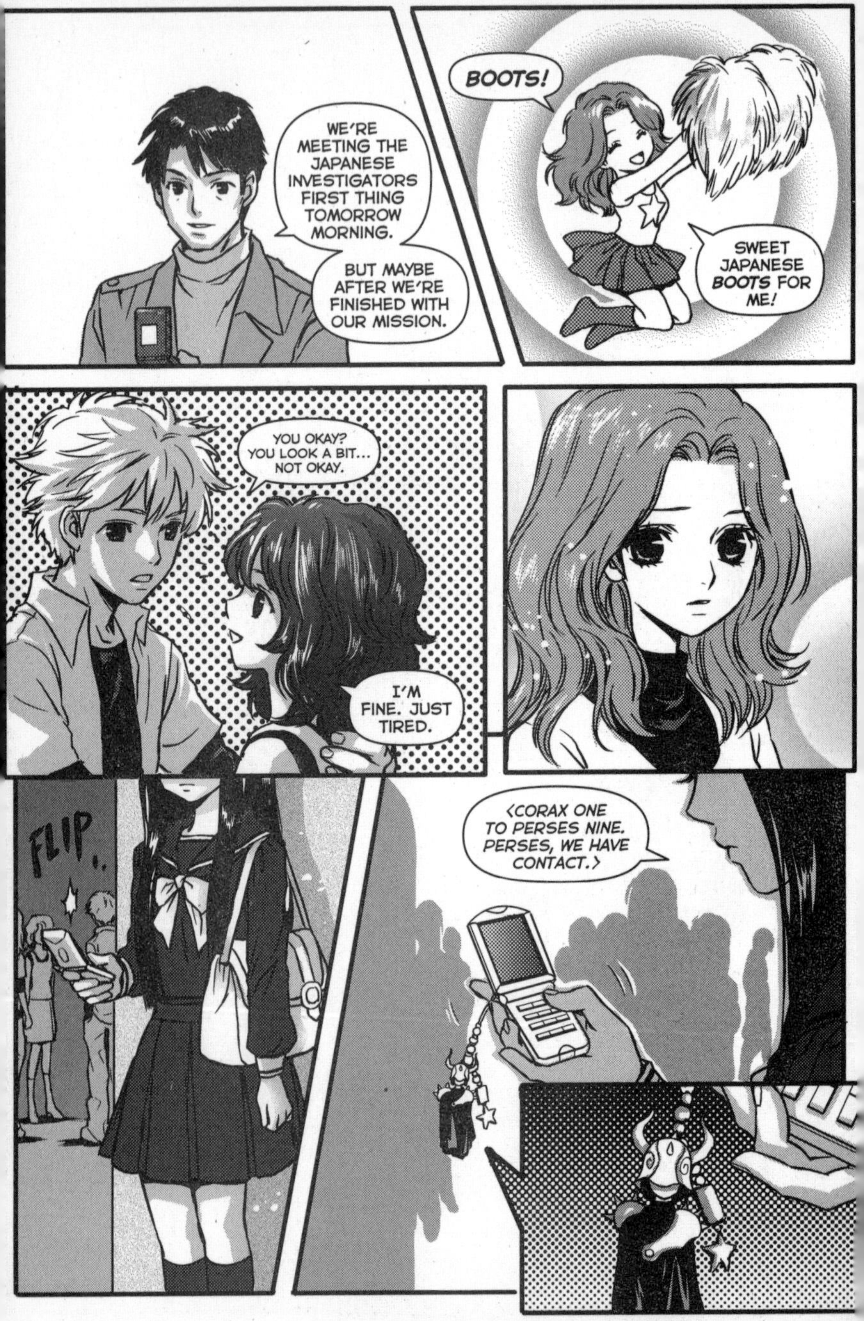
WE'RE MEETING THE JAPANESE INVESTIGATORS FIRST THING TOMORROW MORNING.
BUT MAYBE AFTER WE'RE FINISHED WITH OUR MISSION.
BOOTS!
SWEET JAPANESE BOOTS FOR ME!
YOU OKAY? YOU LOOK A BIT... NOT OKAY.
I'M FINE. JUST TIRED.
FLIP
<CORAX ONE TO PERSES NINE. PERSES, WE HAVE CONTACT.>

Chapter Two

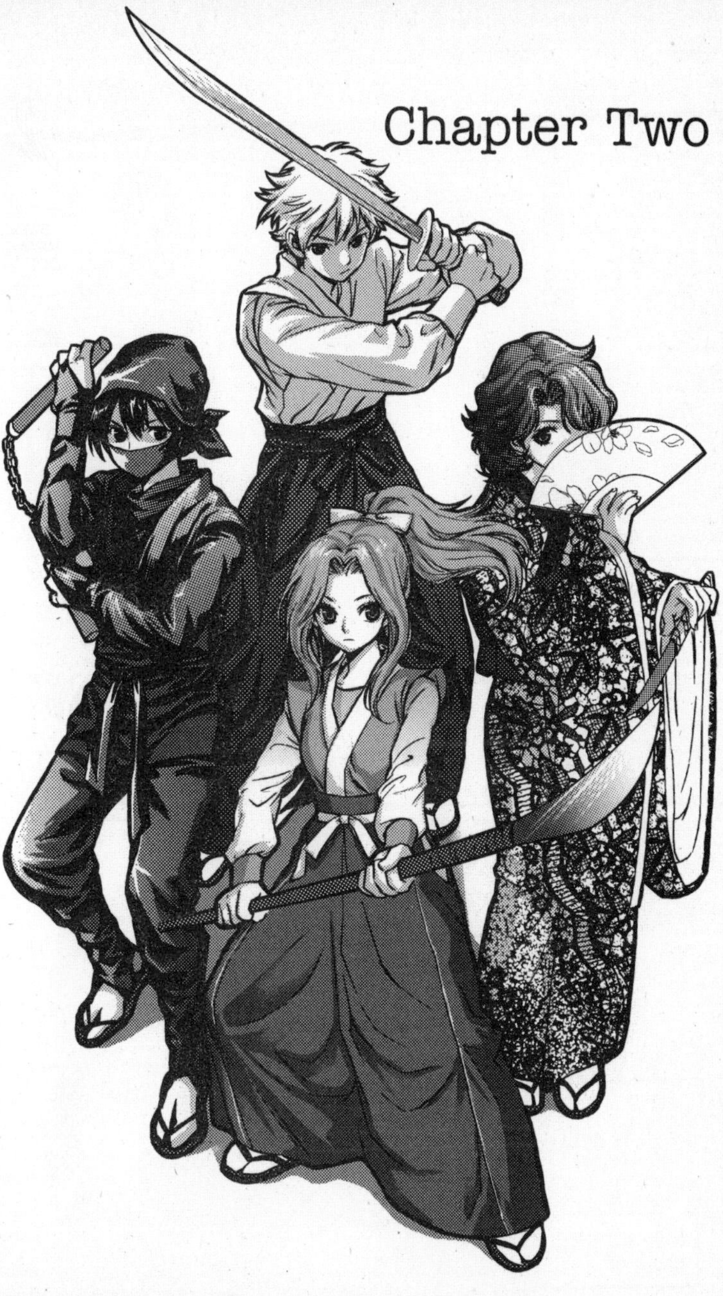

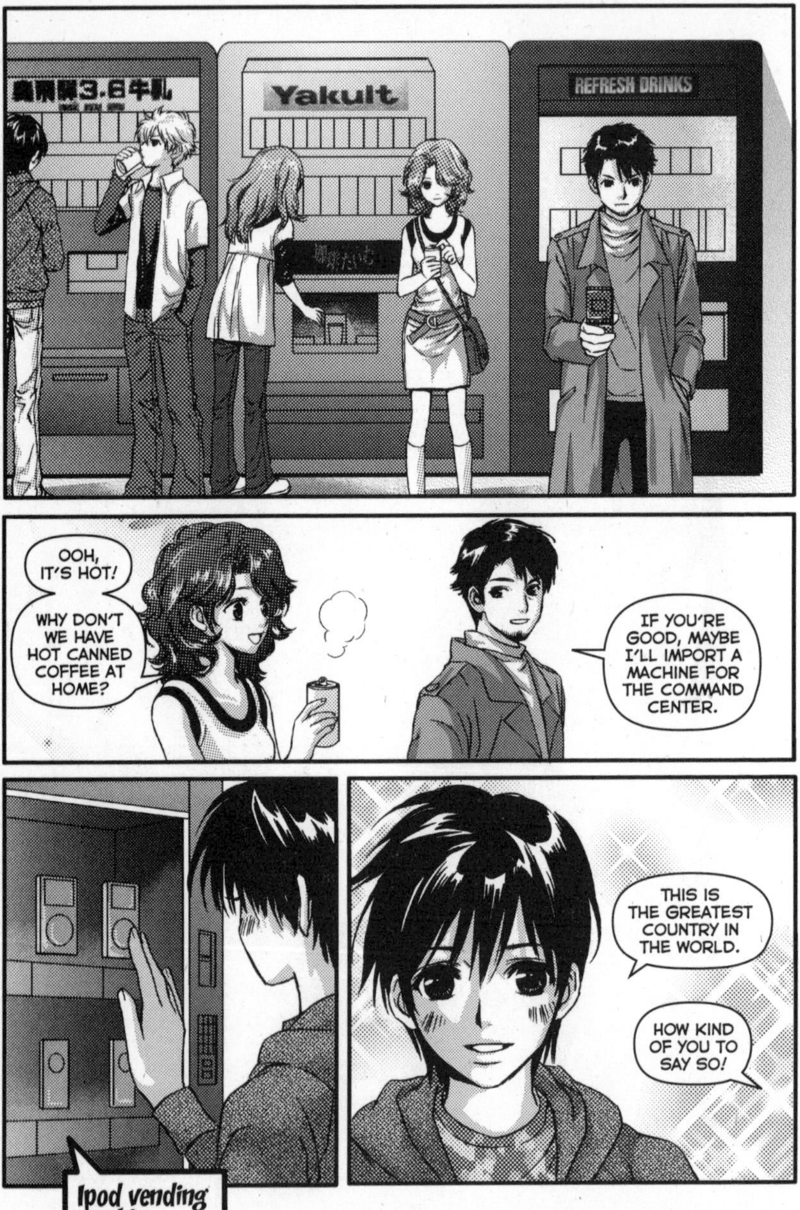
Yakult
REFRESH DRINKS
OOH, IT'S HOT!
WHY DON'T WE HAVE HOT CANNED COFFEE AT HOME?
IF YOU'RE GOOD, MAYBE I'LL IMPORT A MACHINE FOR THE COMMAND CENTER.
Ipod vending machine.
THIS IS THE GREATEST COUNTRY IN THE WORLD.
HOW KIND OF YOU TO SAY SO!

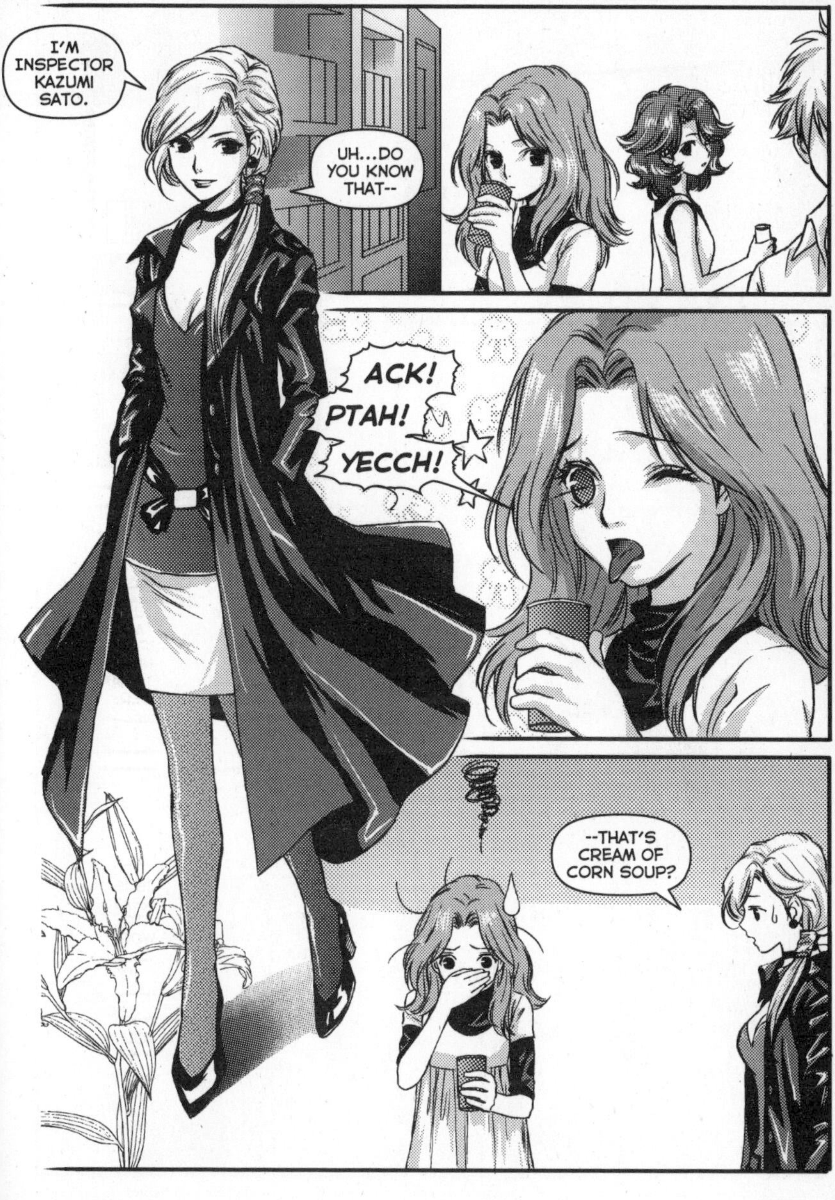
I'M INSPECTOR KAZUMI SATO.
UH...DO YOU KNOW THAT--
ACK!
PTAH!
YECCH!
--THAT'S CREAM OF CORN SOUP?

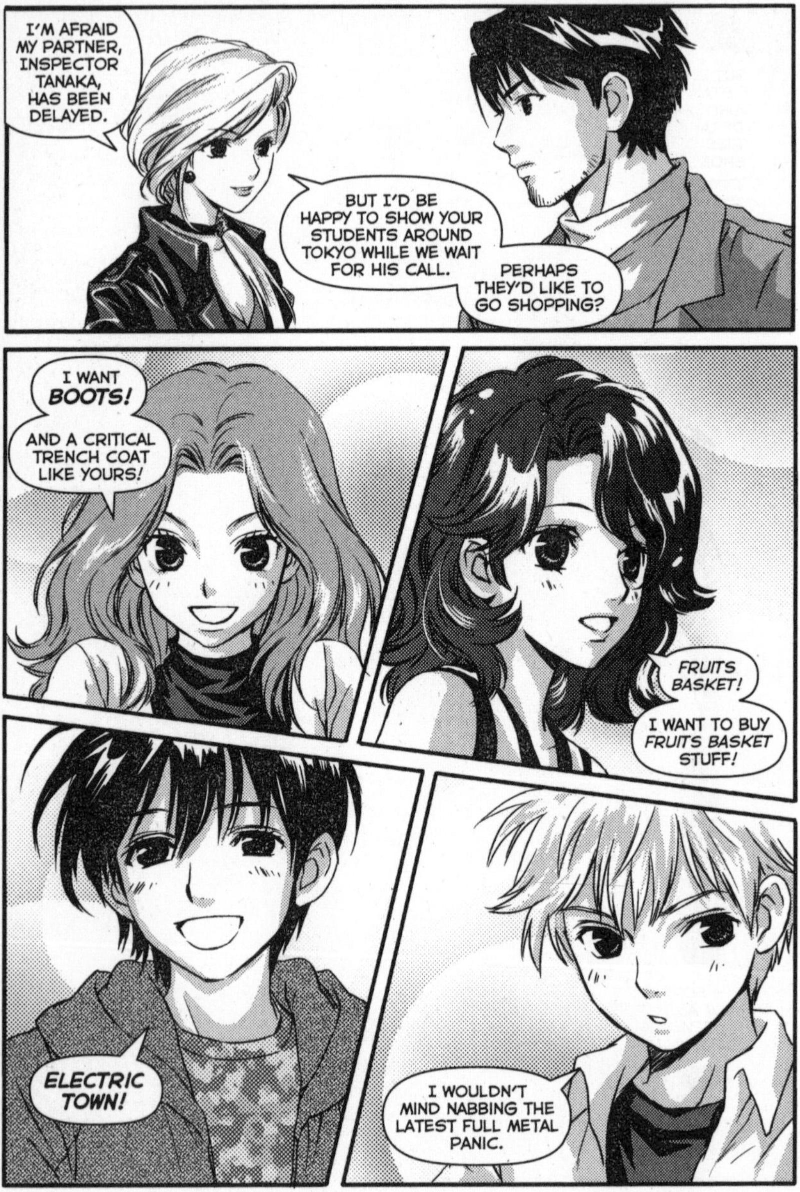
I'M AFRAID MY PARTNER, INSPECTOR TANAKA, HAS BEEN DELAYED.
BUT I'D BE HAPPY TO SHOW YOUR STUDENTS AROUND TOKYO WHILE WE WAIT FOR HIS CALL.
PERHAPS THEY'D LIKE TO GO SHOPPING?
I WANT *BOOTS!*
AND A CRITICAL TRENCH COAT LIKE YOURS!
FRUITS BASKET!
I WANT TO BUY *FRUITS BASKET* STUFF!
ELECTRIC TOWN!
I WOULDN'T MIND NABBING THE LATEST FULL METAL PANIC.

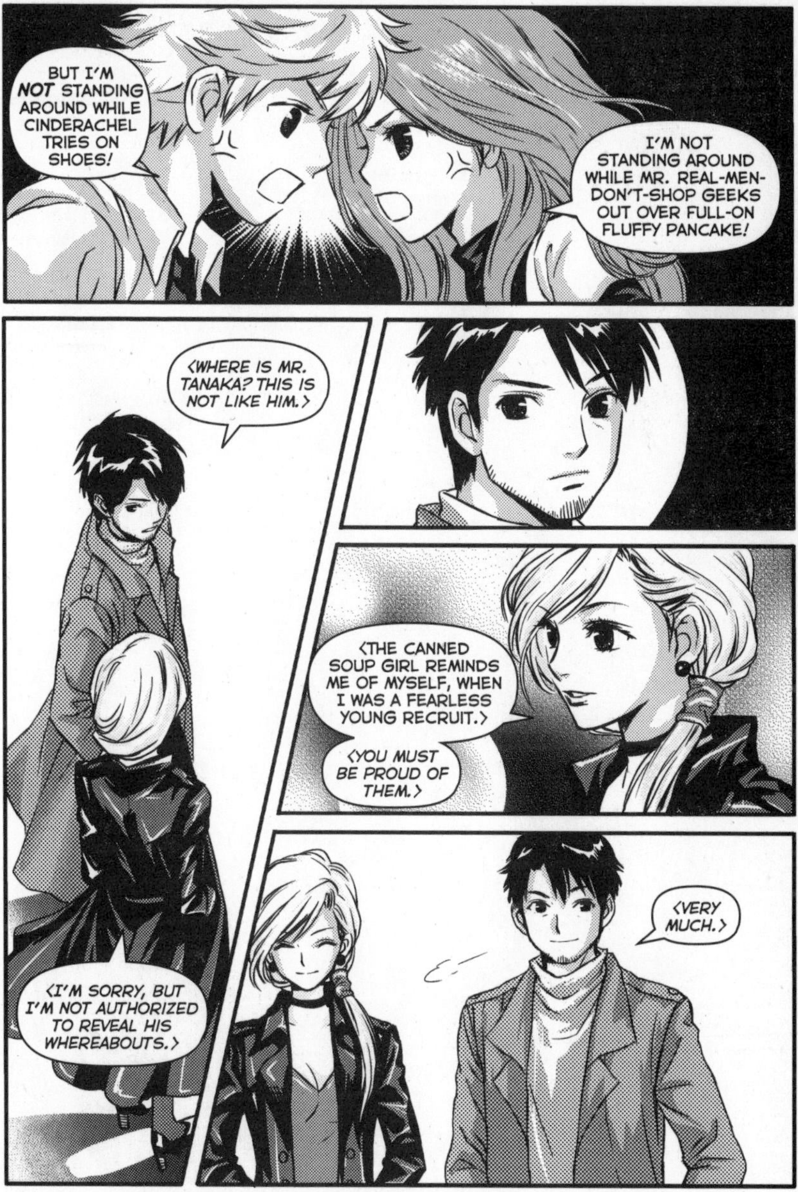
BUT I'M **NOT** STANDING AROUND WHILE CINDERACHEL TRIES ON SHOES!
I'M NOT STANDING AROUND WHILE MR. REAL-MEN-DON'T-SHOP GEEKS OUT OVER FULL-ON FLUFFY PANCAKE!
<WHERE IS MR. TANAKA? THIS IS NOT LIKE HIM.>
<I'M SORRY, BUT I'M NOT AUTHORIZED TO REVEAL HIS WHEREABOUTS.>
<THE CANNED SOUP GIRL REMINDS ME OF MYSELF, WHEN I WAS A FEARLESS YOUNG RECRUIT.>
<YOU MUST BE PROUD OF THEM.>
<VERY MUCH.>

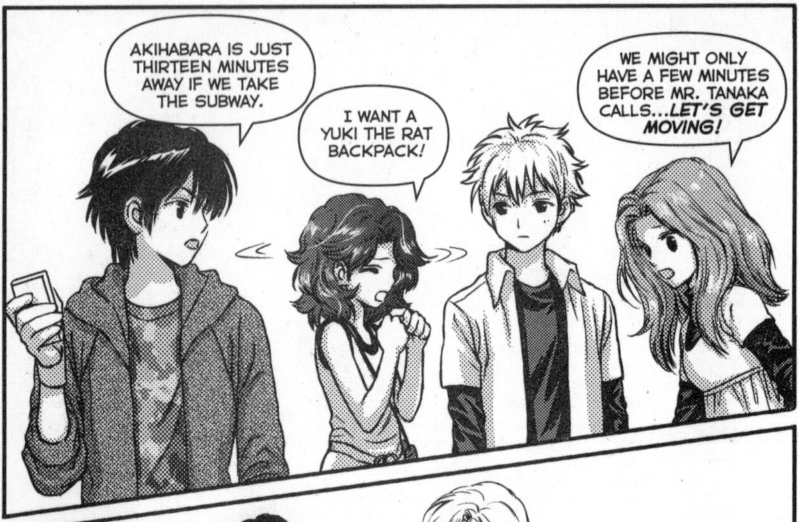
AKIHABARA IS JUST THIRTEEN MINUTES AWAY IF WE TAKE THE SUBWAY.
I WANT A YUKI THE RAT BACKPACK!
WE MIGHT ONLY HAVE A FEW MINUTES BEFORE MR. TANAKA CALLS...*LET'S GET MOVING!*

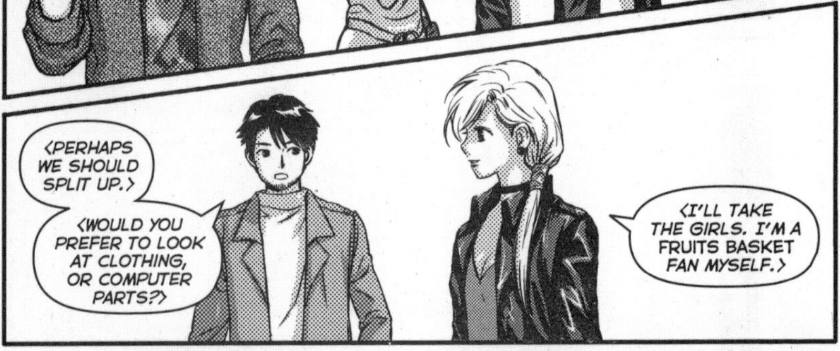
<PERHAPS WE SHOULD SPLIT UP.>
<WOULD YOU PREFER TO LOOK AT CLOTHING, OR COMPUTER PARTS?>
<I'LL TAKE THE GIRLS. I'M A FRUITS BASKET FAN MYSELF.>

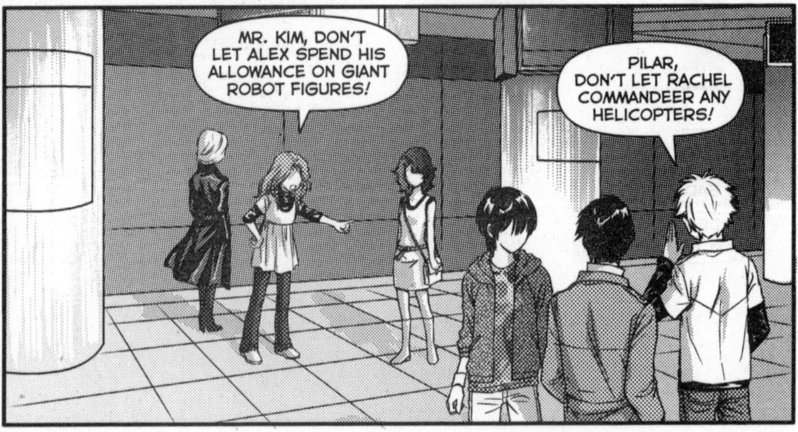
MR. KIM, DON'T LET ALEX SPEND HIS ALLOWANCE ON GIANT ROBOT FIGURES!
PILAR, DON'T LET RACHEL COMMANDEER ANY HELICOPTERS!

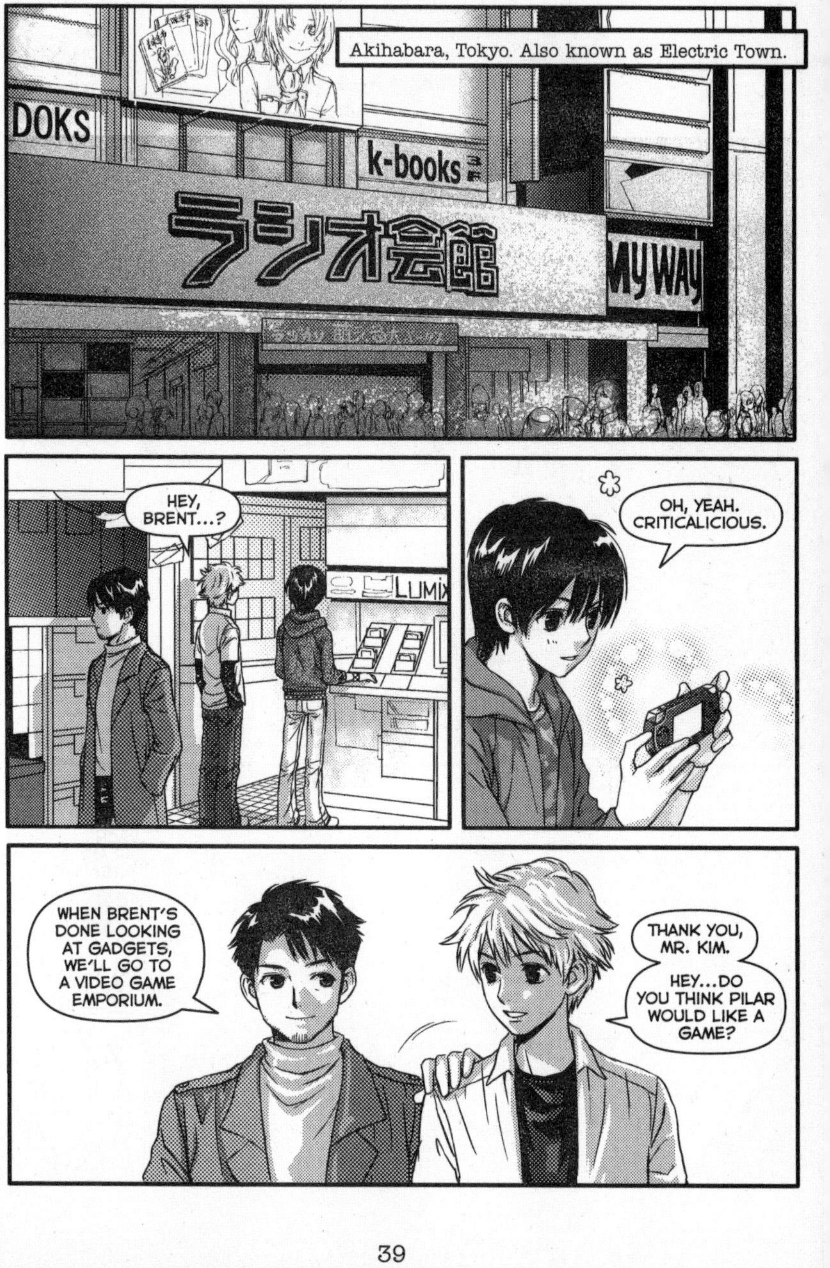
Akihabara, Tokyo. Also known as Electric Town.
DOKS
k-books
ラジオ会館
MY WAY
HEY, BRENT...?
LUMIX
OH, YEAH. CRITICALICIOUS.
WHEN BRENT'S DONE LOOKING AT GADGETS, WE'LL GO TO A VIDEO GAME EMPORIUM.
THANK YOU, MR. KIM.
HEY...DO YOU THINK PILAR WOULD LIKE A GAME?

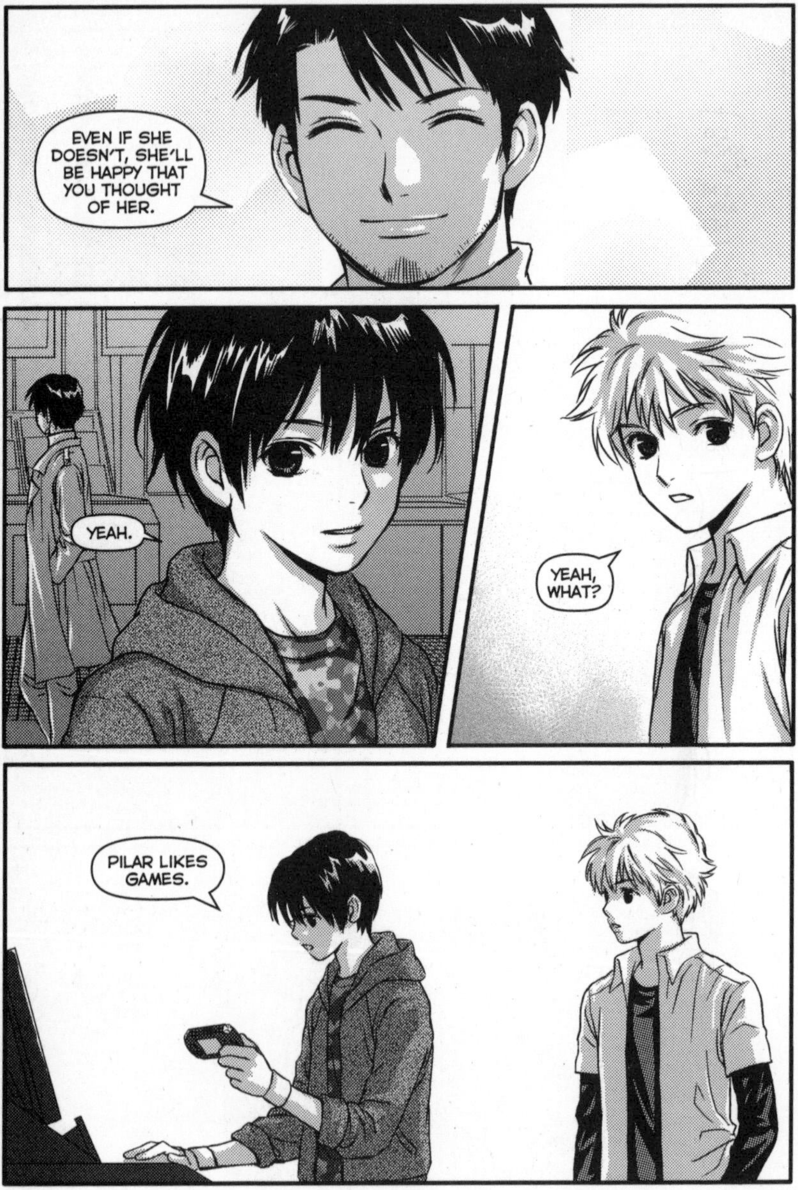
EVEN IF SHE DOESN'T, SHE'LL BE HAPPY THAT YOU THOUGHT OF HER.
YEAH.
YEAH, WHAT?
PILAR LIKES GAMES.

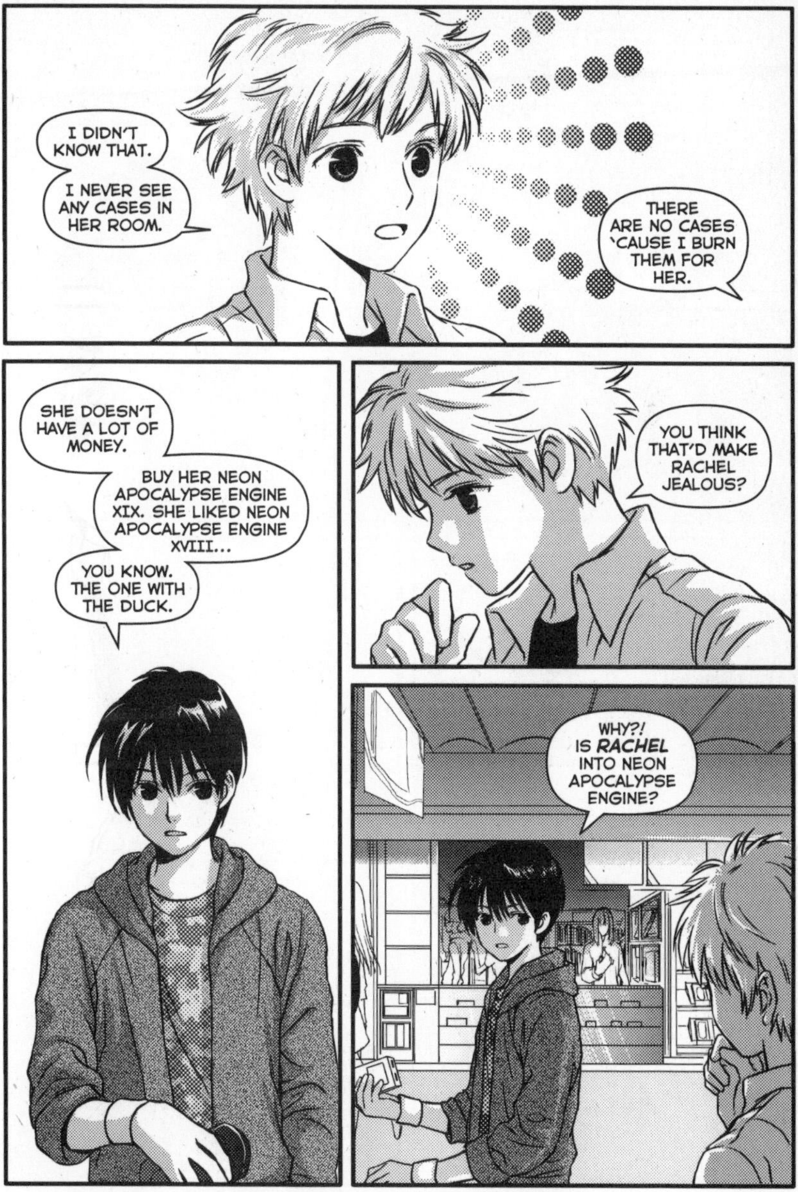
I DIDN'T KNOW THAT.
I NEVER SEE ANY CASES IN HER ROOM.
THERE ARE NO CASES 'CAUSE I BURN THEM FOR HER.
SHE DOESN'T HAVE A LOT OF MONEY.
BUY HER NEON APOCALYPSE ENGINE XIX. SHE LIKED NEON APOCALYPSE ENGINE XVIII...
YOU KNOW. THE ONE WITH THE DUCK.
YOU THINK THAT'D MAKE RACHEL JEALOUS?
WHY?! IS *RACHEL* INTO NEON APOCALYPSE ENGINE?

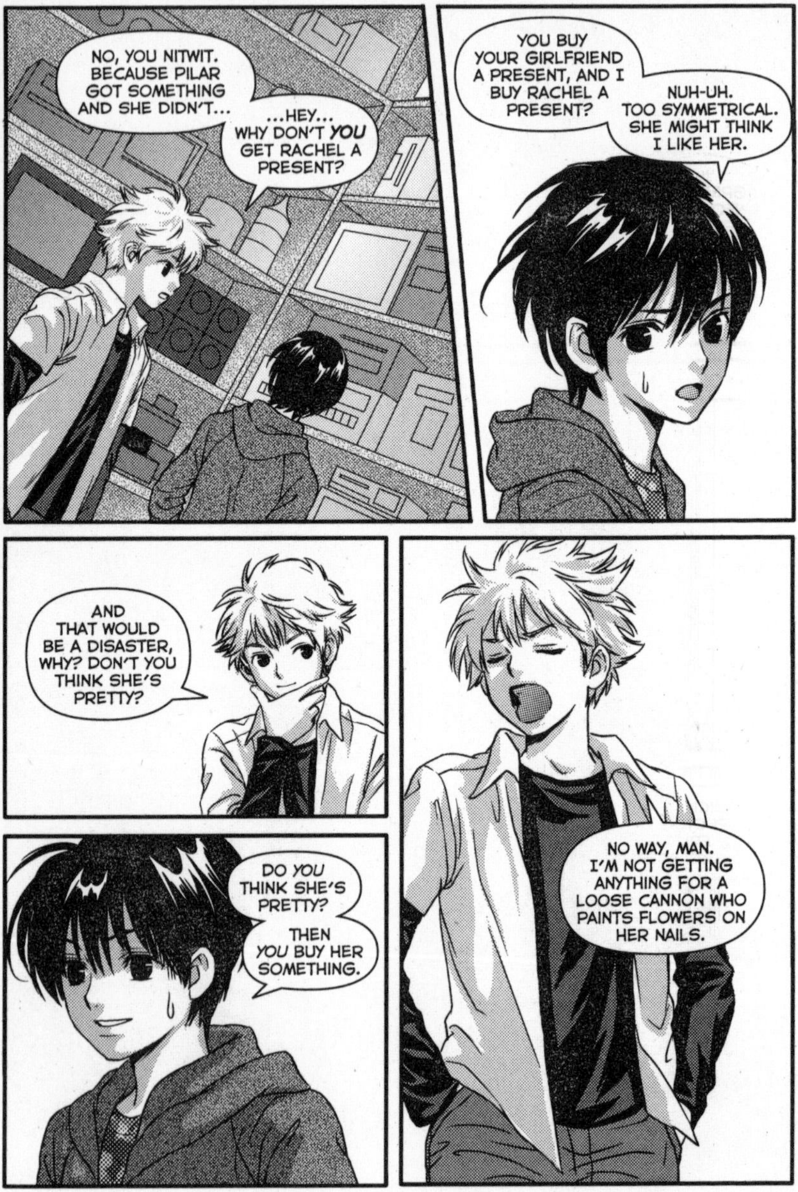
NO, YOU NITWIT. BECAUSE PILAR GOT SOMETHING AND SHE DIDN'T...
...HEY... WHY DON'T *YOU* GET RACHEL A PRESENT?
YOU BUY YOUR GIRLFRIEND A PRESENT, AND I BUY RACHEL A PRESENT?
NUH-UH. TOO SYMMETRICAL. SHE MIGHT THINK I LIKE HER.
AND THAT WOULD BE A DISASTER, WHY? DON'T YOU THINK SHE'S PRETTY?
DO *YOU* THINK SHE'S PRETTY?
THEN *YOU* BUY HER SOMETHING.
NO WAY, MAN. I'M NOT GETTING ANYTHING FOR A LOOSE CANNON WHO PAINTS FLOWERS ON HER NAILS.

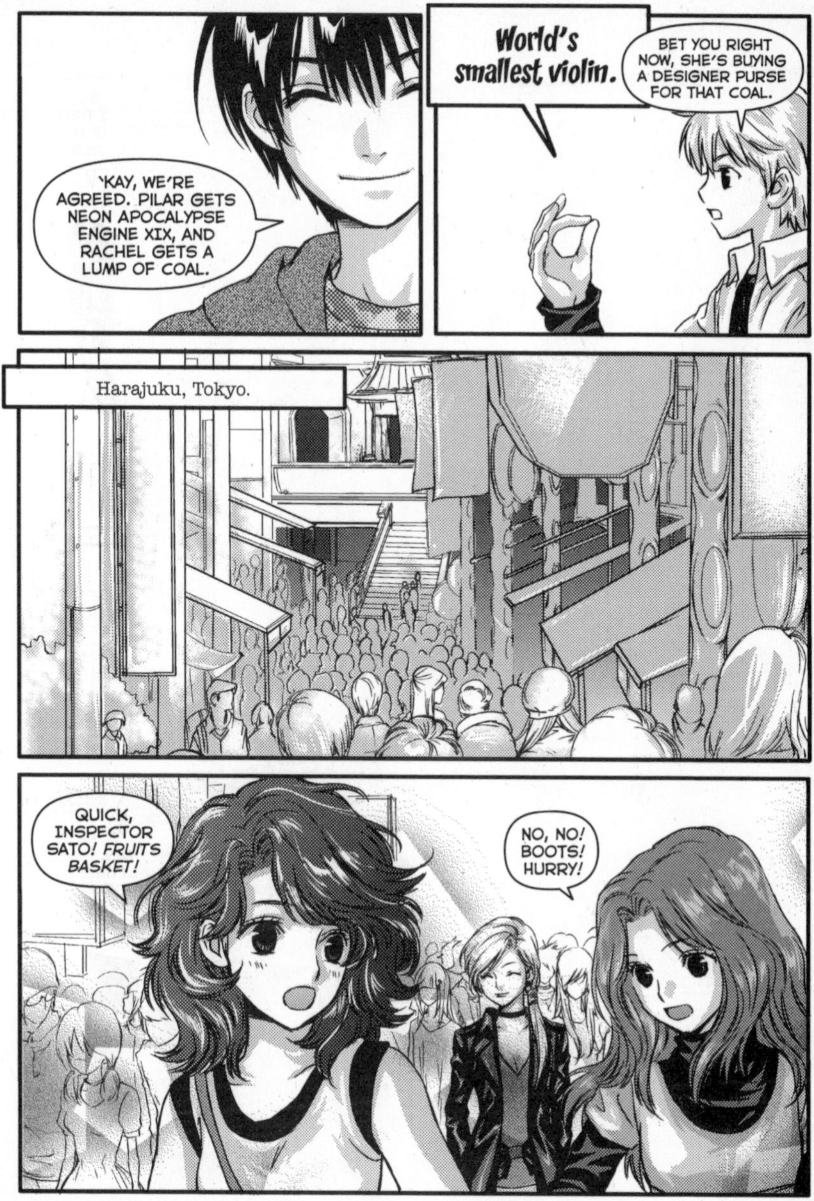
'KAY, WE'RE AGREED. PILAR GETS NEON APOCALYPSE ENGINE XIX, AND RACHEL GETS A LUMP OF COAL.
World's smallest violin.
BET YOU RIGHT NOW, SHE'S BUYING A DESIGNER PURSE FOR THAT COAL.
Harajuku, Tokyo.
QUICK, INSPECTOR SATO! *FRUITS BASKET*!
NO, NO! BOOTS! HURRY!

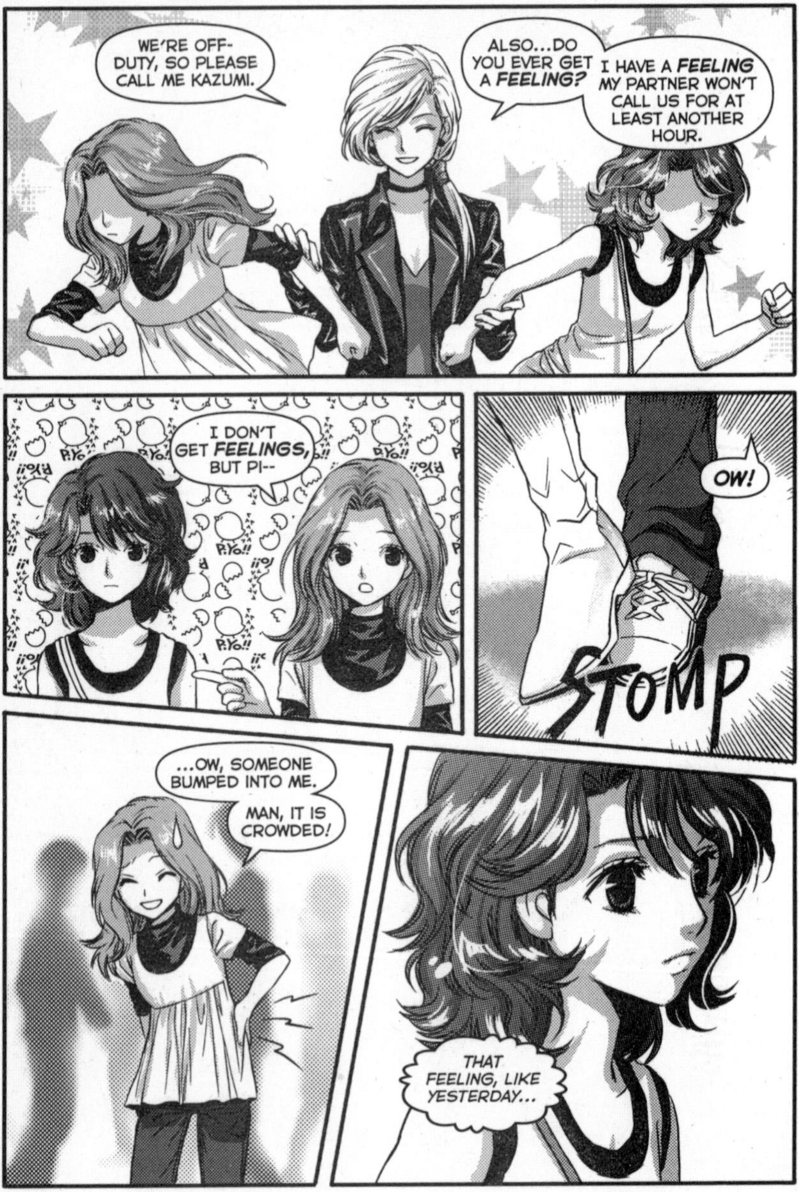
WE'RE OFF-DUTY, SO PLEASE CALL ME KAZUMI.
ALSO...DO YOU EVER GET A *FEELING?*
I HAVE A *FEELING* MY PARTNER WON'T CALL US FOR AT LEAST ANOTHER HOUR.
I DON'T GET *FEELINGS,* BUT PI--
OW!
STOMP
...OW, SOMEONE BUMPED INTO ME.
MAN, IT IS CROWDED!
THAT FEELING, LIKE YESTERDAY...

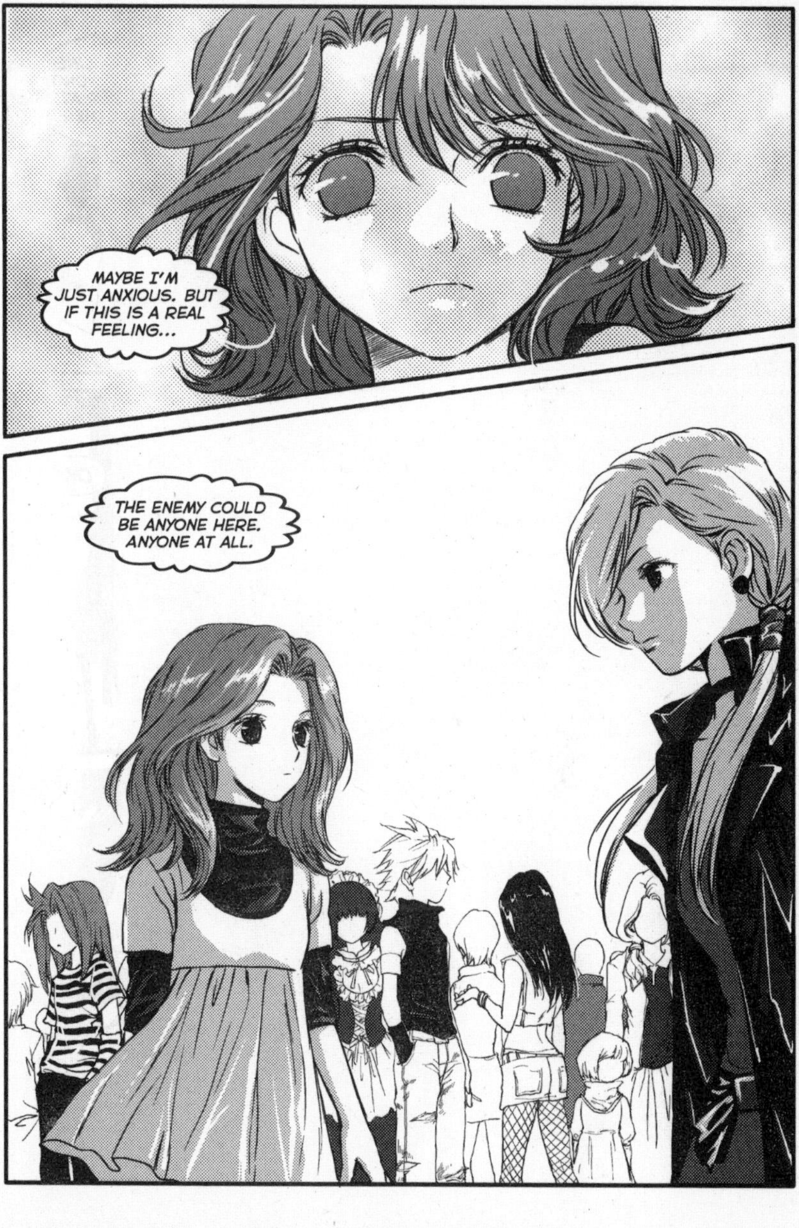
MAYBE I'M JUST ANXIOUS. BUT IF THIS IS A REAL FEELING...
THE ENEMY COULD BE ANYONE HERE. ANYONE AT ALL.

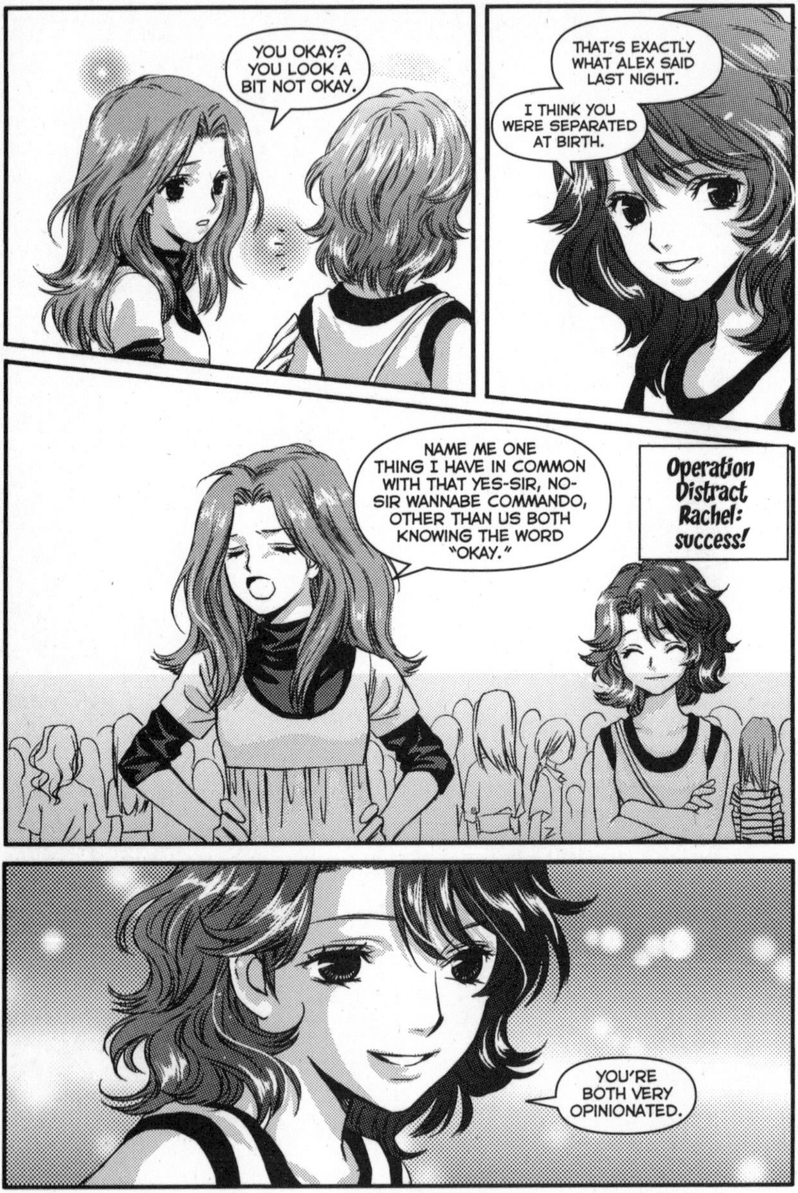
YOU OKAY? YOU LOOK A BIT NOT OKAY.
THAT'S EXACTLY WHAT ALEX SAID LAST NIGHT.
I THINK YOU WERE SEPARATED AT BIRTH.
NAME ME ONE THING I HAVE IN COMMON WITH THAT YES-SIR, NO-SIR WANNABE COMMANDO, OTHER THAN US BOTH KNOWING THE WORD "OKAY."
Operation Distract Rachel: success!
YOU'RE BOTH VERY OPINIONATED.

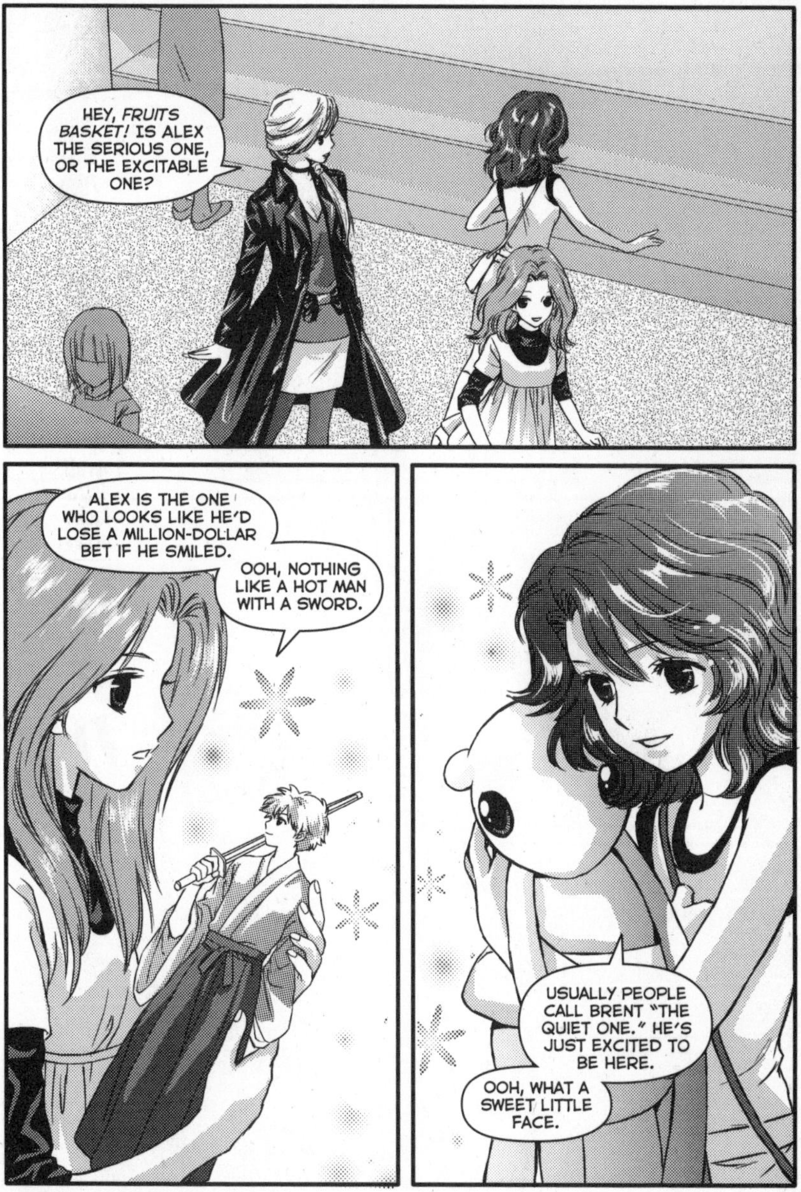
HEY, *FRUITS BASKET!* IS ALEX THE SERIOUS ONE, OR THE EXCITABLE ONE?
ALEX IS THE ONE WHO LOOKS LIKE HE'D LOSE A MILLION-DOLLAR BET IF HE SMILED.
OOH, NOTHING LIKE A HOT MAN WITH A SWORD.
USUALLY PEOPLE CALL BRENT "THE QUIET ONE." HE'S JUST EXCITED TO BE HERE.
OOH, WHAT A SWEET LITTLE FACE.

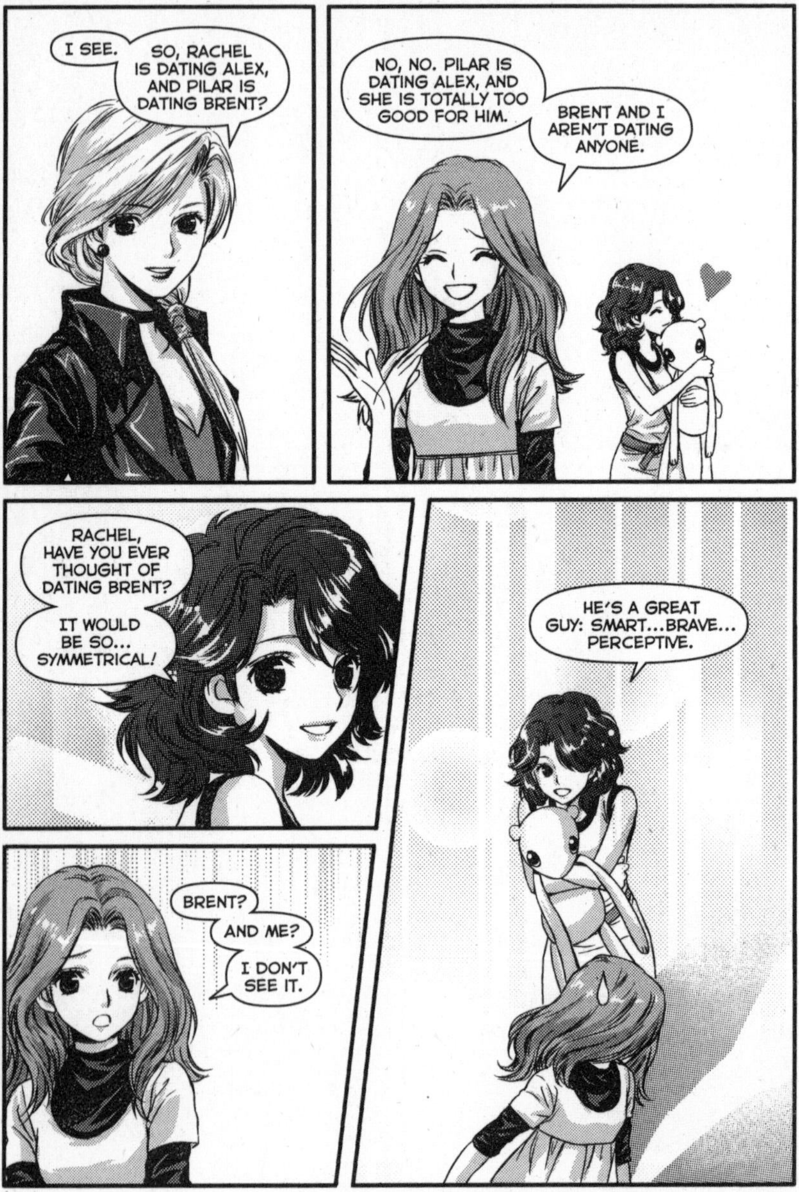
I SEE.
SO, RACHEL IS DATING ALEX, AND PILAR IS DATING BRENT?
NO, NO. PILAR IS DATING ALEX, AND SHE IS TOTALLY TOO GOOD FOR HIM.
BRENT AND I AREN'T DATING ANYONE.
RACHEL, HAVE YOU EVER THOUGHT OF DATING BRENT?
IT WOULD BE SO... SYMMETRICAL!
BRENT?
AND ME?
I DON'T SEE IT.
HE'S A GREAT GUY: SMART...BRAVE... PERCEPTIVE.

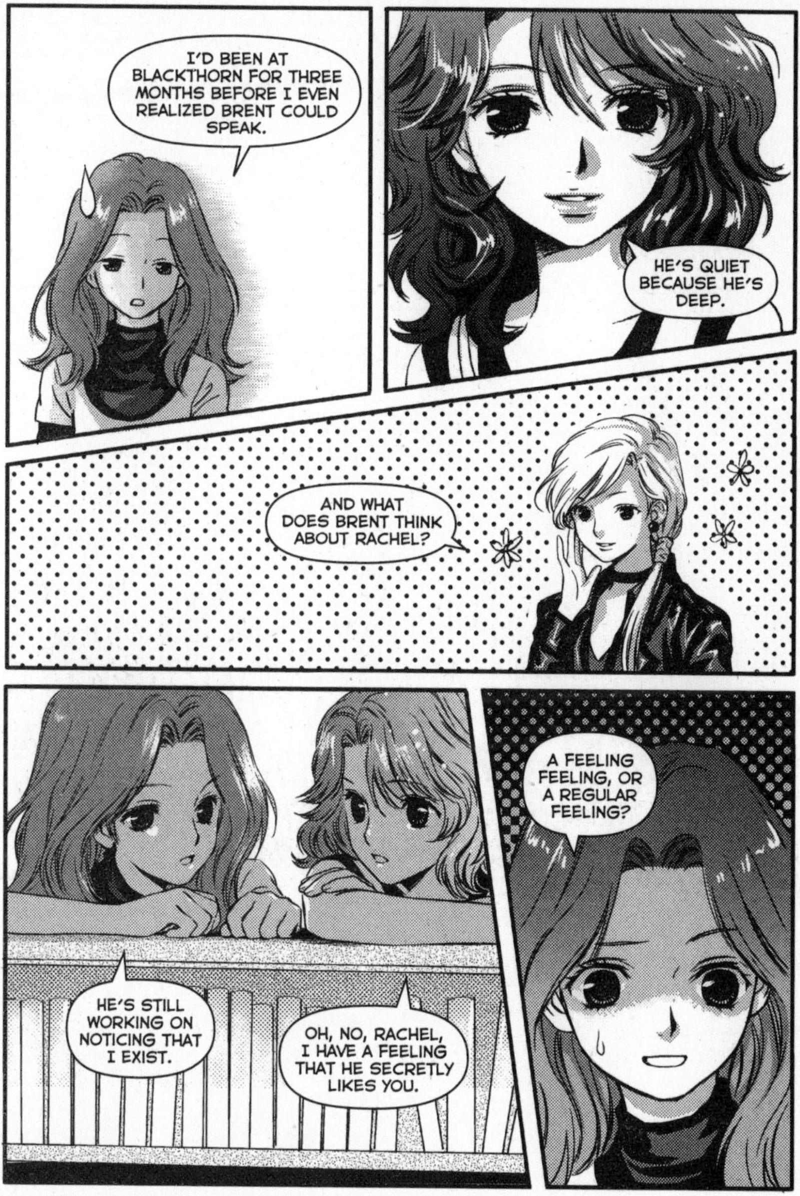
I'D BEEN AT BLACKTHORN FOR THREE MONTHS BEFORE I EVEN REALIZED BRENT COULD SPEAK.
HE'S QUIET BECAUSE HE'S DEEP.
AND WHAT DOES BRENT THINK ABOUT RACHEL?
HE'S STILL WORKING ON NOTICING THAT I EXIST.
OH, NO, RACHEL, I HAVE A FEELING THAT HE SECRETLY LIKES YOU.
A FEELING FEELING, OR A REGULAR FEELING?

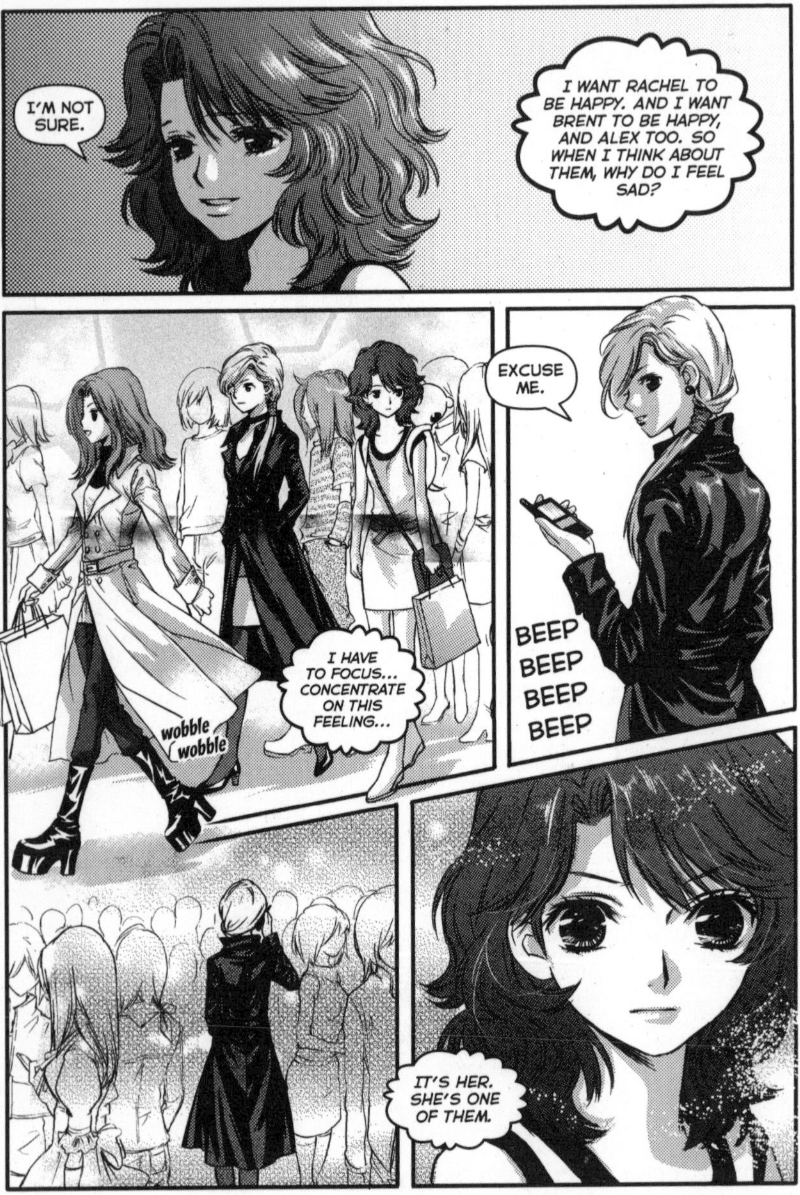
I'M NOT SURE.
I WANT RACHEL TO BE HAPPY. AND I WANT BRENT TO BE HAPPY, AND ALEX TOO. SO WHEN I THINK ABOUT THEM, WHY DO I FEEL SAD?
wobble wobble
I HAVE TO FOCUS... CONCENTRATE ON THIS FEELING...
EXCUSE ME.
BEEP BEEP BEEP BEEP
IT'S HER. SHE'S ONE OF THEM.

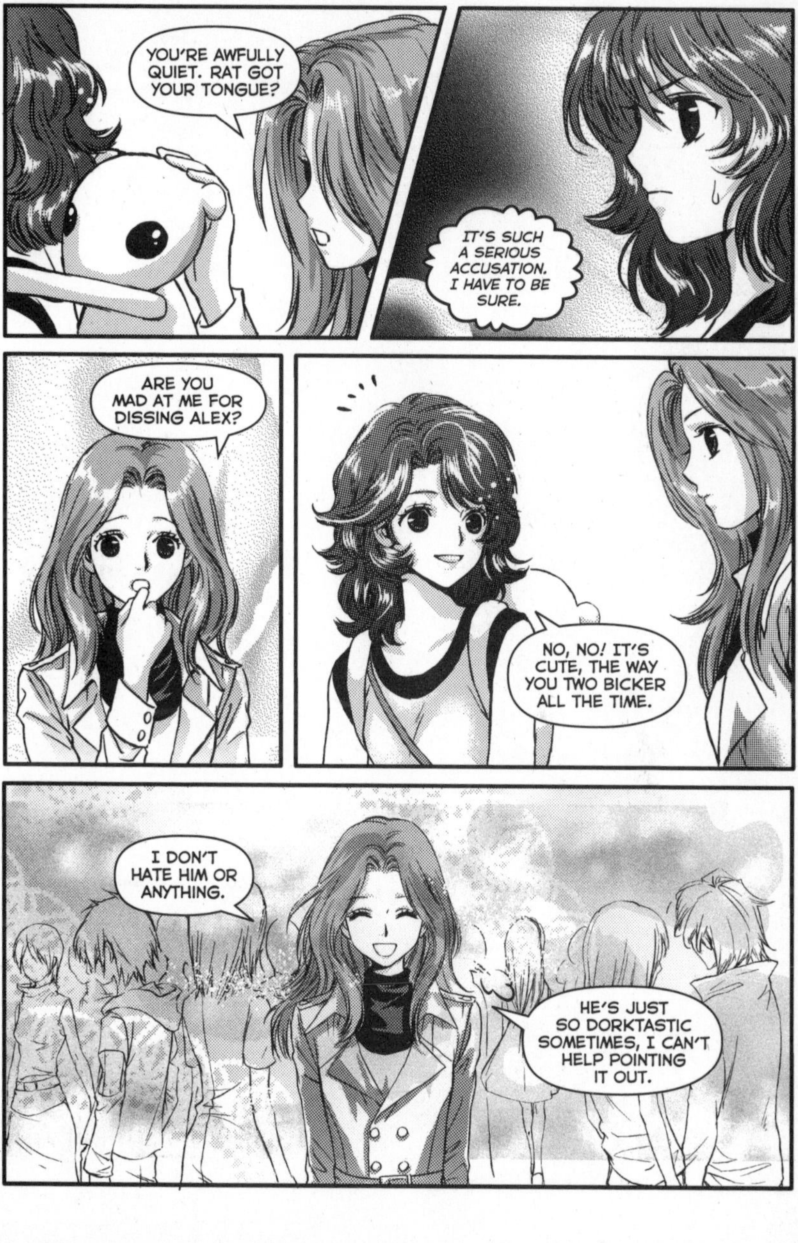
YOU'RE AWFULLY QUIET. RAT GOT YOUR TONGUE?
IT'S SUCH A SERIOUS ACCUSATION. I HAVE TO BE SURE.
ARE YOU MAD AT ME FOR DISSING ALEX?
NO, NO! IT'S CUTE, THE WAY YOU TWO BICKER ALL THE TIME.
I DON'T HATE HIM OR ANYTHING.
HE'S JUST SO DORKTASTIC SOMETIMES, I CAN'T HELP POINTING IT OUT.

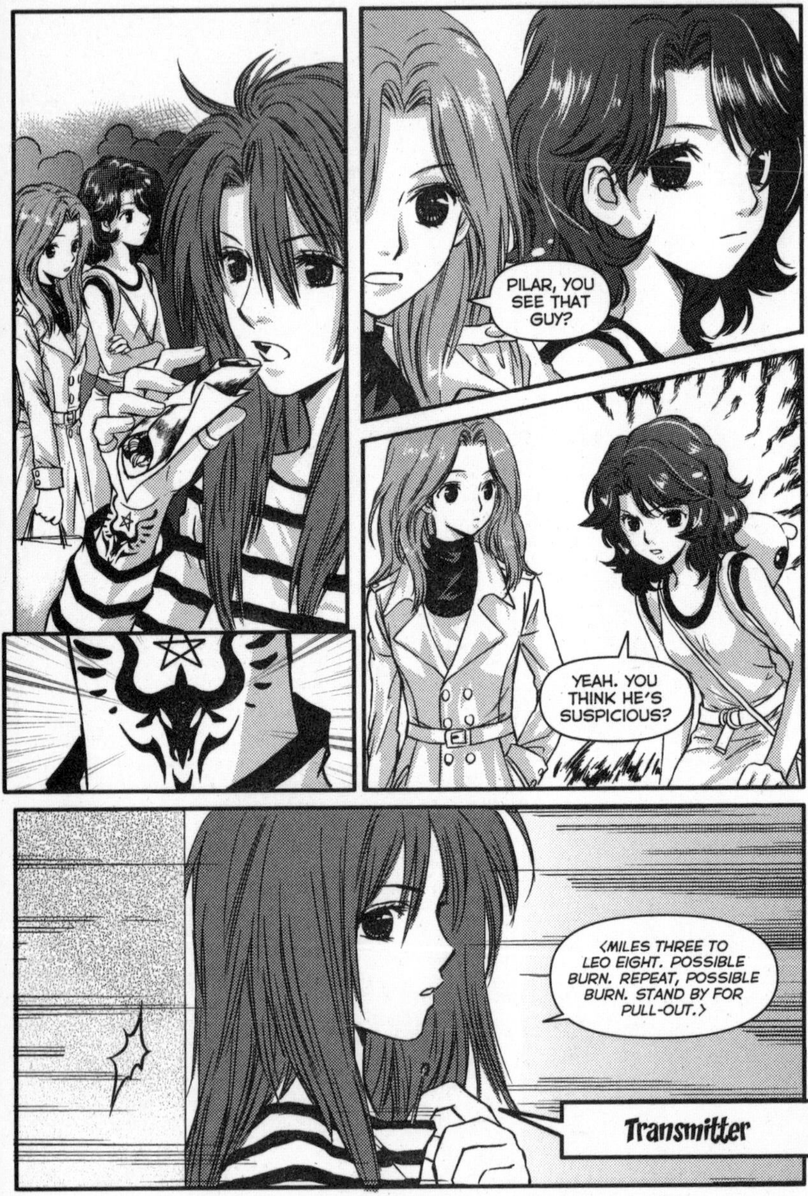
PILAR, YOU SEE THAT GUY?
YEAH. YOU THINK HE'S SUSPICIOUS?
<MILES THREE TO LEO EIGHT. POSSIBLE BURN. REPEAT, POSSIBLE BURN. STAND BY FOR PULL-OUT.>
Transmitter

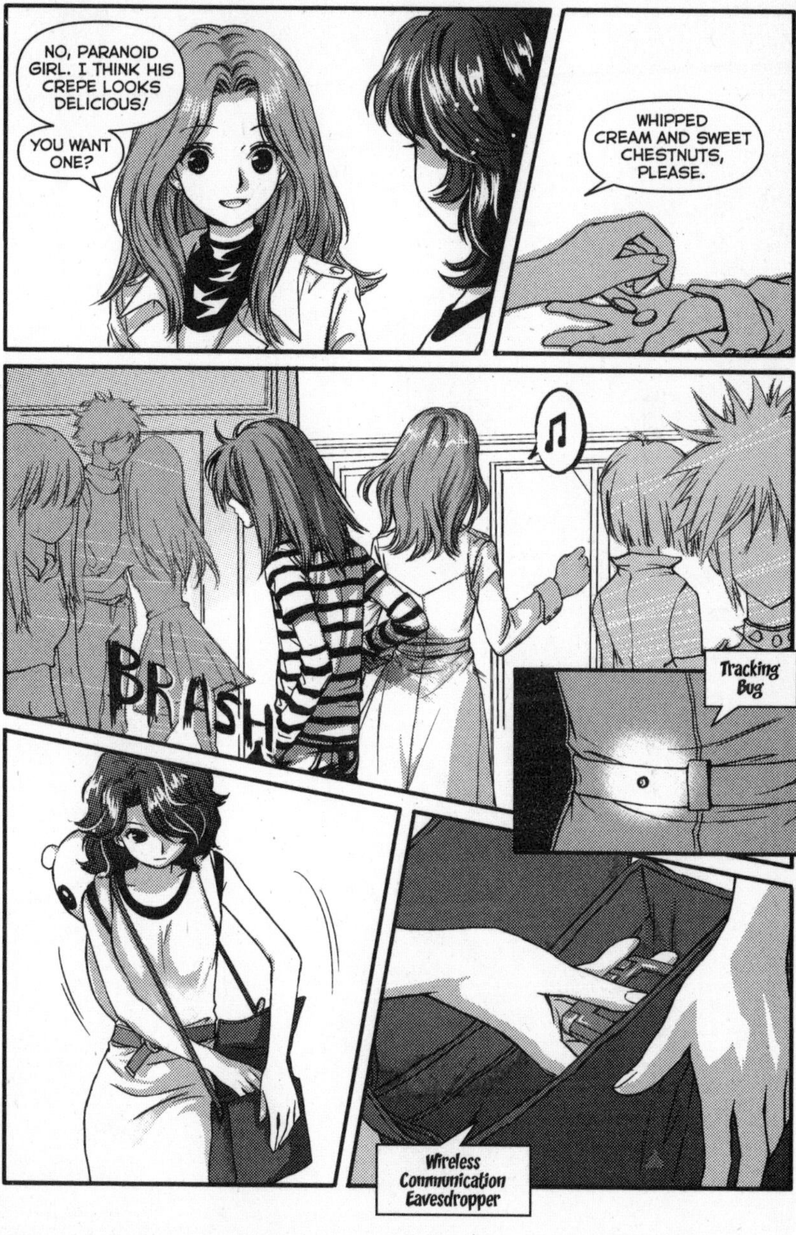
NO, PARANOID GIRL. I THINK HIS CREPE LOOKS DELICIOUS!
YOU WANT ONE?
WHIPPED CREAM AND SWEET CHESTNUTS, PLEASE.
♫
BRASH
Tracking Bug
Wireless Communication Eavesdropper

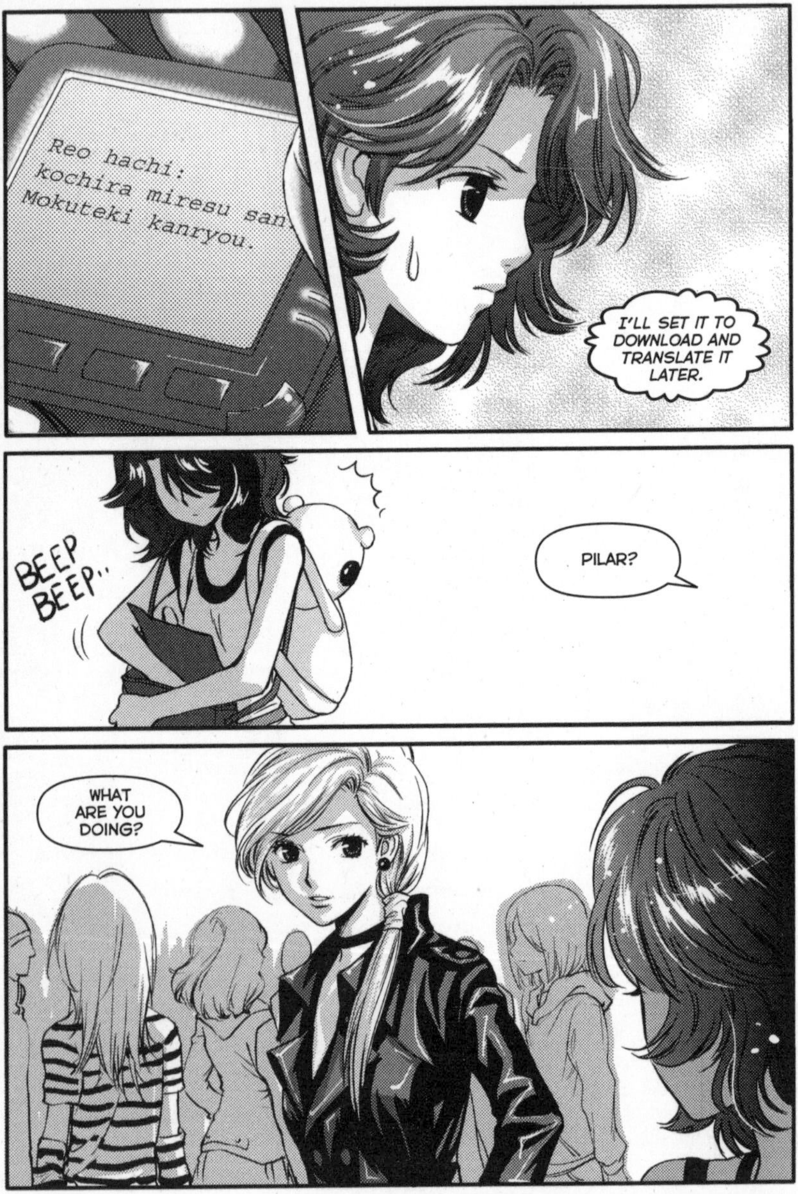
Reo hachi:
kochira miresu san.
Mokuteki kanryou.
I'LL SET IT TO DOWNLOAD AND TRANSLATE IT LATER.
BEEP BEEP..
PILAR?
WHAT ARE YOU DOING?

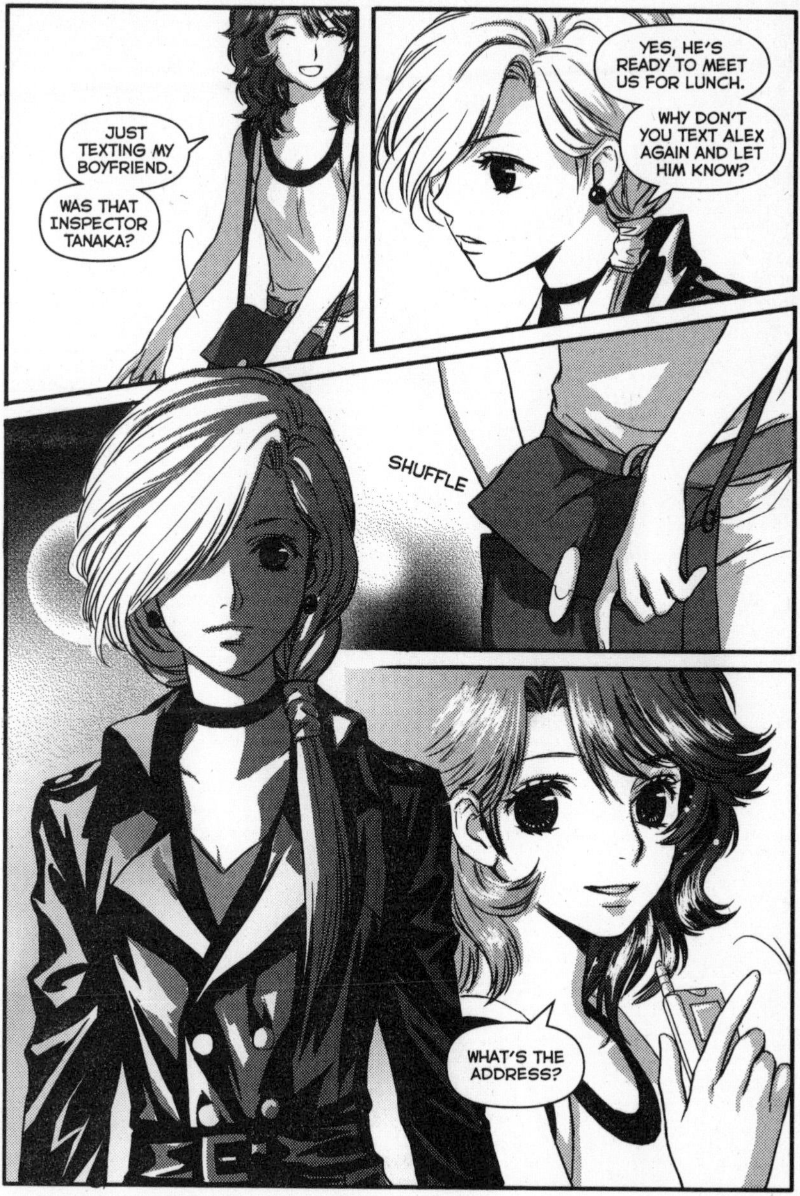
JUST TEXTING MY BOYFRIEND.
WAS THAT INSPECTOR TANAKA?
YES, HE'S READY TO MEET US FOR LUNCH.
WHY DON'T YOU TEXT ALEX AGAIN AND LET HIM KNOW?
SHUFFLE
WHAT'S THE ADDRESS?

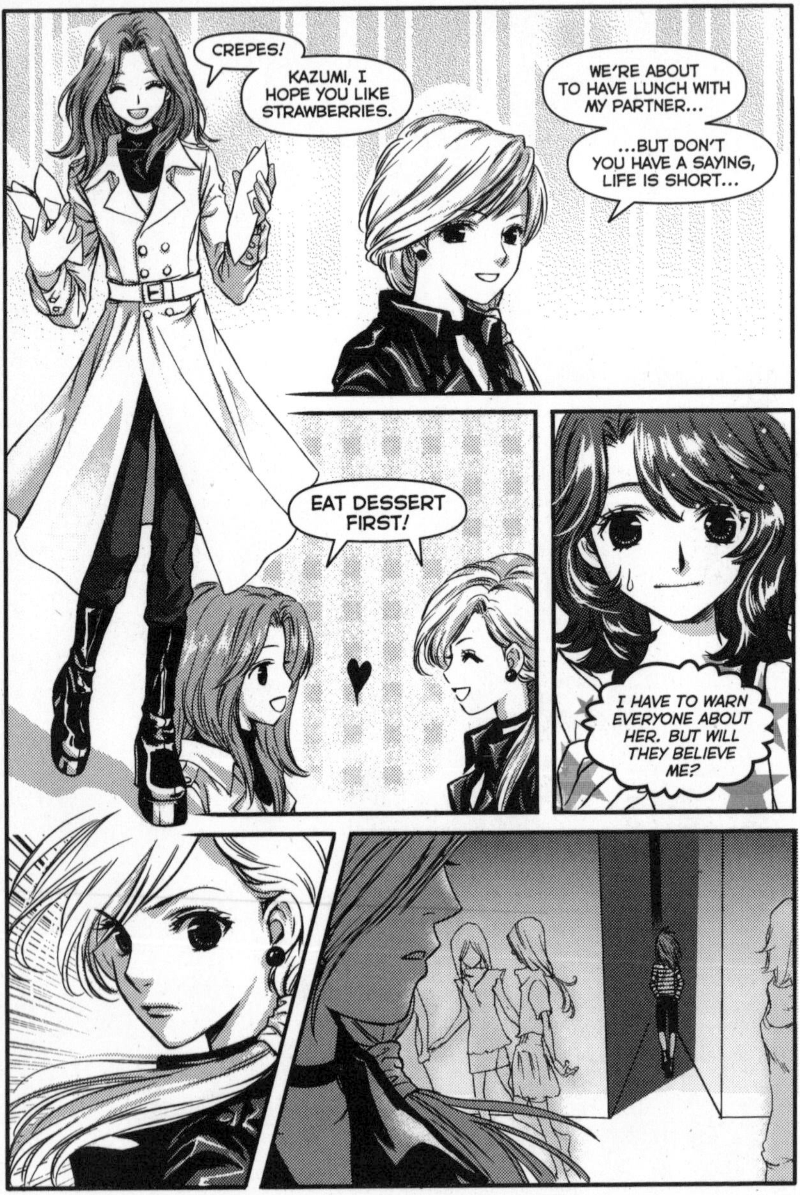
CREPES!
KAZUMI, I HOPE YOU LIKE STRAWBERRIES.
WE'RE ABOUT TO HAVE LUNCH WITH MY PARTNER...
...BUT DON'T YOU HAVE A SAYING, LIFE IS SHORT...
EAT DESSERT FIRST!
I HAVE TO WARN EVERYONE ABOUT HER. BUT WILL THEY BELIEVE ME?

Chapter Three

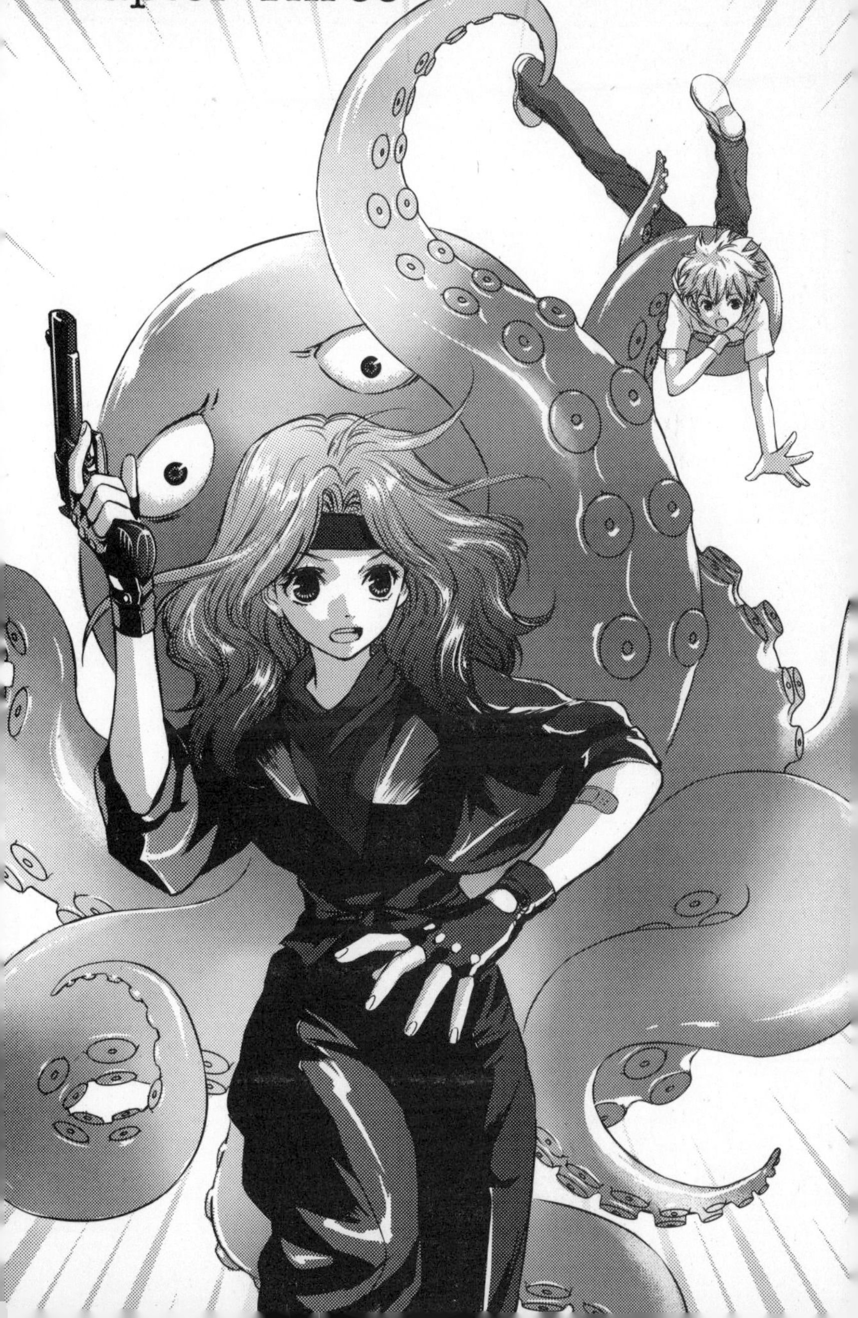

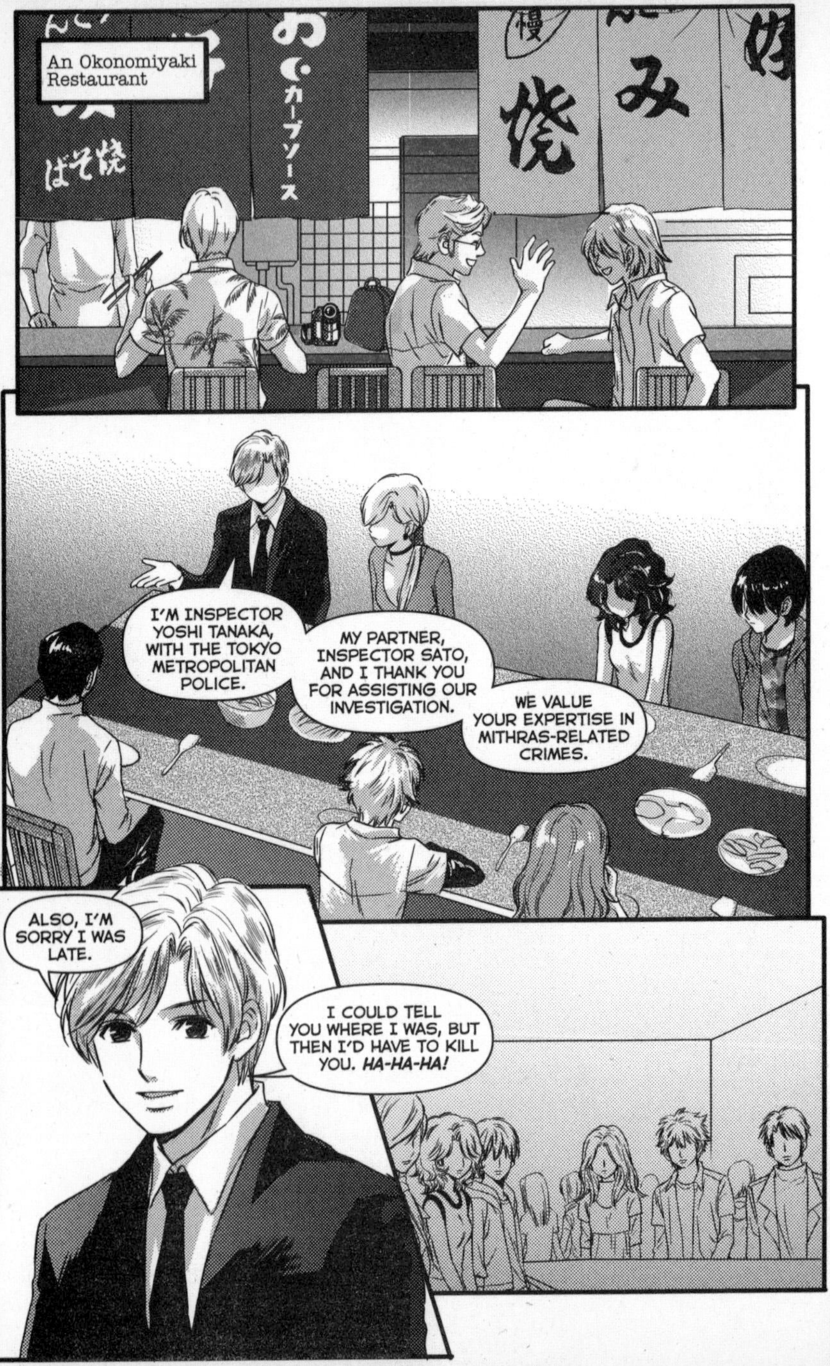
An Okonomiyaki Restaurant
カープソース
I'M INSPECTOR YOSHI TANAKA, WITH THE TOKYO METROPOLITAN POLICE.
MY PARTNER, INSPECTOR SATO, AND I THANK YOU FOR ASSISTING OUR INVESTIGATION.
WE VALUE YOUR EXPERTISE IN MITHRAS-RELATED CRIMES.
ALSO, I'M SORRY I WAS LATE.
I COULD TELL YOU WHERE I WAS, BUT THEN I'D HAVE TO KILL YOU. *HA-HA-HA!*

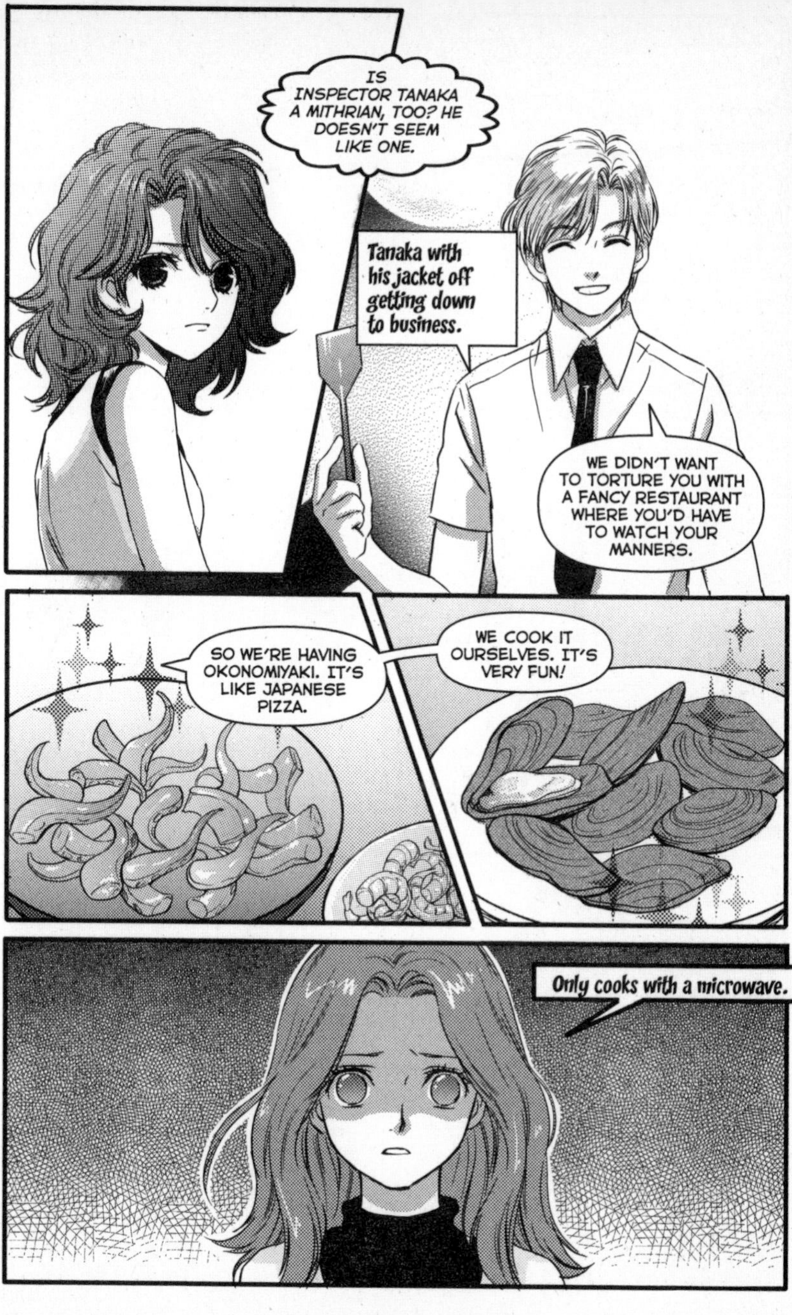
IS INSPECTOR TANAKA A MITHRIAN, TOO? HE DOESN'T SEEM LIKE ONE.
Tanaka with his jacket off getting down to business.
WE DIDN'T WANT TO TORTURE YOU WITH A FANCY RESTAURANT WHERE YOU'D HAVE TO WATCH YOUR MANNERS.
SO WE'RE HAVING OKONOMIYAKI. IT'S LIKE JAPANESE PIZZA.
WE COOK IT OURSELVES. IT'S VERY FUN!
Only cooks with a microwave.

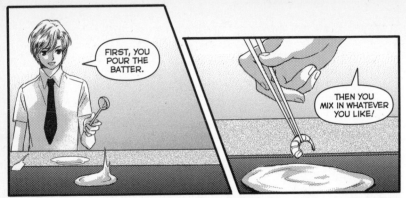

FIRST, YOU POUR THE BATTER.

THEN YOU MIX IN WHATEVER YOU LIKE!

Oh!

Ooooooo!

Mmmmmmm!

Hm? What?

ABOUT SECURITY AT THE MUSEUM...

SIZZLE..

SLITHER..

60

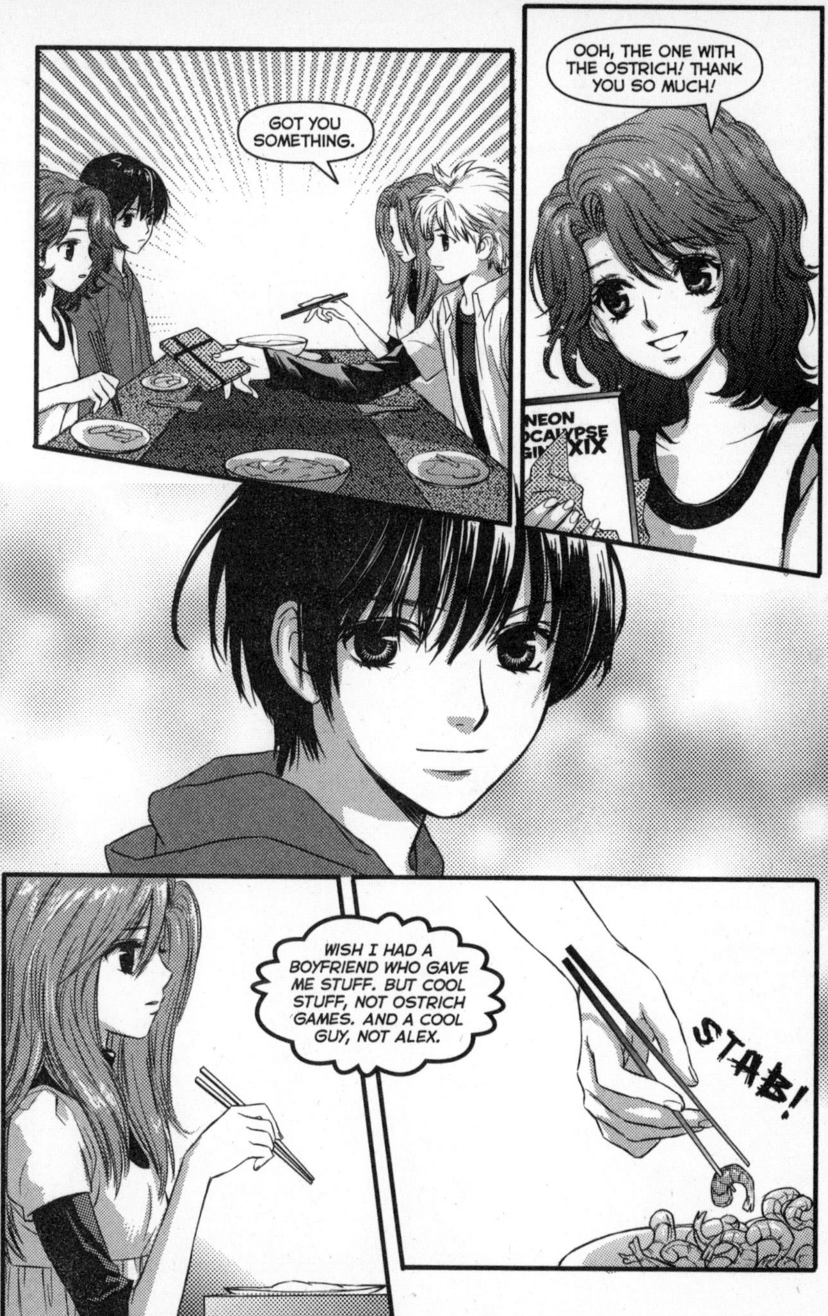
GOT YOU SOMETHING.
OOH, THE ONE WITH THE OSTRICH! THANK YOU SO MUCH!
NEON
WISH I HAD A BOYFRIEND WHO GAVE ME STUFF. BUT COOL STUFF, NOT OSTRICH GAMES. AND A COOL GUY, NOT ALEX.
STAB!

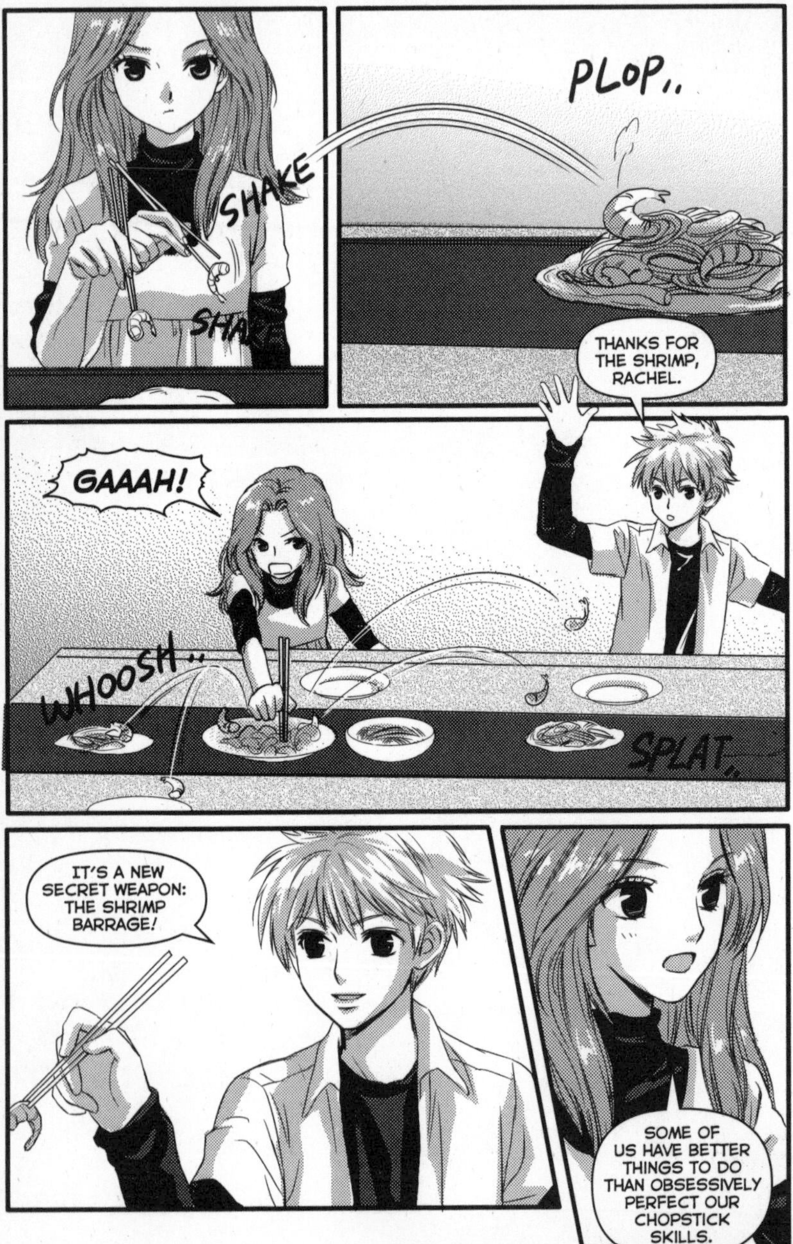
SHAKE
SHAKE
PLOP..
THANKS FOR THE SHRIMP, RACHEL.
GAAAH!
WHOOSH..
SPLAT..
IT'S A NEW SECRET WEAPON: THE SHRIMP BARRAGE!
SOME OF US HAVE BETTER THINGS TO DO THAN OBSESSIVELY PERFECT OUR CHOPSTICK SKILLS.

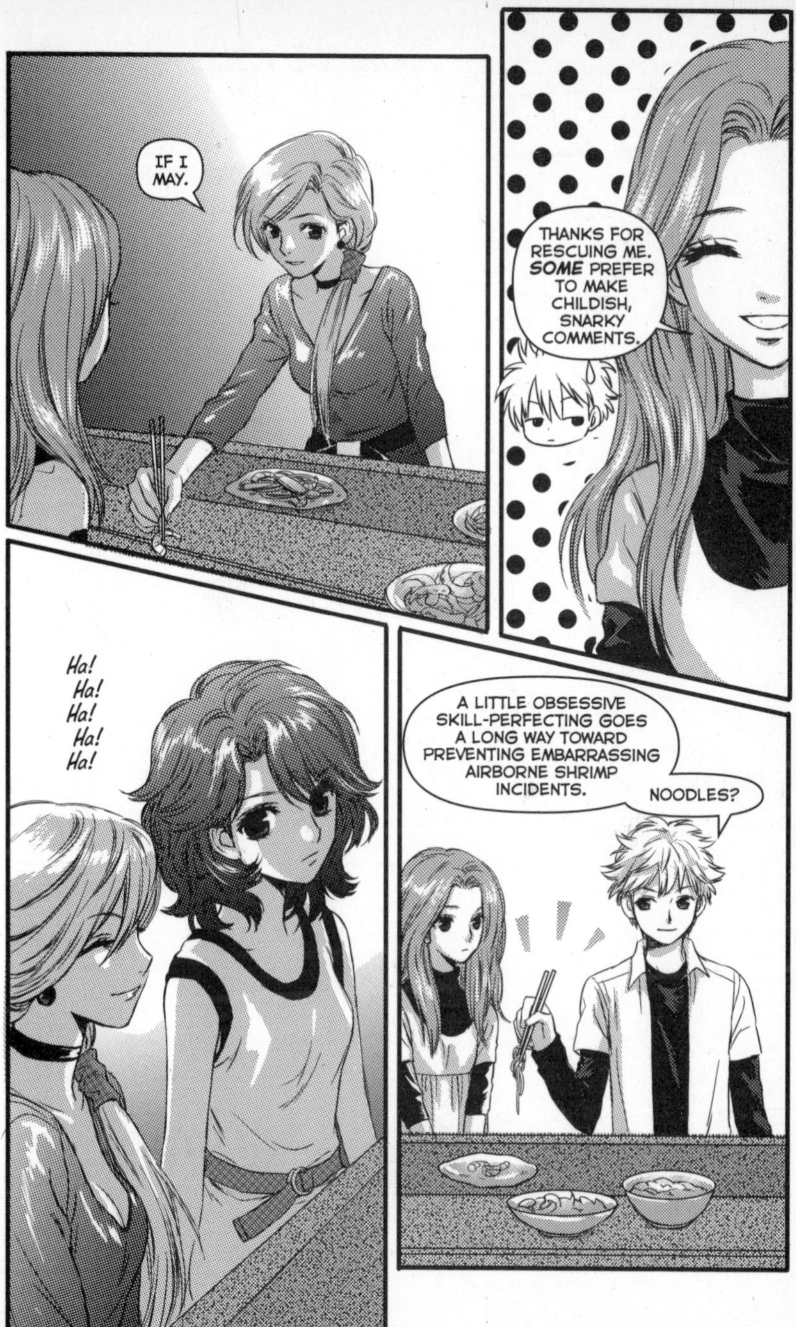
IF I MAY.
THANKS FOR RESCUING ME. SOME PREFER TO MAKE CHILDISH, SNARKY COMMENTS.
Ha! Ha! Ha! Ha! Ha!
A LITTLE OBSESSIVE SKILL-PERFECTING GOES A LONG WAY TOWARD PREVENTING EMBARRASSING AIRBORNE SHRIMP INCIDENTS.
NOODLES?

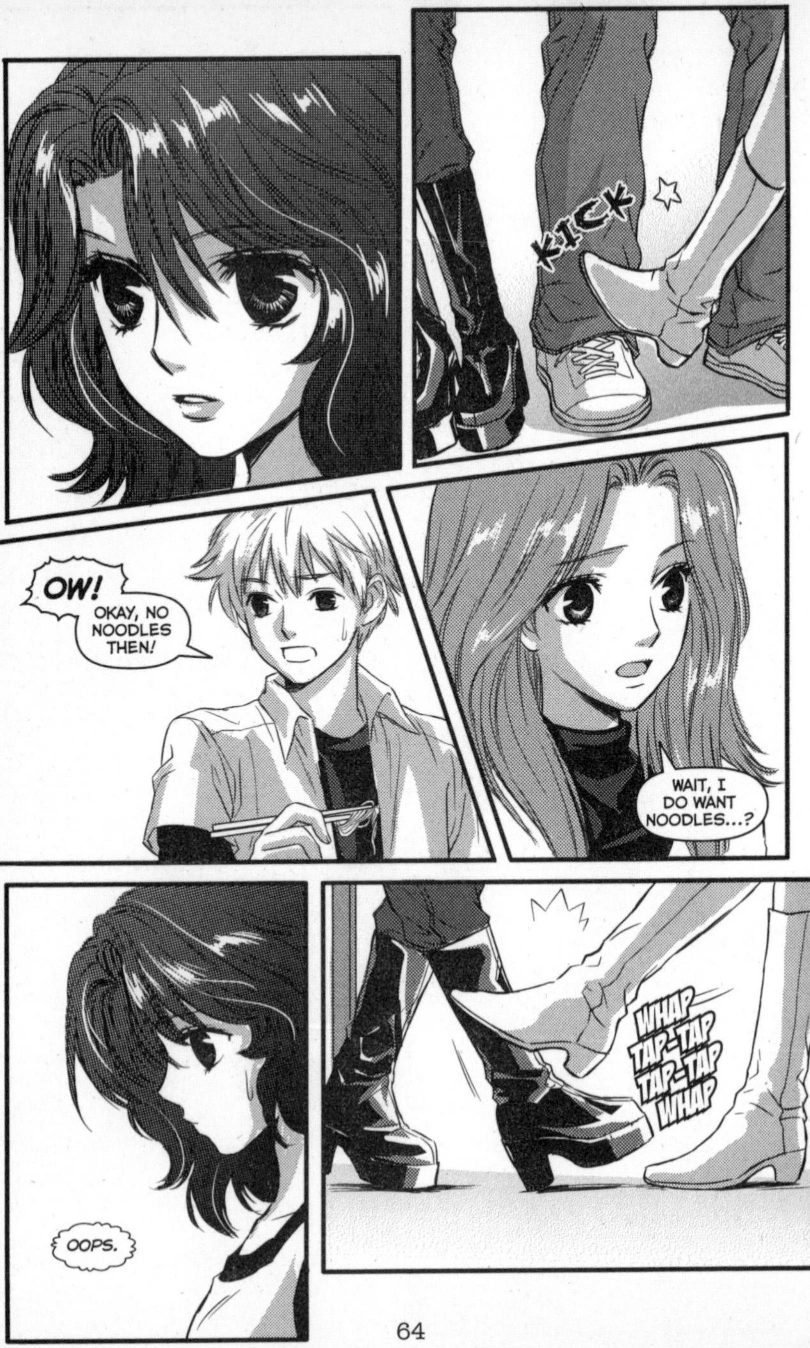
KICK
OW! OKAY, NO NOODLES THEN!
WAIT, I DO WANT NOODLES...?
OOPS.
WHAP TAP-TAP TAP-TAP WHAP

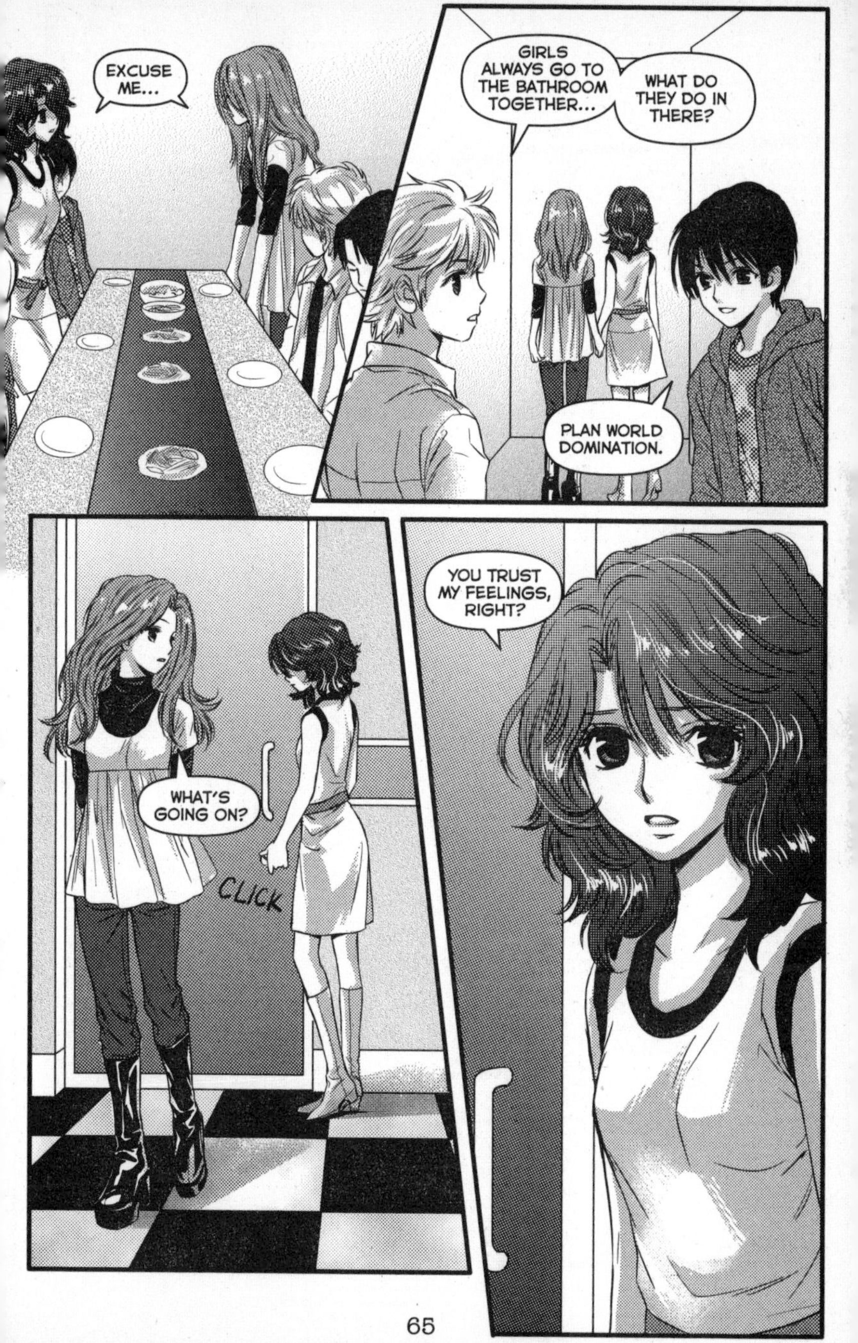
EXCUSE ME...
GIRLS ALWAYS GO TO THE BATHROOM TOGETHER...
WHAT DO THEY DO IN THERE?
PLAN WORLD DOMINATION.
WHAT'S GOING ON?
CLICK
YOU TRUST MY FEELINGS, RIGHT?

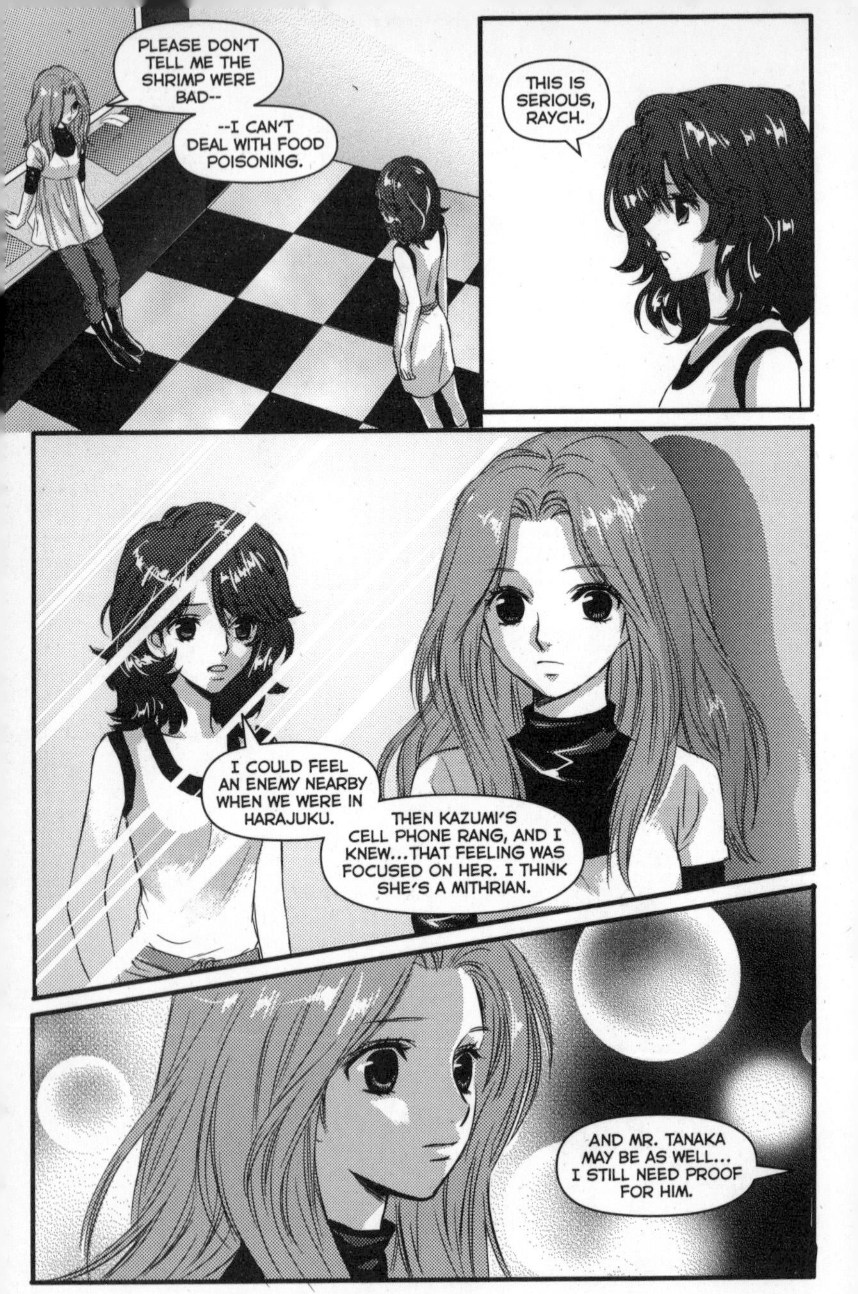
PLEASE DON'T TELL ME THE SHRIMP WERE BAD--
--I CAN'T DEAL WITH FOOD POISONING.
THIS IS SERIOUS, RAYCH.
I COULD FEEL AN ENEMY NEARBY WHEN WE WERE IN HARAJUKU.
THEN KAZUMI'S CELL PHONE RANG, AND I KNEW...THAT FEELING WAS FOCUSED ON HER. I THINK SHE'S A MITHRIAN.
AND MR. TANAKA MAY BE AS WELL... I STILL NEED PROOF FOR HIM.

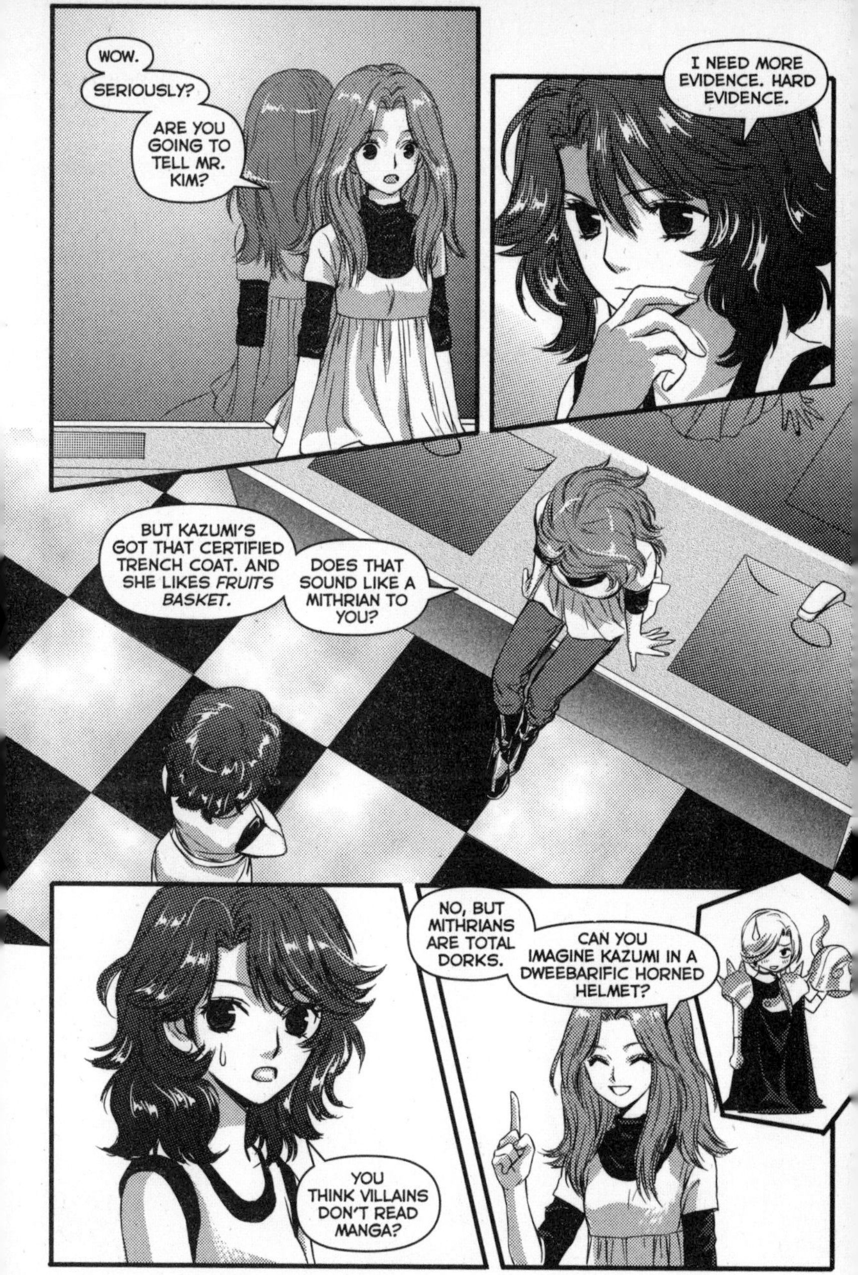
WOW.
SERIOUSLY?
ARE YOU GOING TO TELL MR. KIM?
I NEED MORE EVIDENCE. HARD EVIDENCE.
BUT KAZUMI'S GOT THAT CERTIFIED TRENCH COAT. AND SHE LIKES *FRUITS BASKET*.
DOES THAT SOUND LIKE A MITHRIAN TO YOU?
YOU THINK VILLAINS DON'T READ MANGA?
NO, BUT MITHRIANS ARE TOTAL DORKS.
CAN YOU IMAGINE KAZUMI IN A DWEEBARIFIC HORNED HELMET?

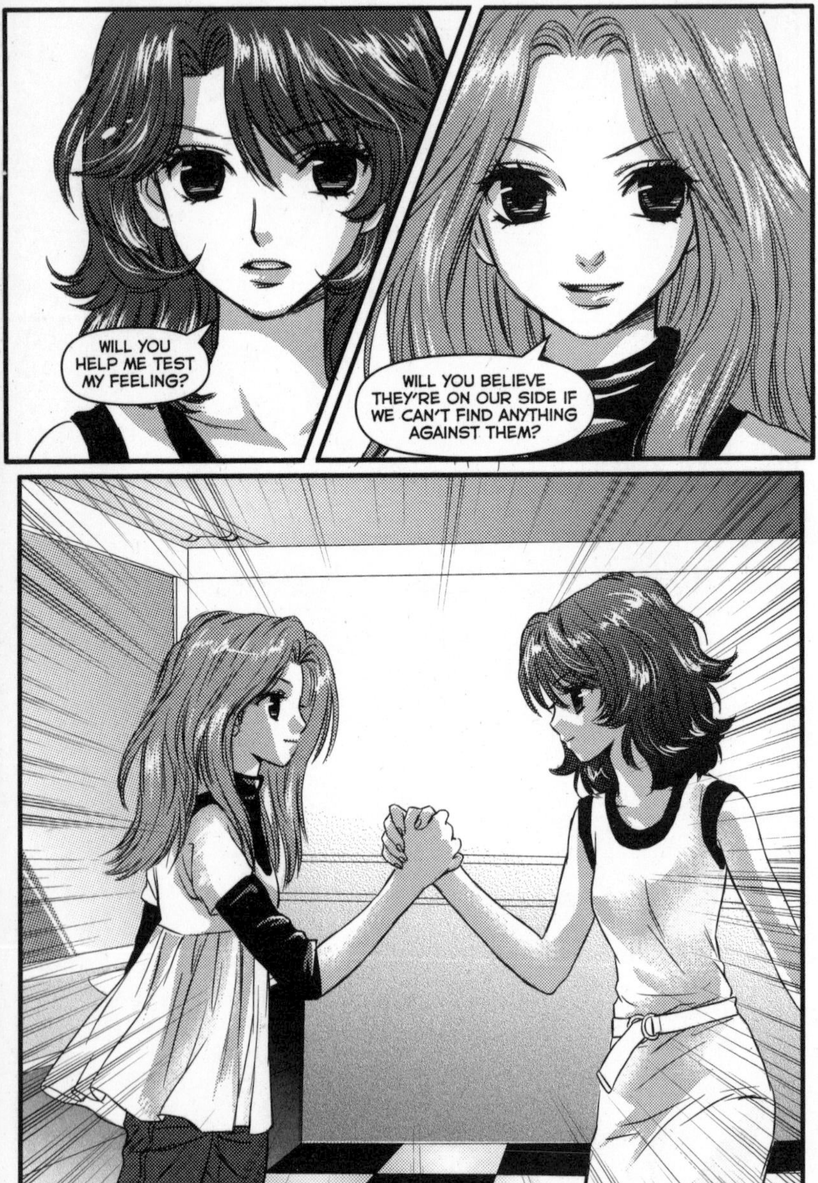
WILL YOU HELP ME TEST MY FEELING?
WILL YOU BELIEVE THEY'RE ON OUR SIDE IF WE CAN'T FIND ANYTHING AGAINST THEM?

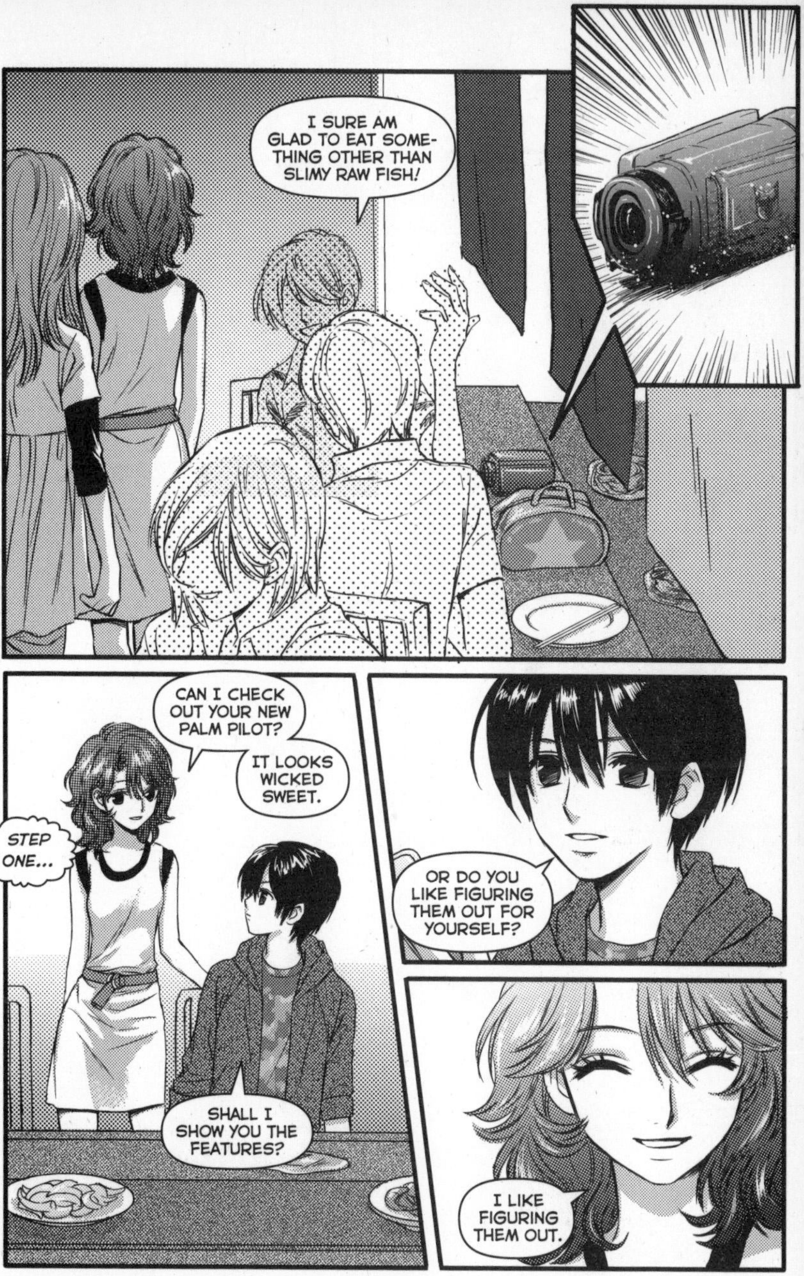
I SURE AM GLAD TO EAT SOMETHING OTHER THAN SLIMY RAW FISH!
CAN I CHECK OUT YOUR NEW PALM PILOT?
IT LOOKS WICKED SWEET.
STEP ONE...
SHALL I SHOW YOU THE FEATURES?
OR DO YOU LIKE FIGURING THEM OUT FOR YOURSELF?
I LIKE FIGURING THEM OUT.

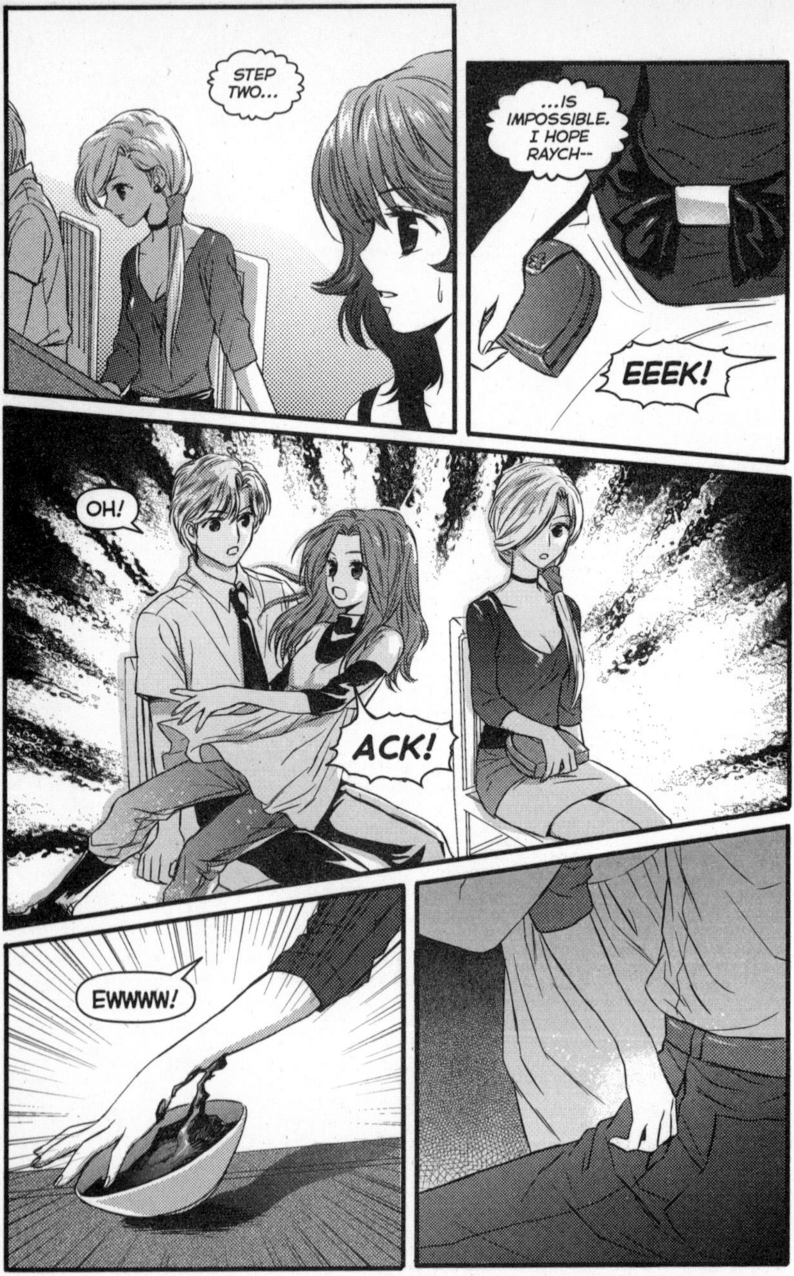
STEP TWO...
...IS IMPOSSIBLE. I HOPE RAYCH--
EEEK!
OH!
ACK!
EWWWW!

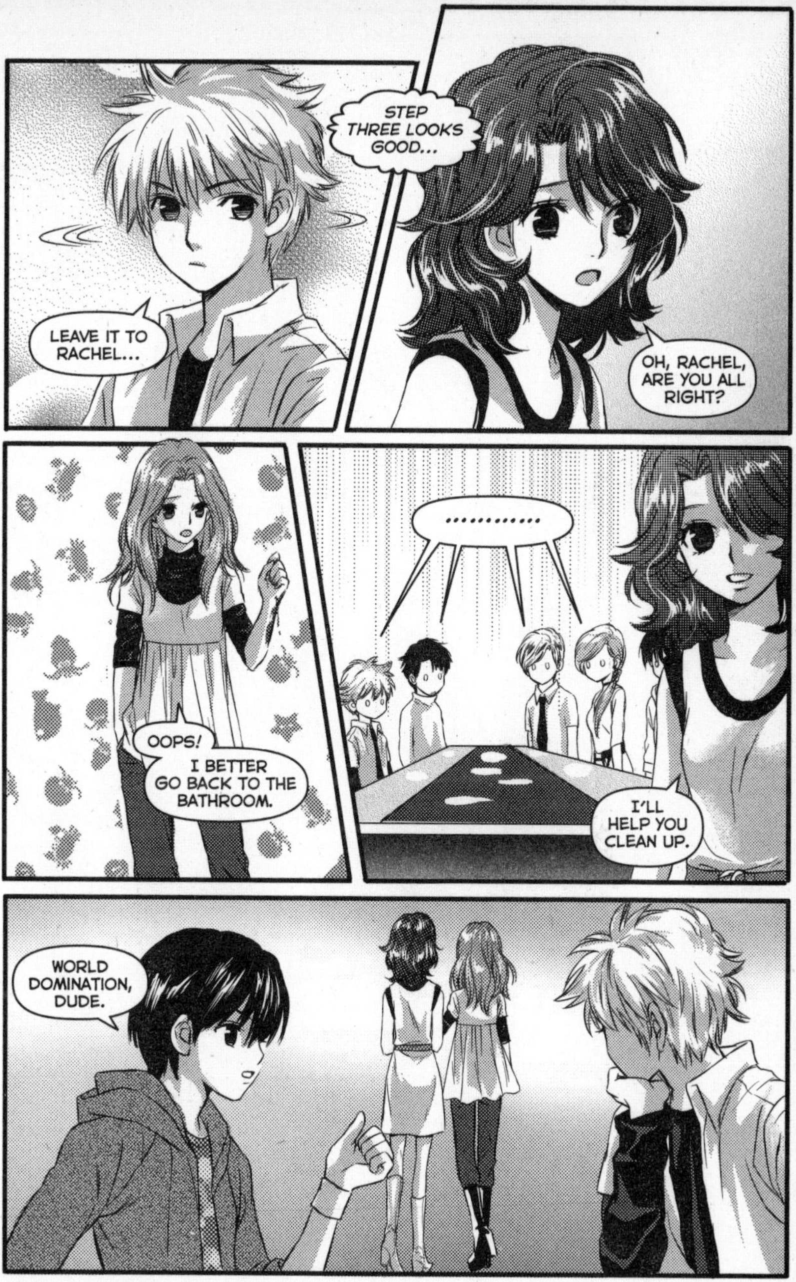
STEP THREE LOOKS GOOD...
LEAVE IT TO RACHEL...
OH, RACHEL, ARE YOU ALL RIGHT?
OOPS! I BETTER GO BACK TO THE BATHROOM.
....
I'LL HELP YOU CLEAN UP.
WORLD DOMINATION, DUDE.

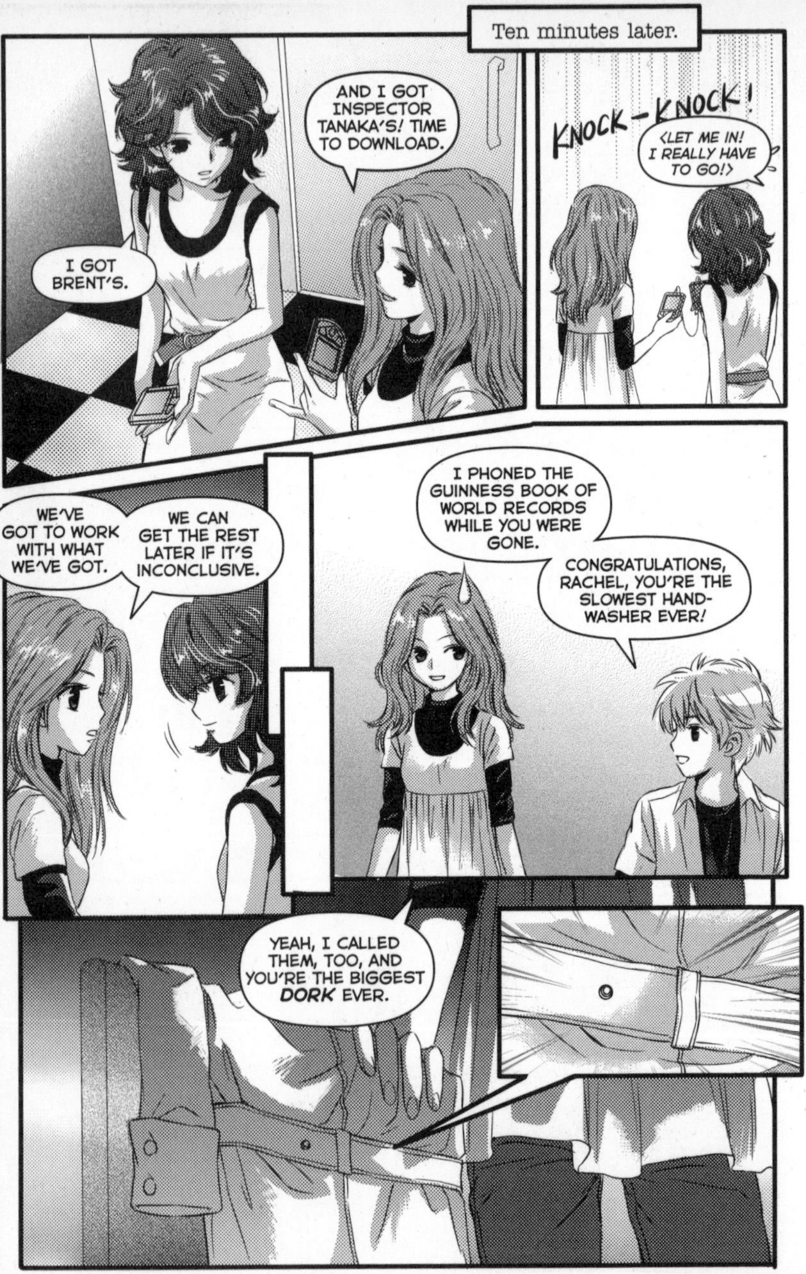
Ten minutes later.
I GOT BRENT'S.
AND I GOT INSPECTOR TANAKA'S! TIME TO DOWNLOAD.
KNOCK-KNOCK!
<LET ME IN! I REALLY HAVE TO GO!>
WE'VE GOT TO WORK WITH WHAT WE'VE GOT.
WE CAN GET THE REST LATER IF IT'S INCONCLUSIVE.
I PHONED THE GUINNESS BOOK OF WORLD RECORDS WHILE YOU WERE GONE.
CONGRATULATIONS, RACHEL, YOU'RE THE SLOWEST HAND-WASHER EVER!
YEAH, I CALLED THEM, TOO, AND YOU'RE THE BIGGEST **DORK** EVER.

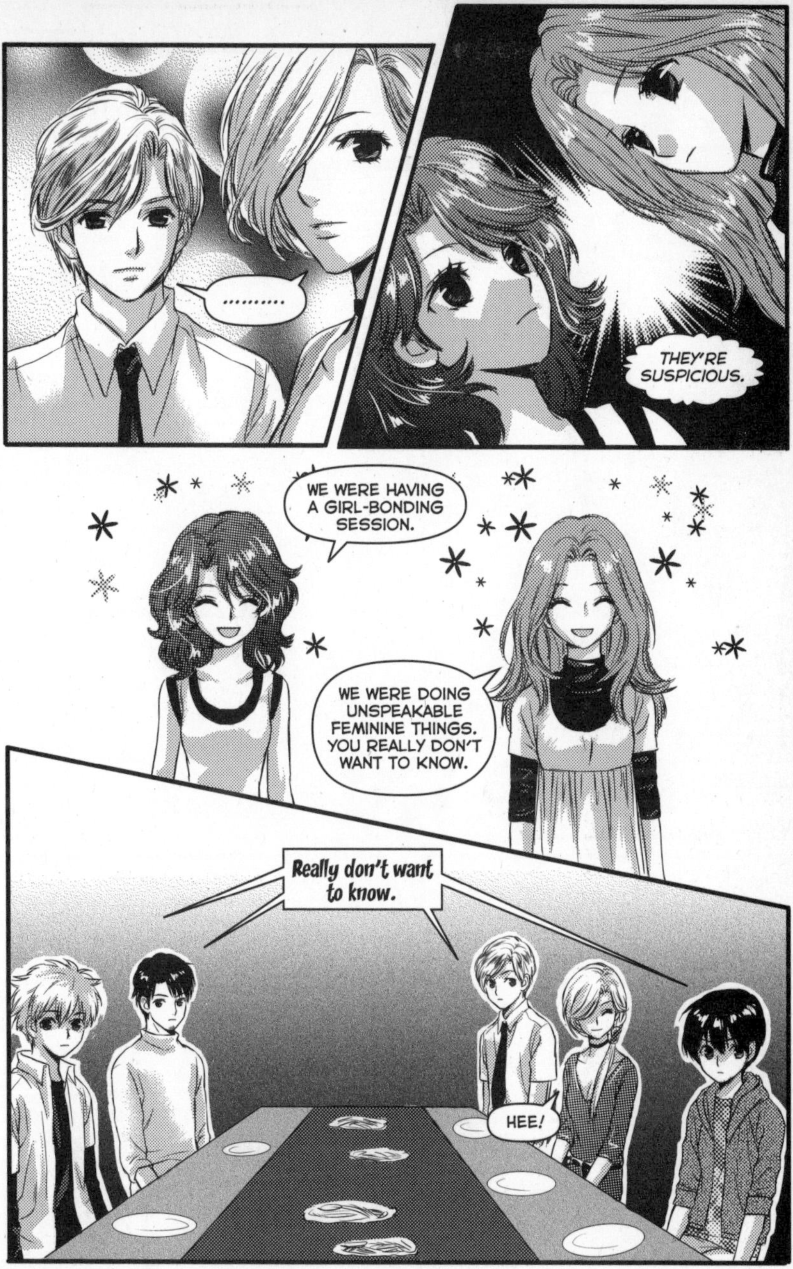
....
THEY'RE SUSPICIOUS.
WE WERE HAVING A GIRL-BONDING SESSION.
WE WERE DOING UNSPEAKABLE FEMININE THINGS. YOU REALLY DON'T WANT TO KNOW.
Really don't want to know.
HEE!

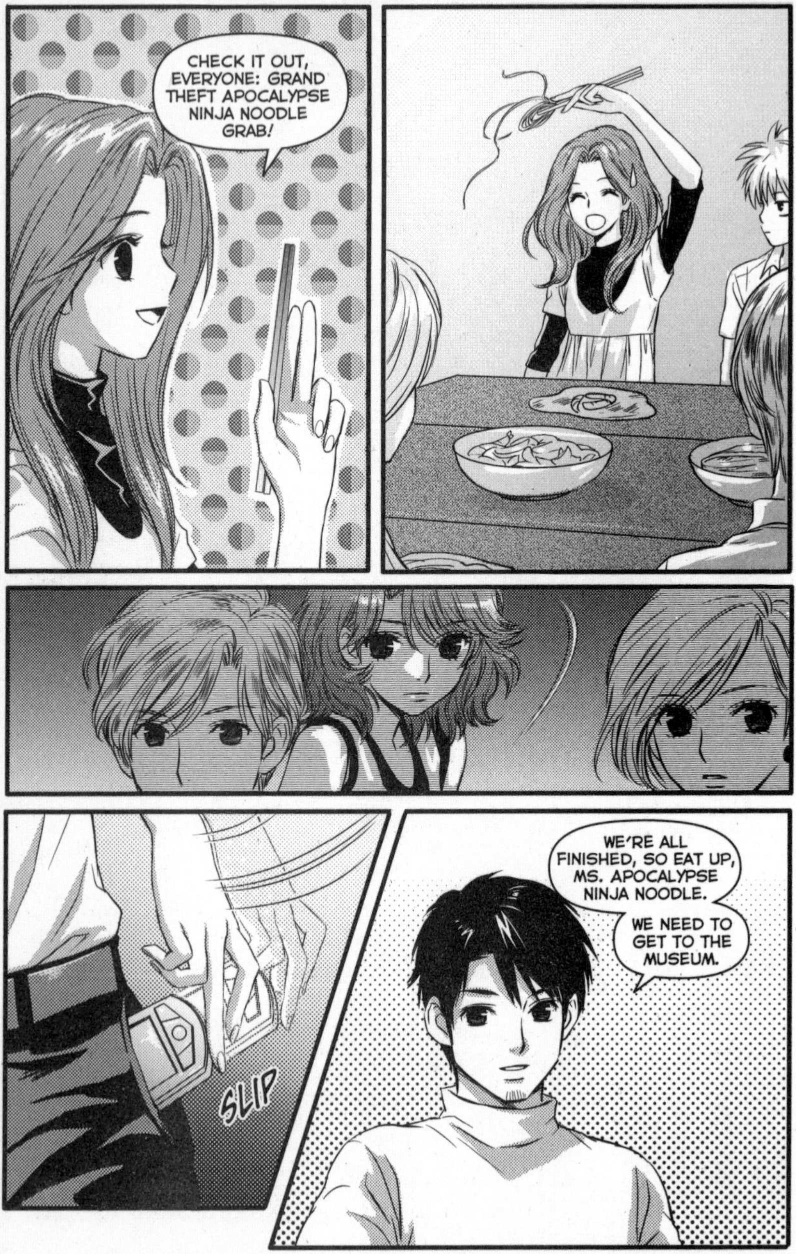
CHECK IT OUT, EVERYONE: GRAND THEFT APOCALYPSE NINJA NOODLE GRAB!
SLIP
WE'RE ALL FINISHED, SO EAT UP, MS. APOCALYPSE NINJA NOODLE.
WE NEED TO GET TO THE MUSEUM.

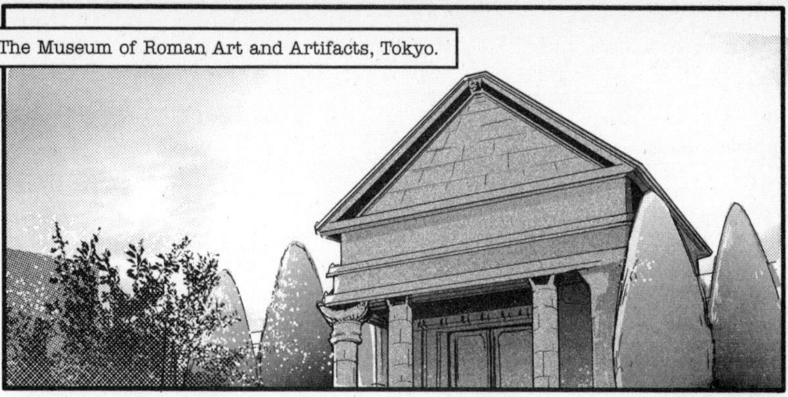
The Museum of Roman Art and Artifacts, Tokyo.
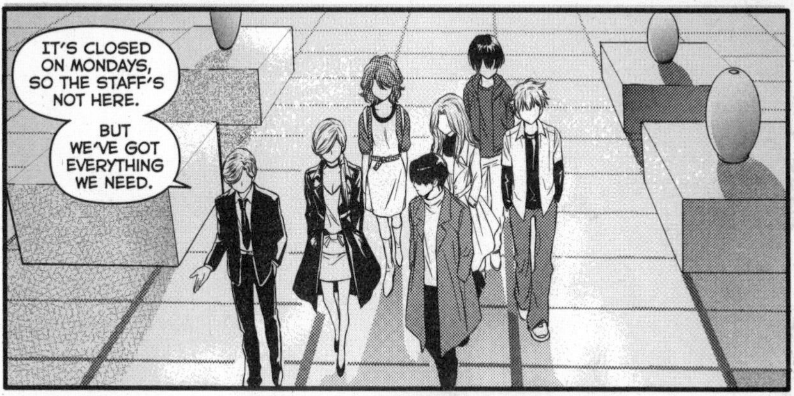
IT'S CLOSED ON MONDAYS, SO THE STAFF'S NOT HERE.
BUT WE'VE GOT EVERYTHING WE NEED.
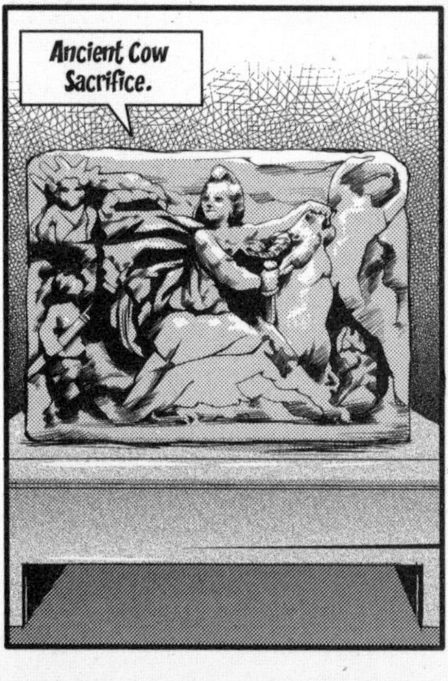
Ancient Cow Sacrifice.
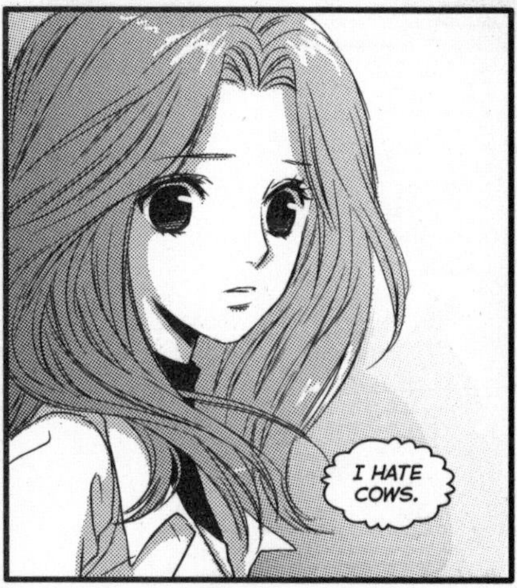
I HATE COWS.

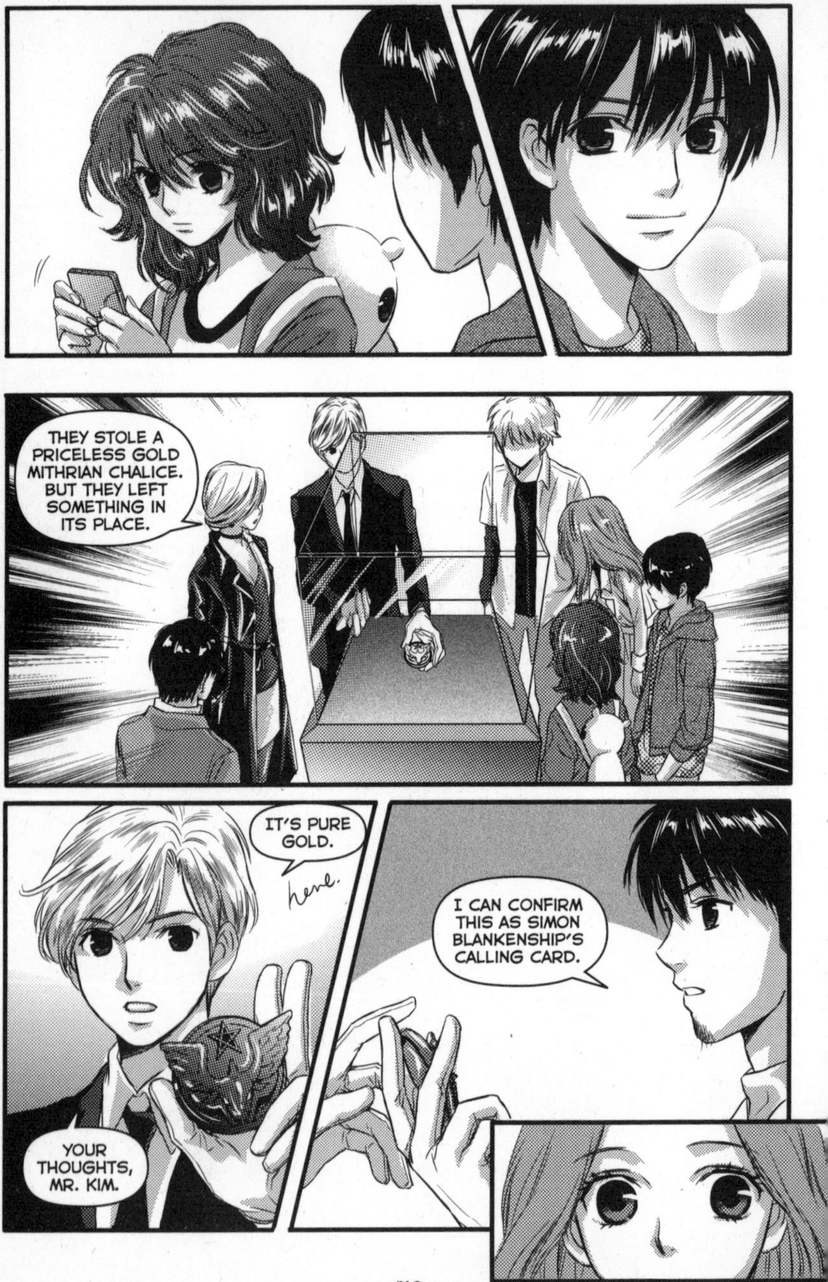
THEY STOLE A PRICELESS GOLD MITHRIAN CHALICE. BUT THEY LEFT SOMETHING IN ITS PLACE.
IT'S PURE GOLD.
here.
YOUR THOUGHTS, MR. KIM.
I CAN CONFIRM THIS AS SIMON BLANKENSHIP'S CALLING CARD.

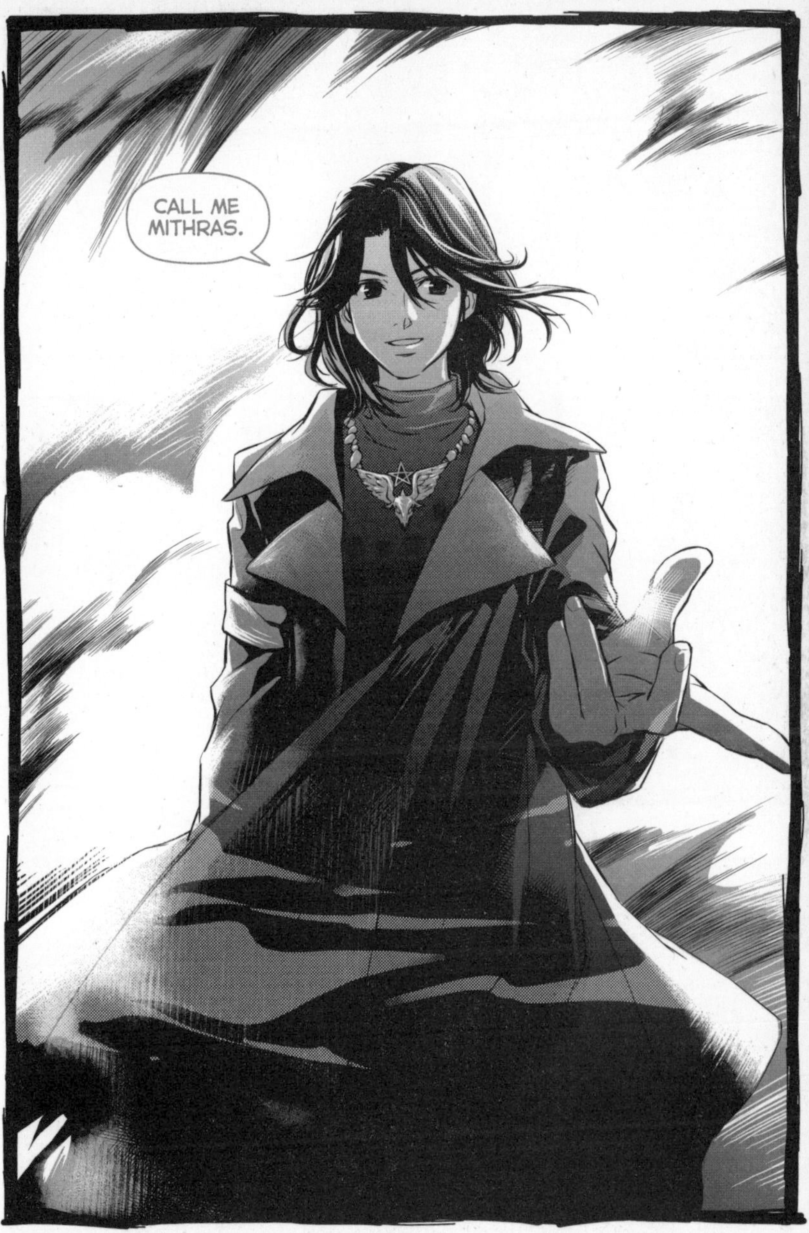
CALL ME MITHRAS.

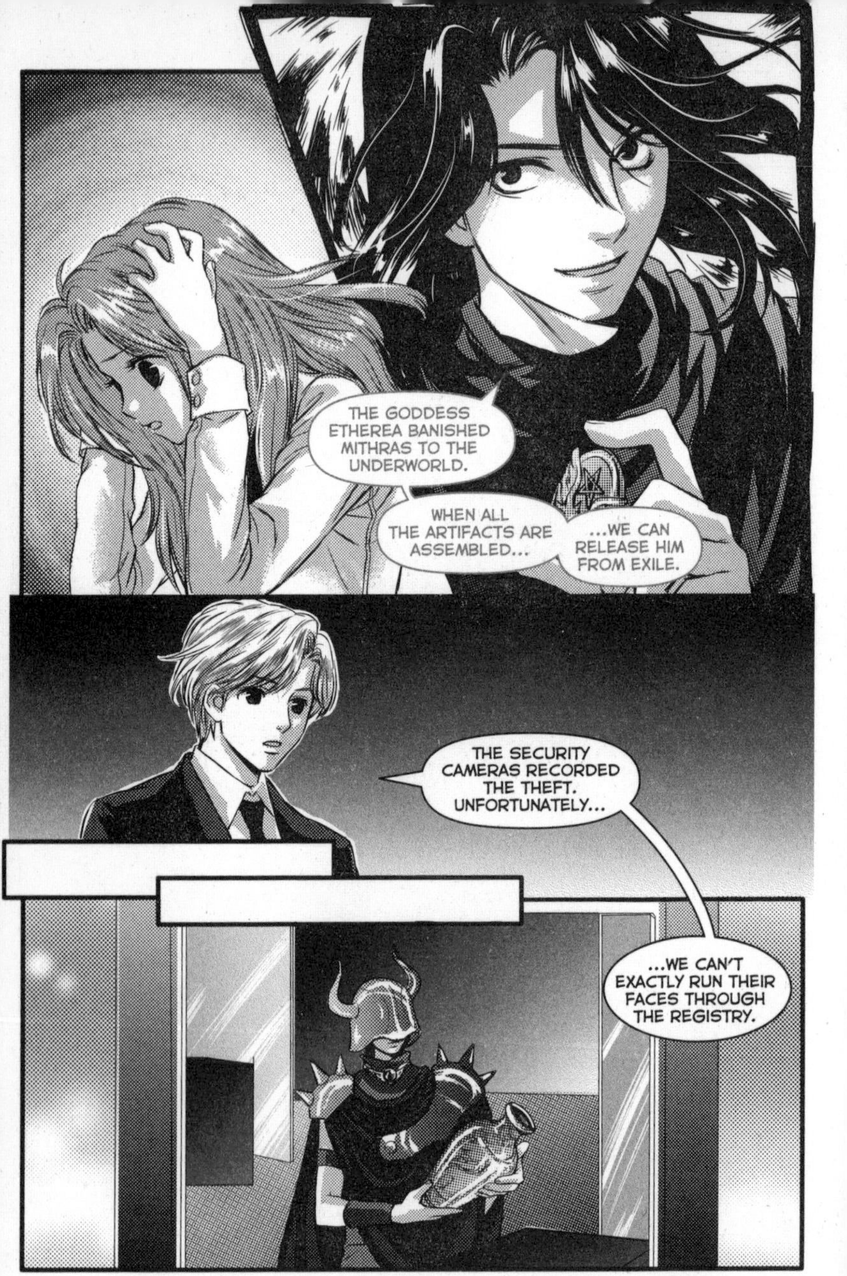
THE GODDESS ETHEREA BANISHED MITHRAS TO THE UNDERWORLD.
WHEN ALL THE ARTIFACTS ARE ASSEMBLED...
...WE CAN RELEASE HIM FROM EXILE.
THE SECURITY CAMERAS RECORDED THE THEFT. UNFORTUNATELY...
...WE CAN'T EXACTLY RUN THEIR FACES THROUGH THE REGISTRY.

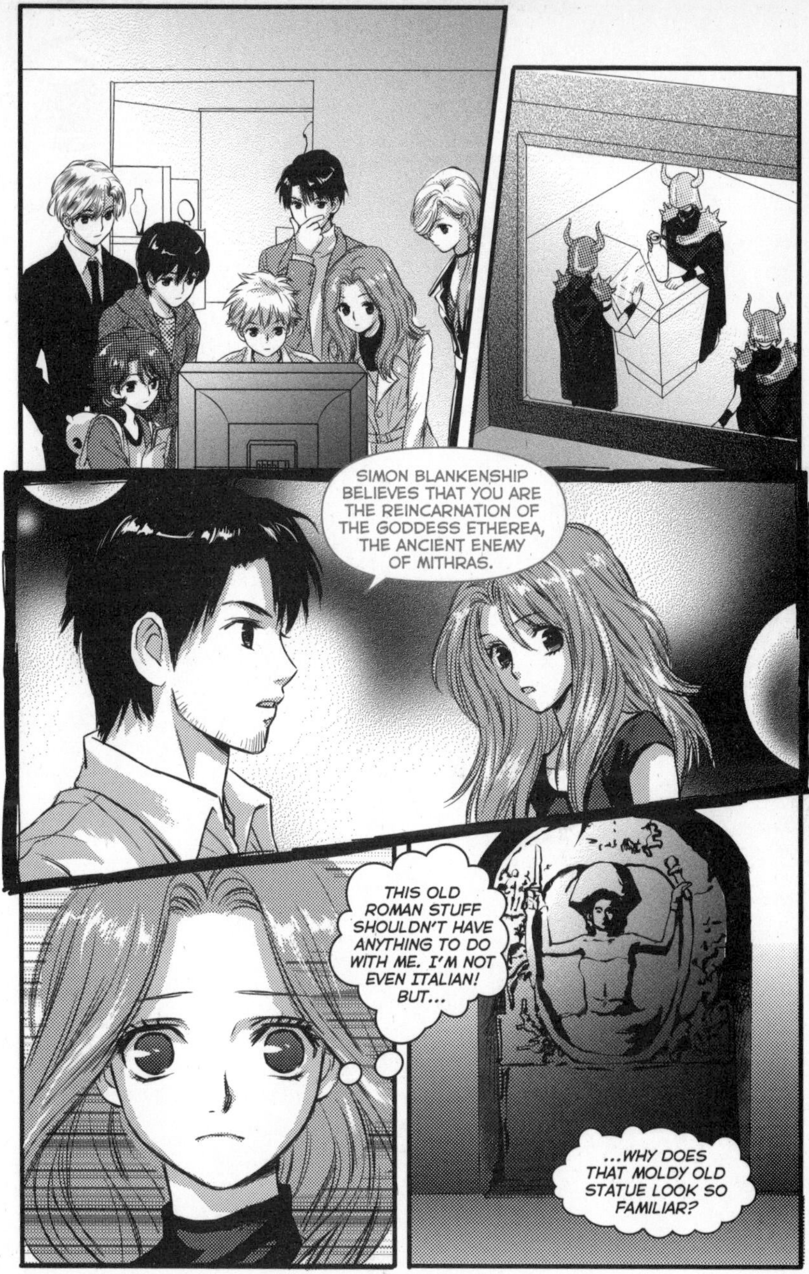
SIMON BLANKENSHIP BELIEVES THAT YOU ARE THE REINCARNATION OF THE GODDESS ETHEREA, THE ANCIENT ENEMY OF MITHRAS.
THIS OLD ROMAN STUFF SHOULDN'T HAVE ANYTHING TO DO WITH ME. I'M NOT EVEN ITALIAN! BUT...
...WHY DOES THAT MOLDY OLD STATUE LOOK SO FAMILIAR?

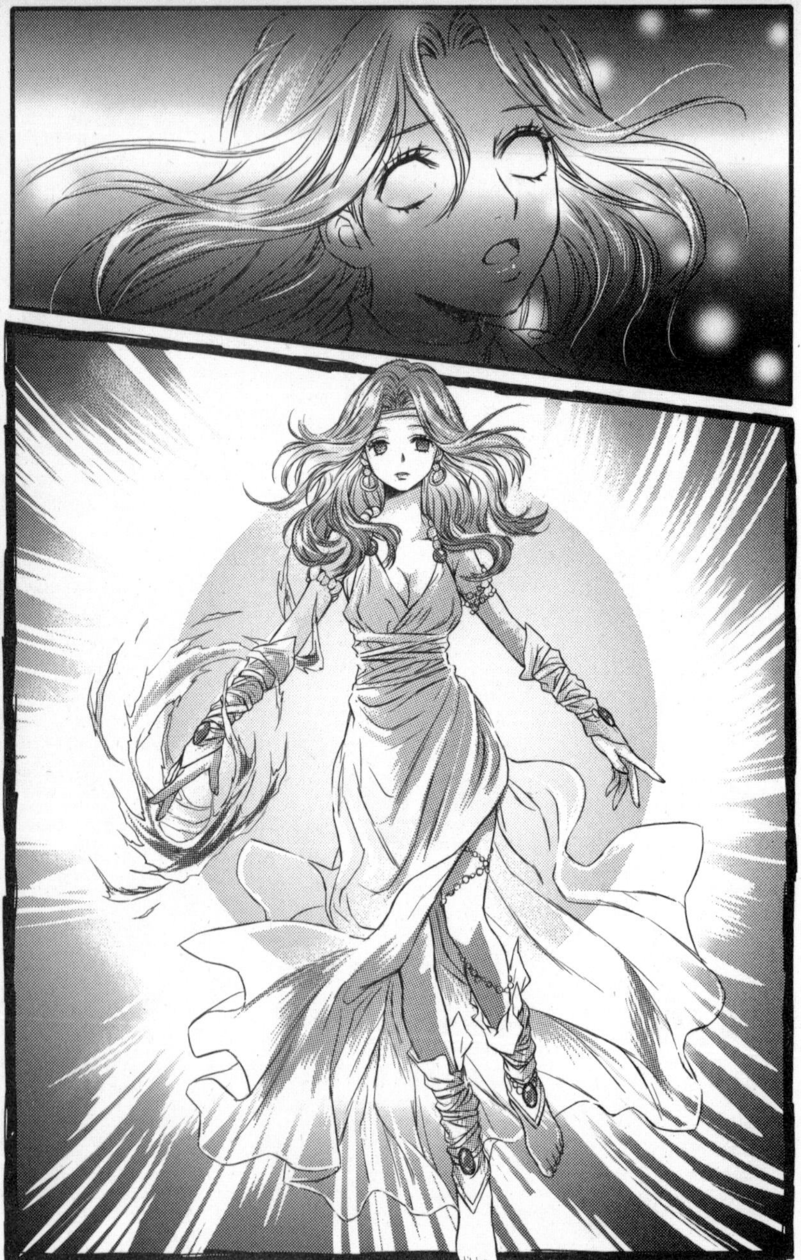

Chapter Four

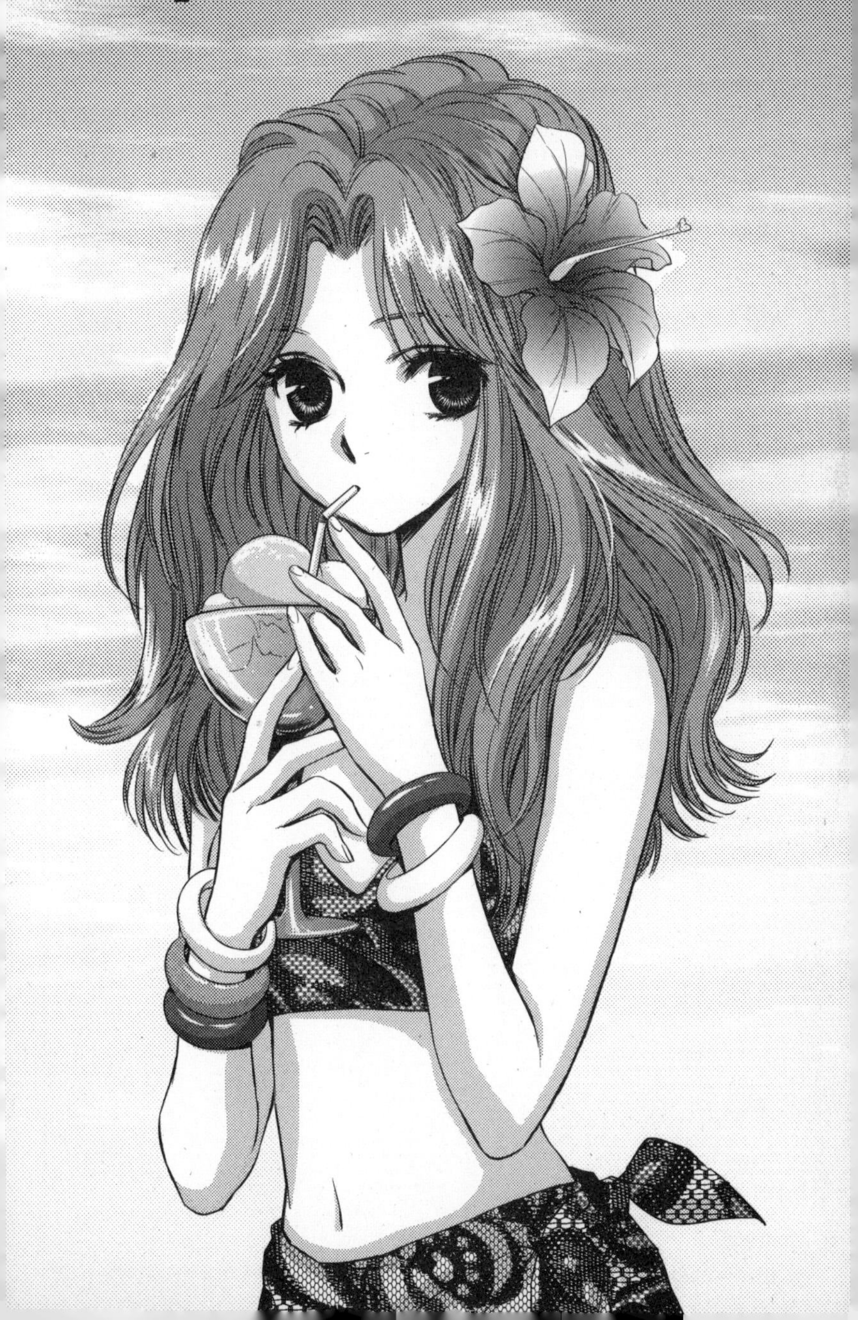

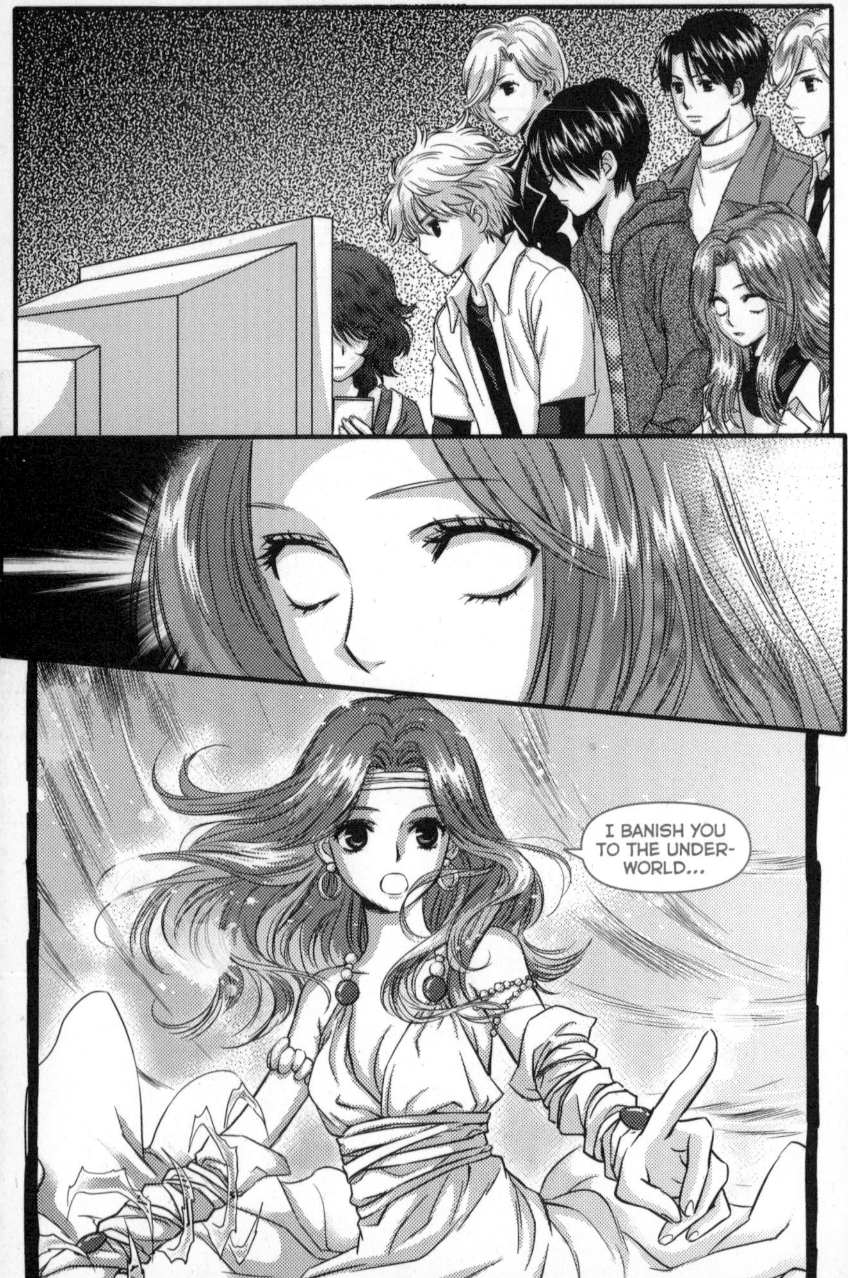
I BANISH YOU TO THE UNDER-WORLD...

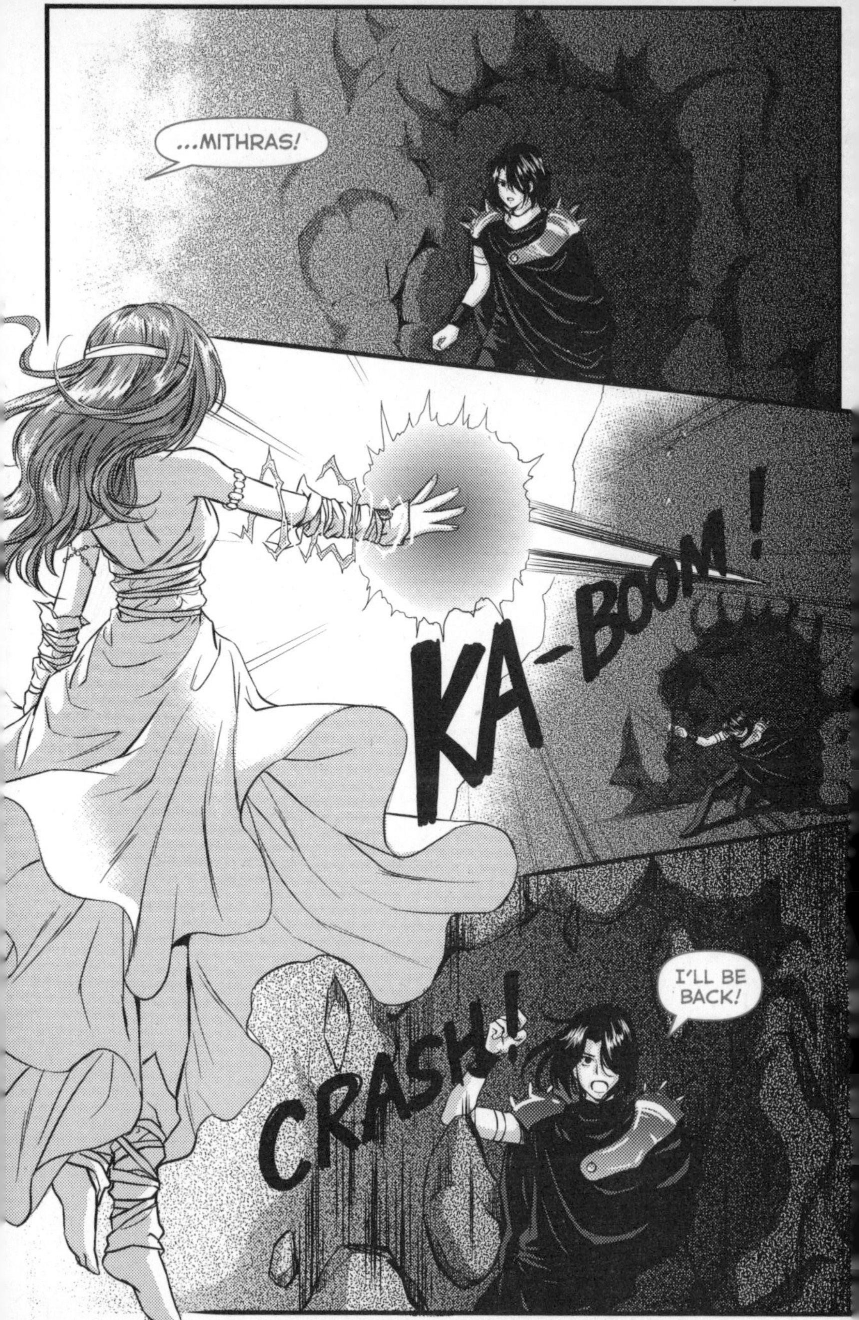
...MITHRAS!
KA-BOOM!
CRASH!
I'LL BE BACK!

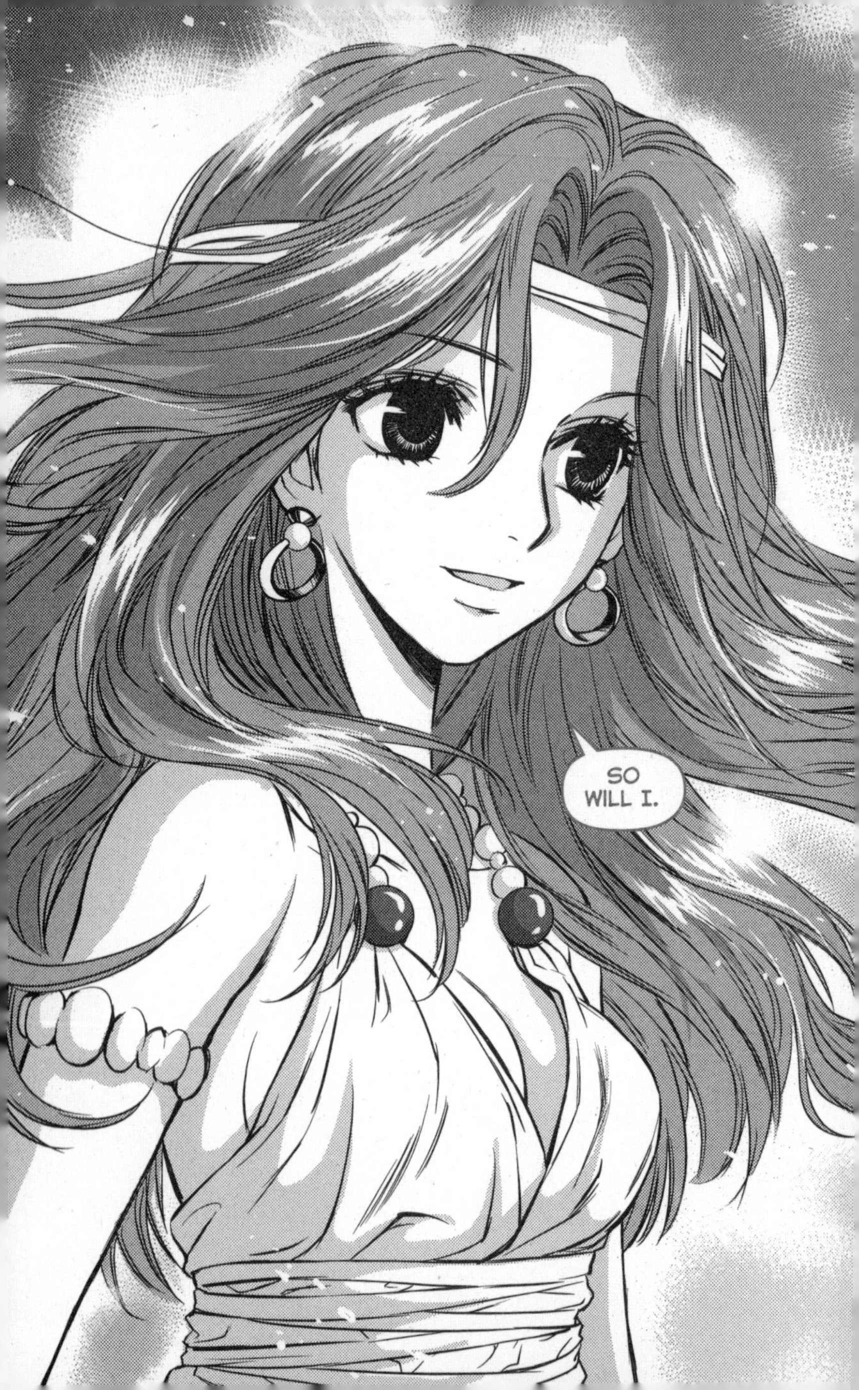
SO WILL I.

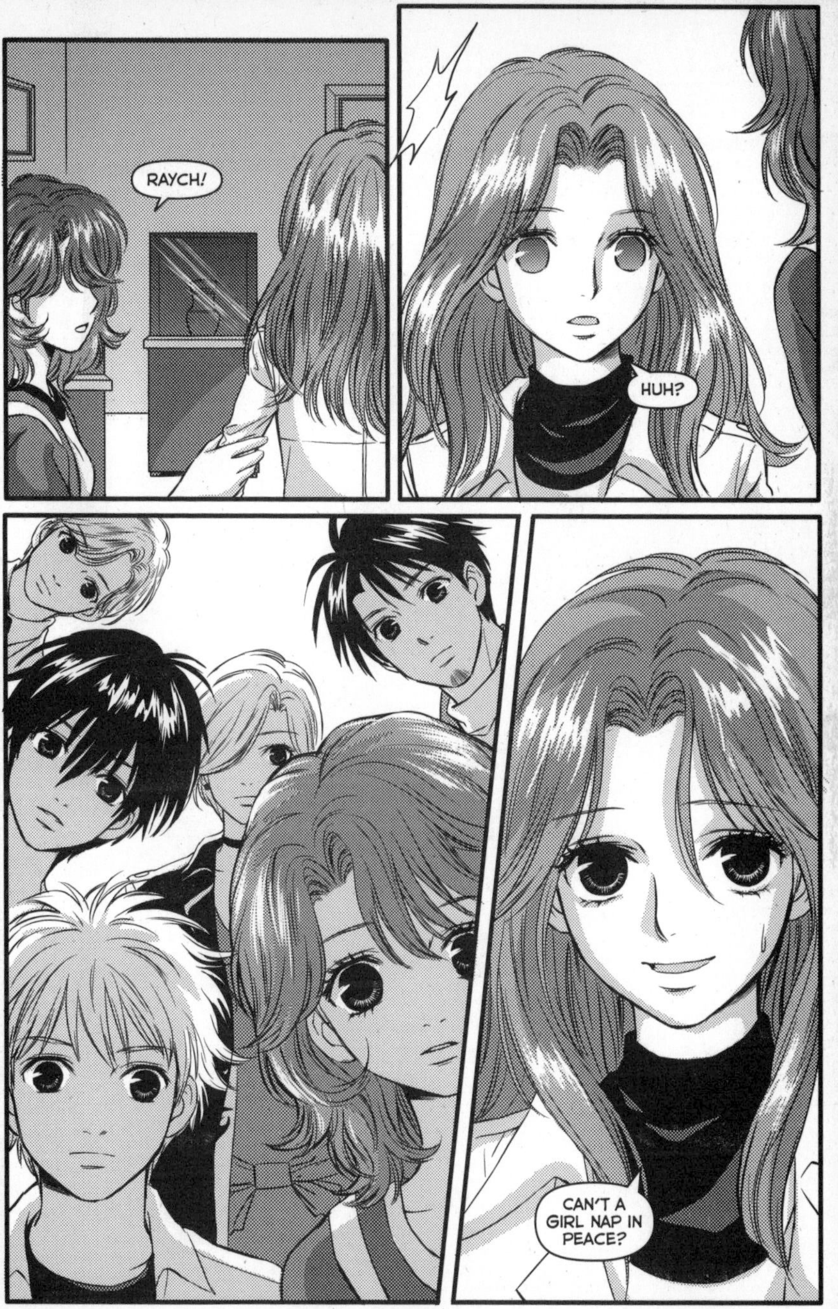
RAYCH!
HUH?
CAN'T A GIRL NAP IN PEACE?

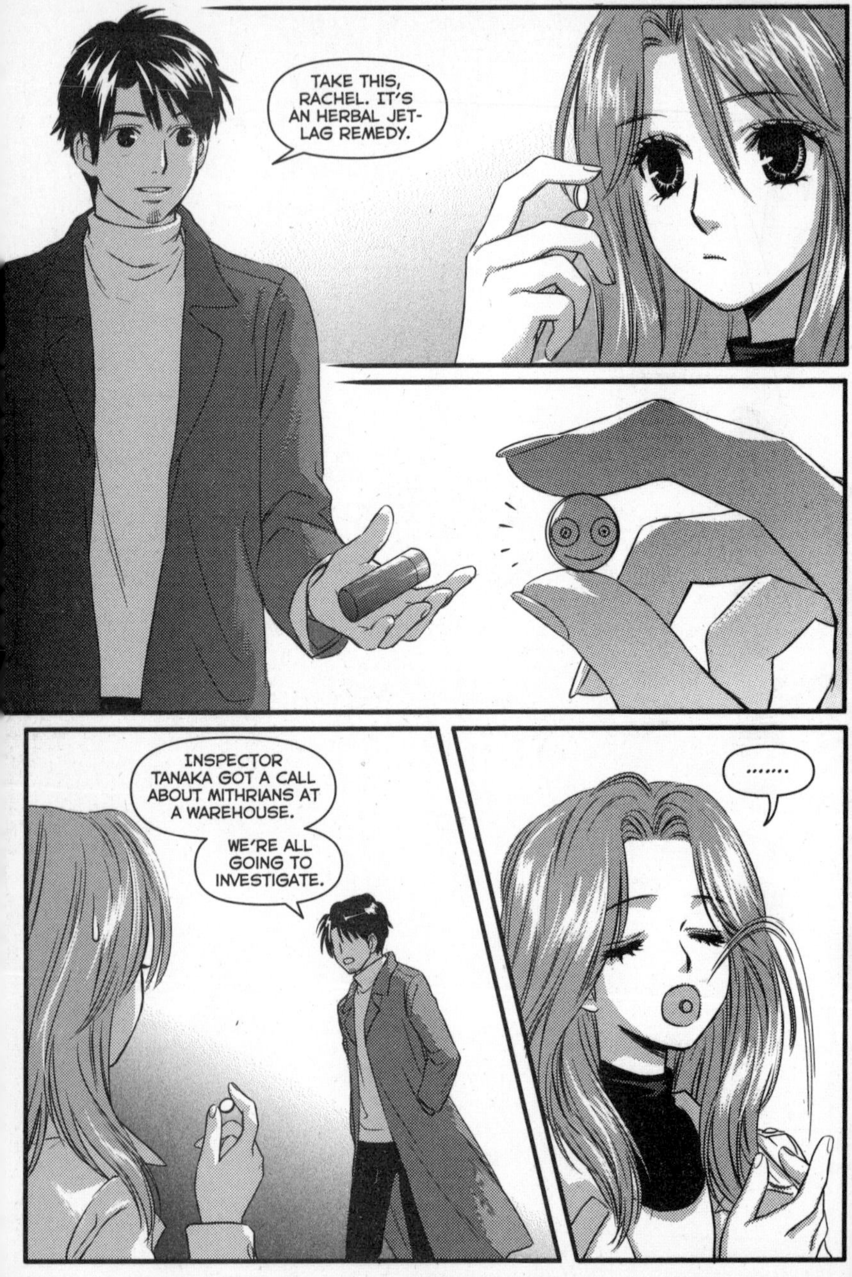
TAKE THIS, RACHEL. IT'S AN HERBAL JET-LAG REMEDY.
INSPECTOR TANAKA GOT A CALL ABOUT MITHRIANS AT A WAREHOUSE.
WE'RE ALL GOING TO INVESTIGATE.
....

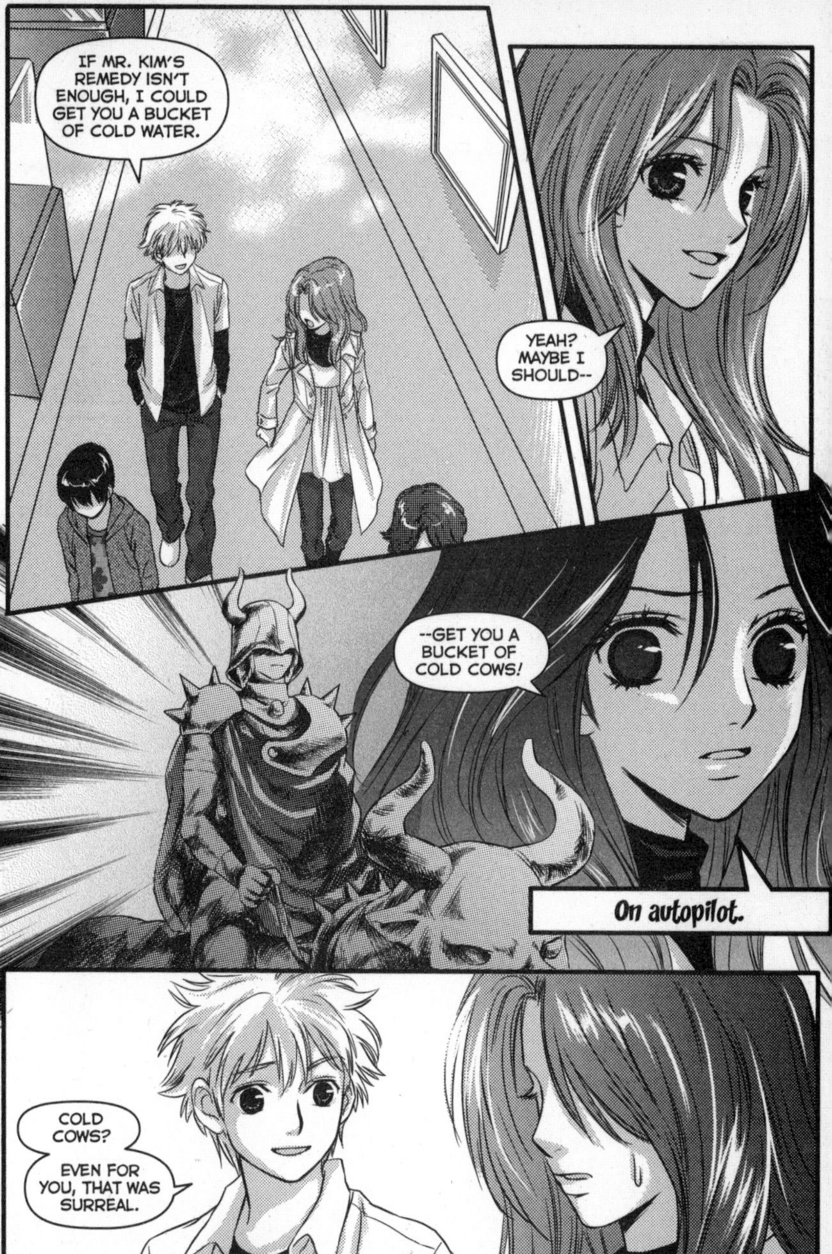
IF MR. KIM'S REMEDY ISN'T ENOUGH, I COULD GET YOU A BUCKET OF COLD WATER.
YEAH? MAYBE I SHOULD--
--GET YOU A BUCKET OF COLD COWS!
On autopilot.
COLD COWS?
EVEN FOR YOU, THAT WAS SURREAL.

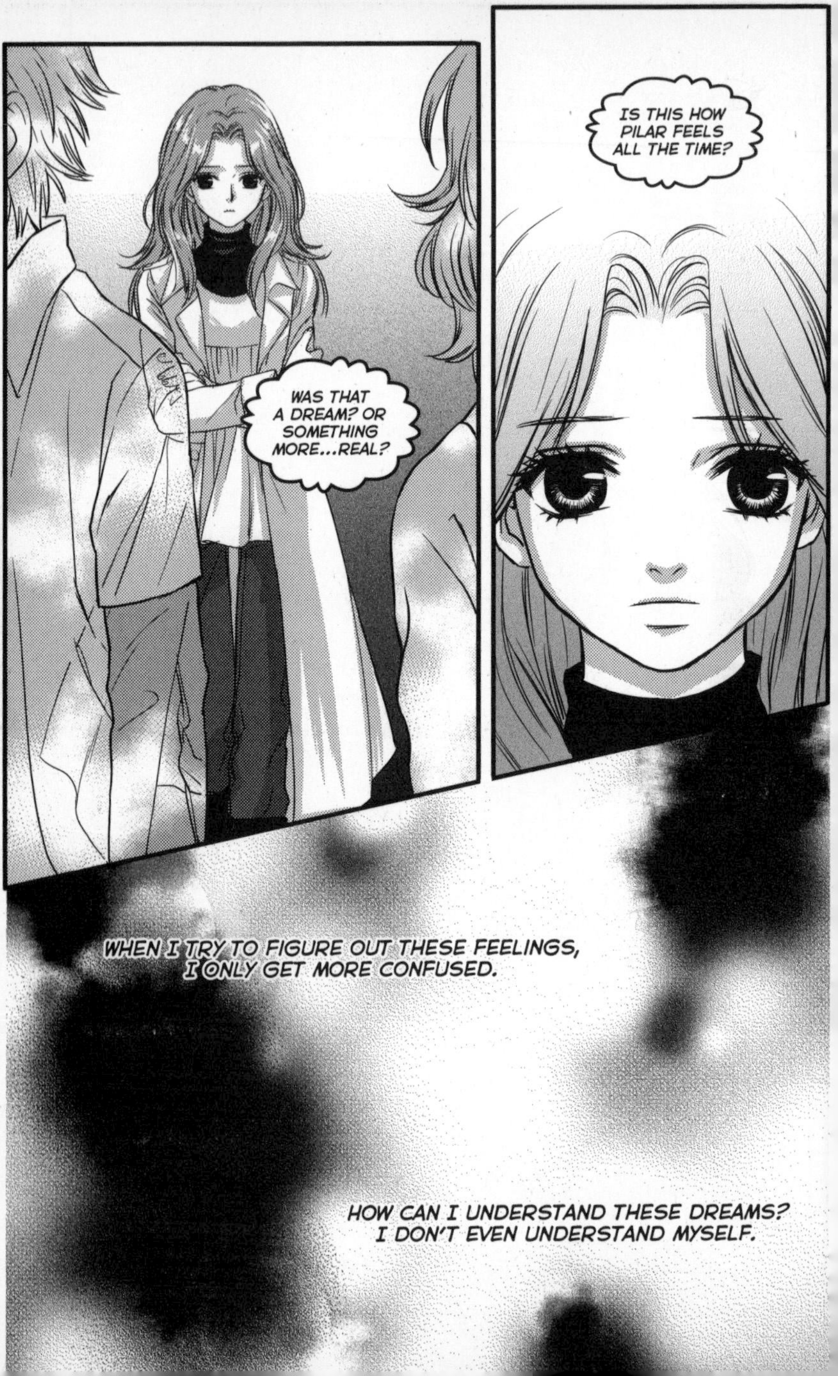
WAS THAT A DREAM? OR SOMETHING MORE...REAL?
IS THIS HOW PILAR FEELS ALL THE TIME?
WHEN I TRY TO FIGURE OUT THESE FEELINGS, I ONLY GET MORE CONFUSED.
HOW CAN I UNDERSTAND THESE DREAMS? I DON'T EVEN UNDERSTAND MYSELF.

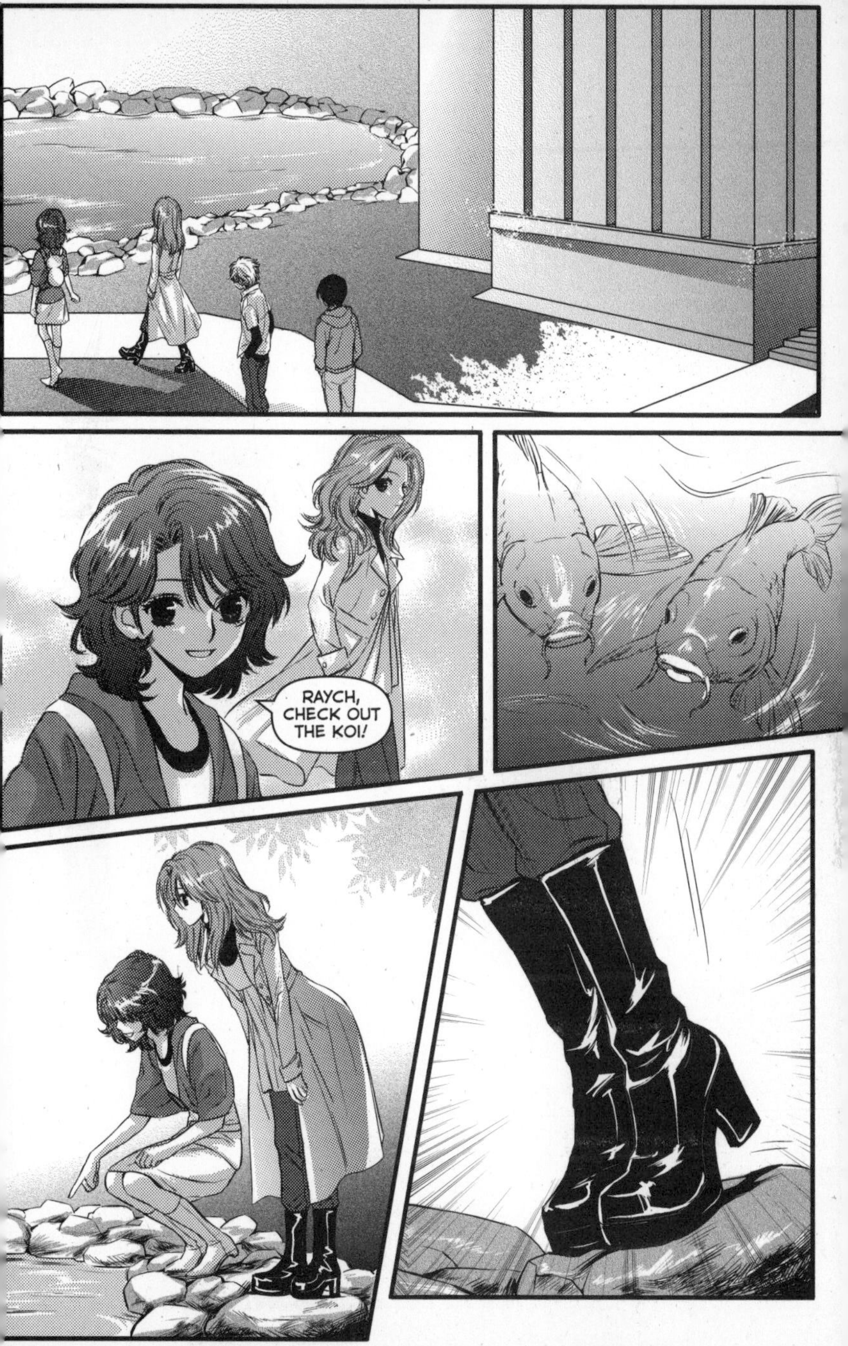
RAYCH, CHECK OUT THE KOI!

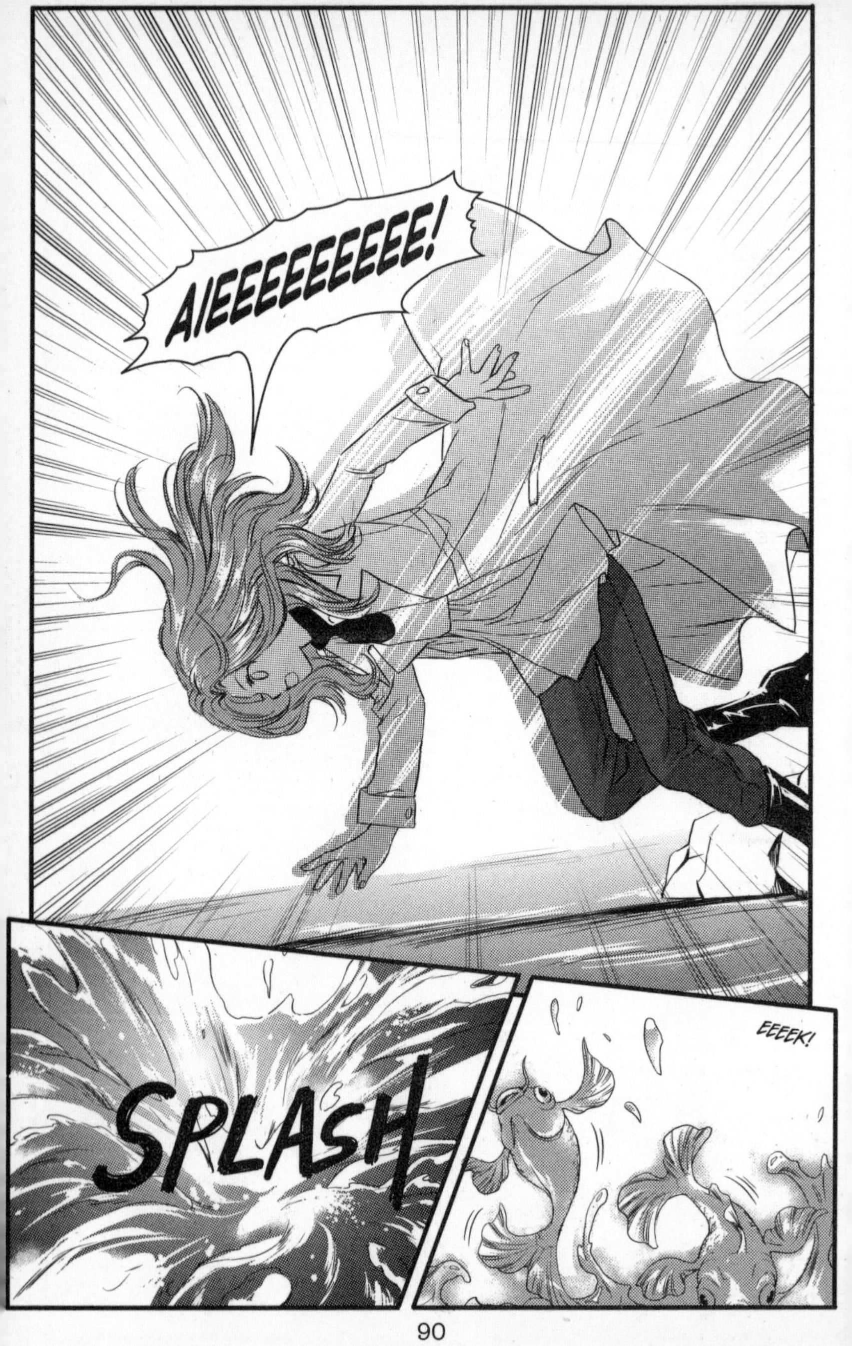
AIEEEEEEEEEE!
SPLASH
EEEEK!

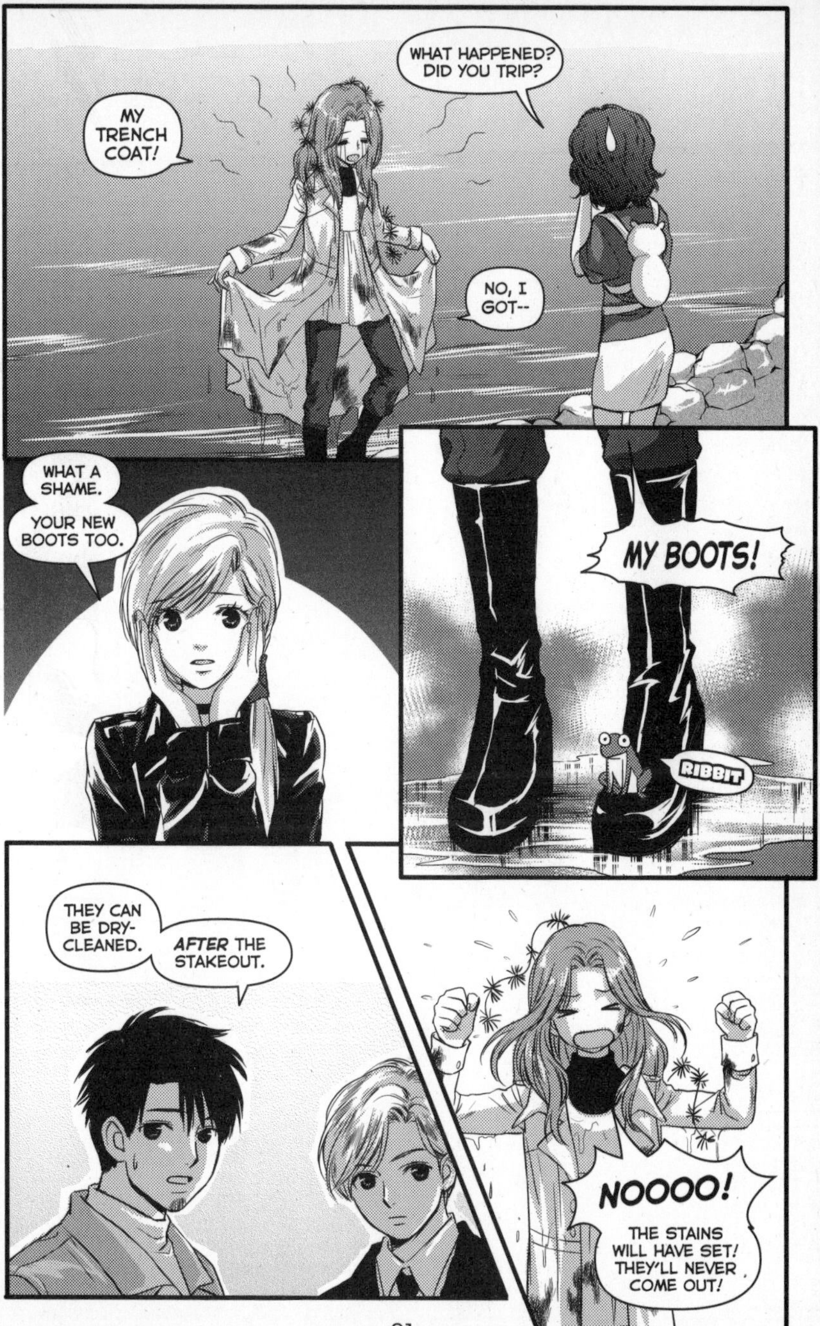
MY TRENCH COAT!
WHAT HAPPENED? DID YOU TRIP?
NO, I GOT--
WHAT A SHAME.
YOUR NEW BOOTS TOO.
MY BOOTS!
RIBBIT
THEY CAN BE DRY-CLEANED.
AFTER THE STAKEOUT.
NOOOO!
THE STAINS WILL HAVE SET! THEY'LL NEVER COME OUT!

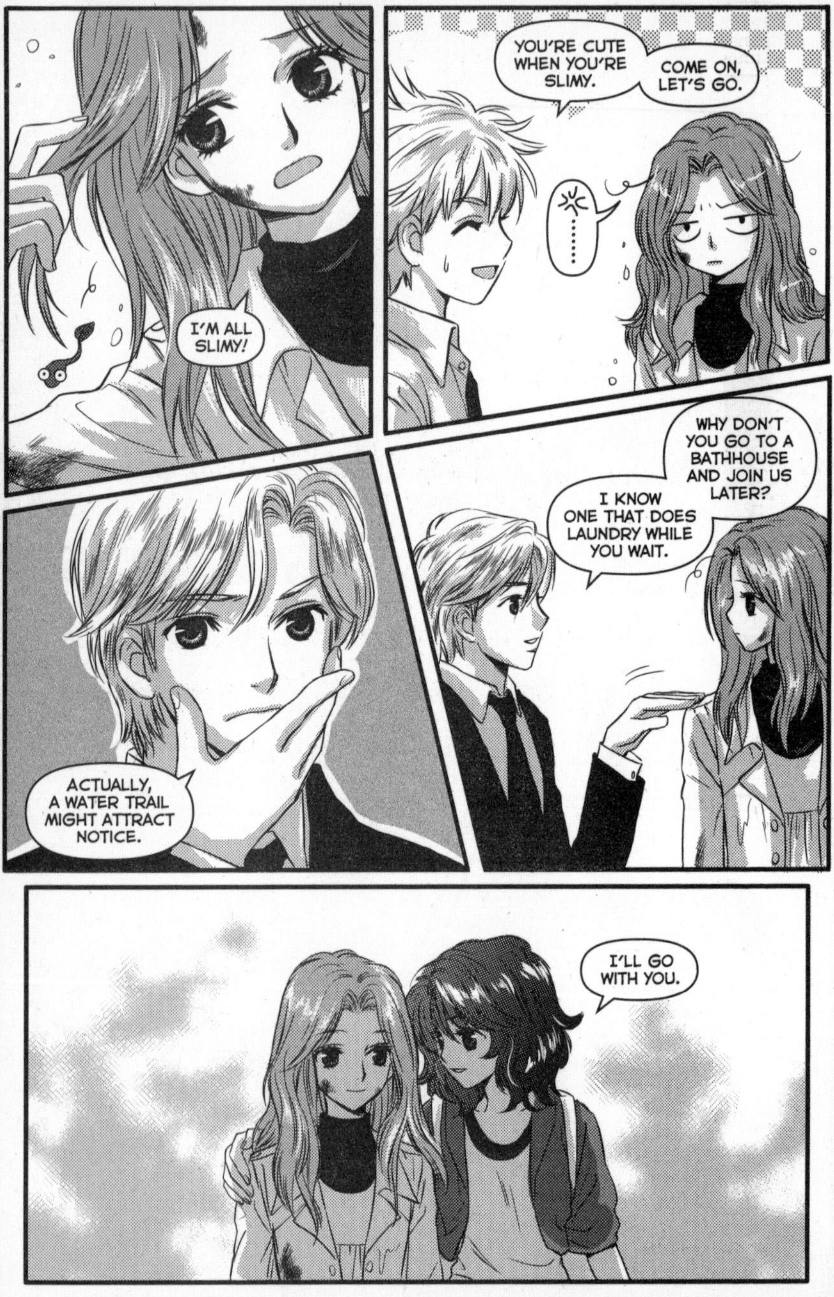
I'M ALL SLIMY!
YOU'RE CUTE WHEN YOU'RE SLIMY.
COME ON, LET'S GO.
......
ACTUALLY, A WATER TRAIL MIGHT ATTRACT NOTICE.
WHY DON'T YOU GO TO A BATHHOUSE AND JOIN US LATER?
I KNOW ONE THAT DOES LAUNDRY WHILE YOU WAIT.
I'LL GO WITH YOU.

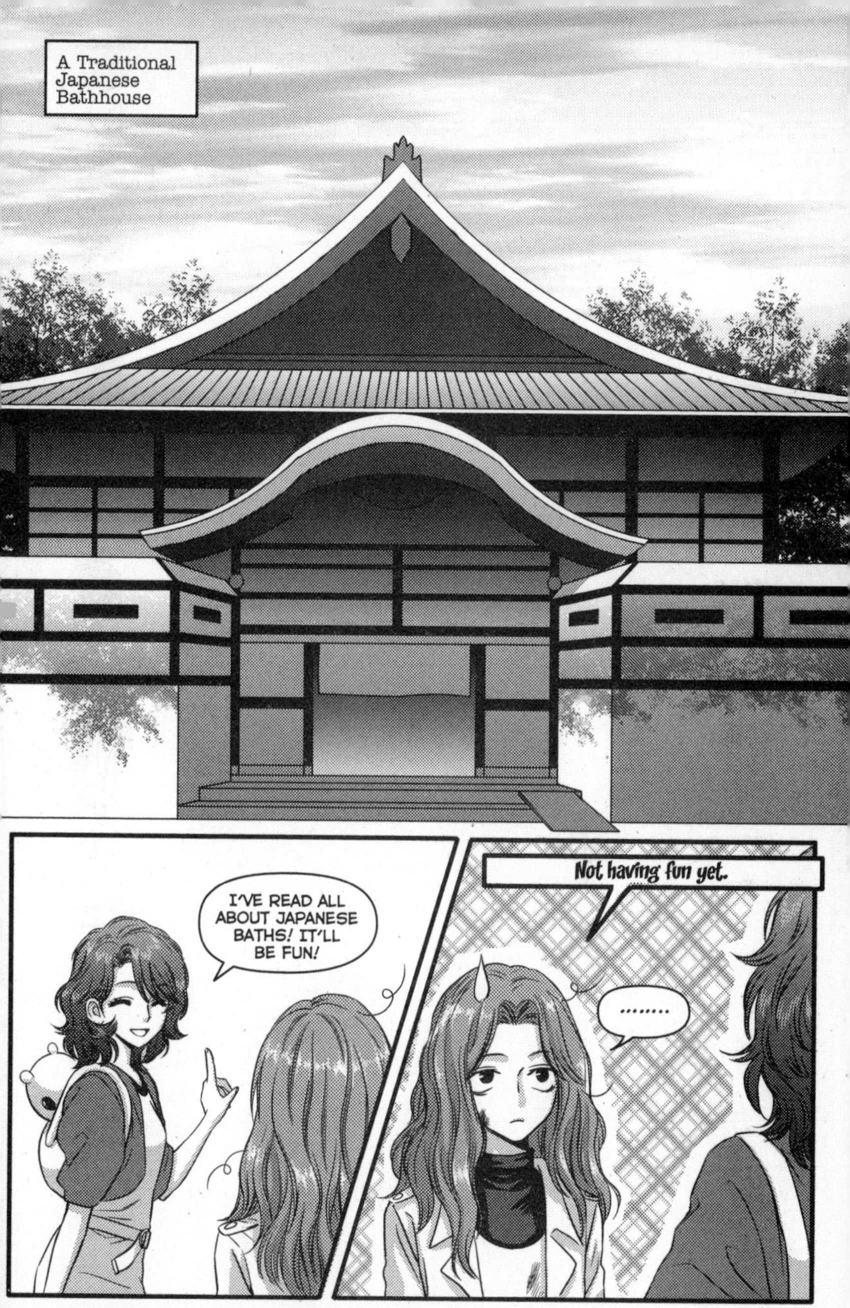
A Traditional Japanese Bathhouse
I'VE READ ALL ABOUT JAPANESE BATHS! IT'LL BE FUN!
Not having fun yet.
....

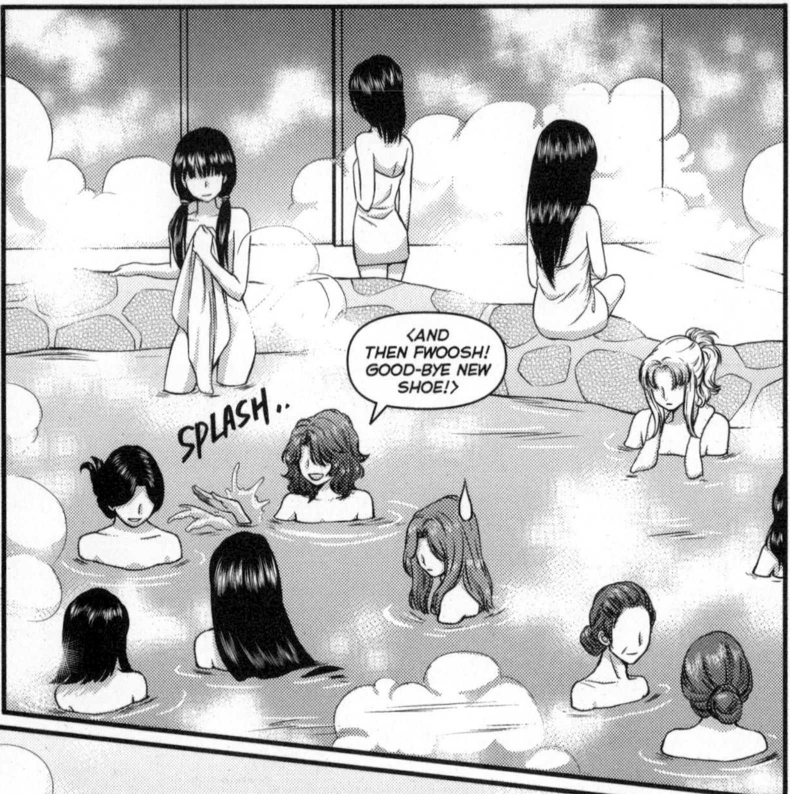
<AND THEN FWOOSH! GOOD-BYE NEW SHOE!>
SPLASH..

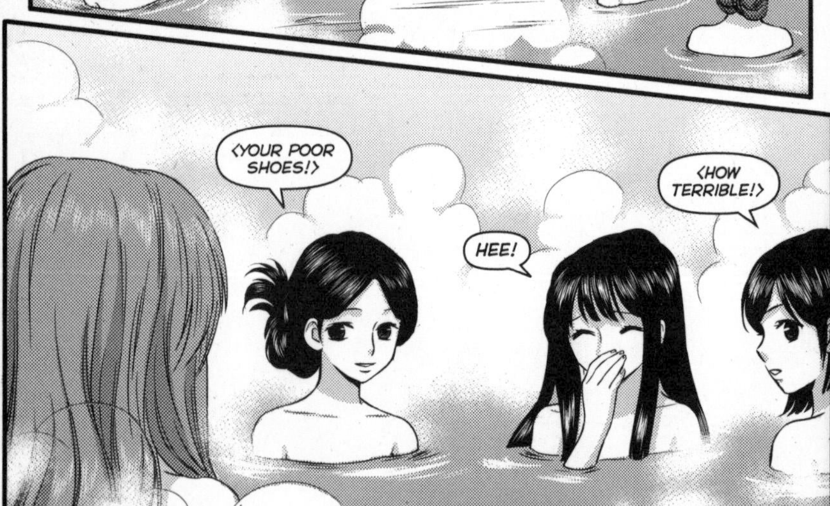
<YOUR POOR SHOES!>
HEE!
<HOW TERRIBLE!>

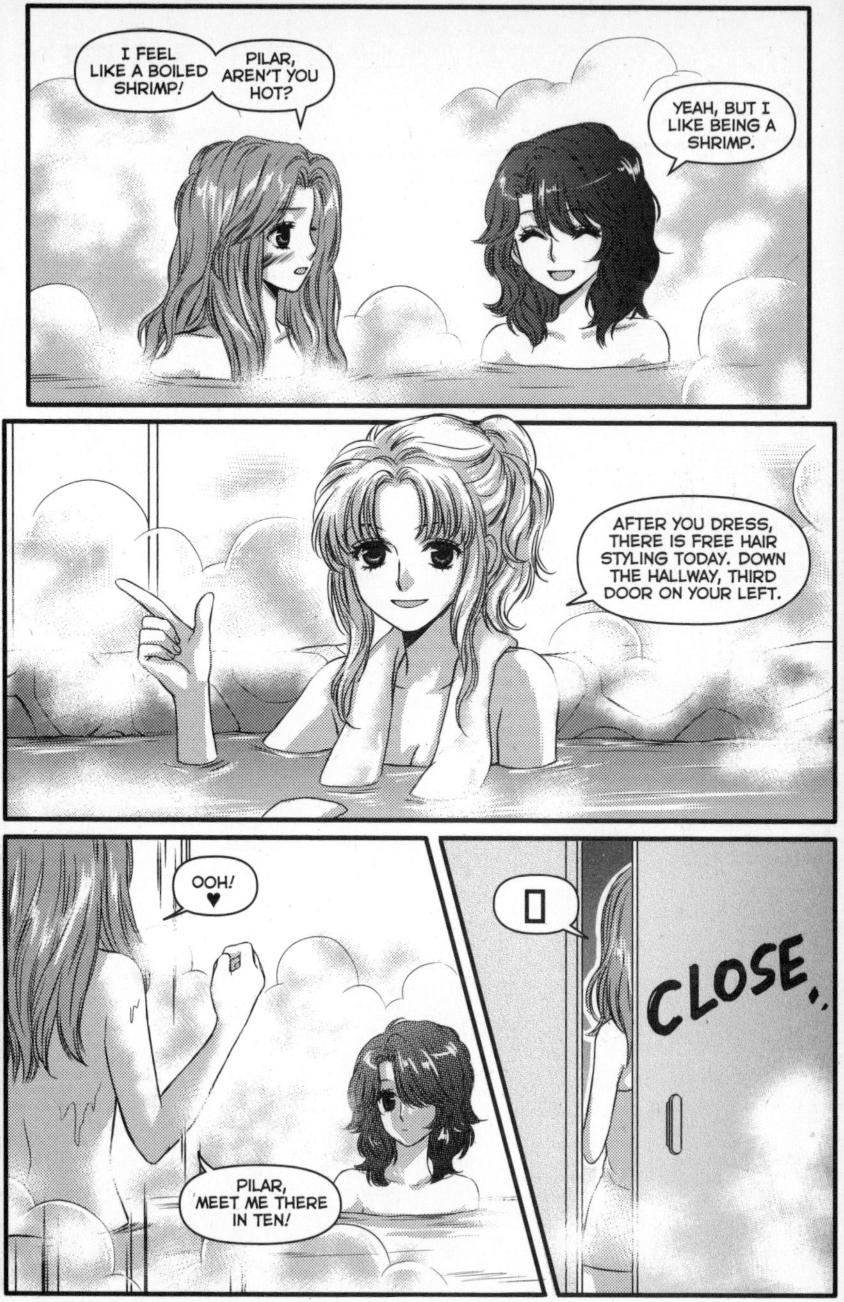
I FEEL LIKE A BOILED SHRIMP!
PILAR, AREN'T YOU HOT?
YEAH, BUT I LIKE BEING A SHRIMP.
AFTER YOU DRESS, THERE IS FREE HAIR STYLING TODAY. DOWN THE HALLWAY, THIRD DOOR ON YOUR LEFT.
OOH! ♥
PILAR, MEET ME THERE IN TEN!
CLOSE..

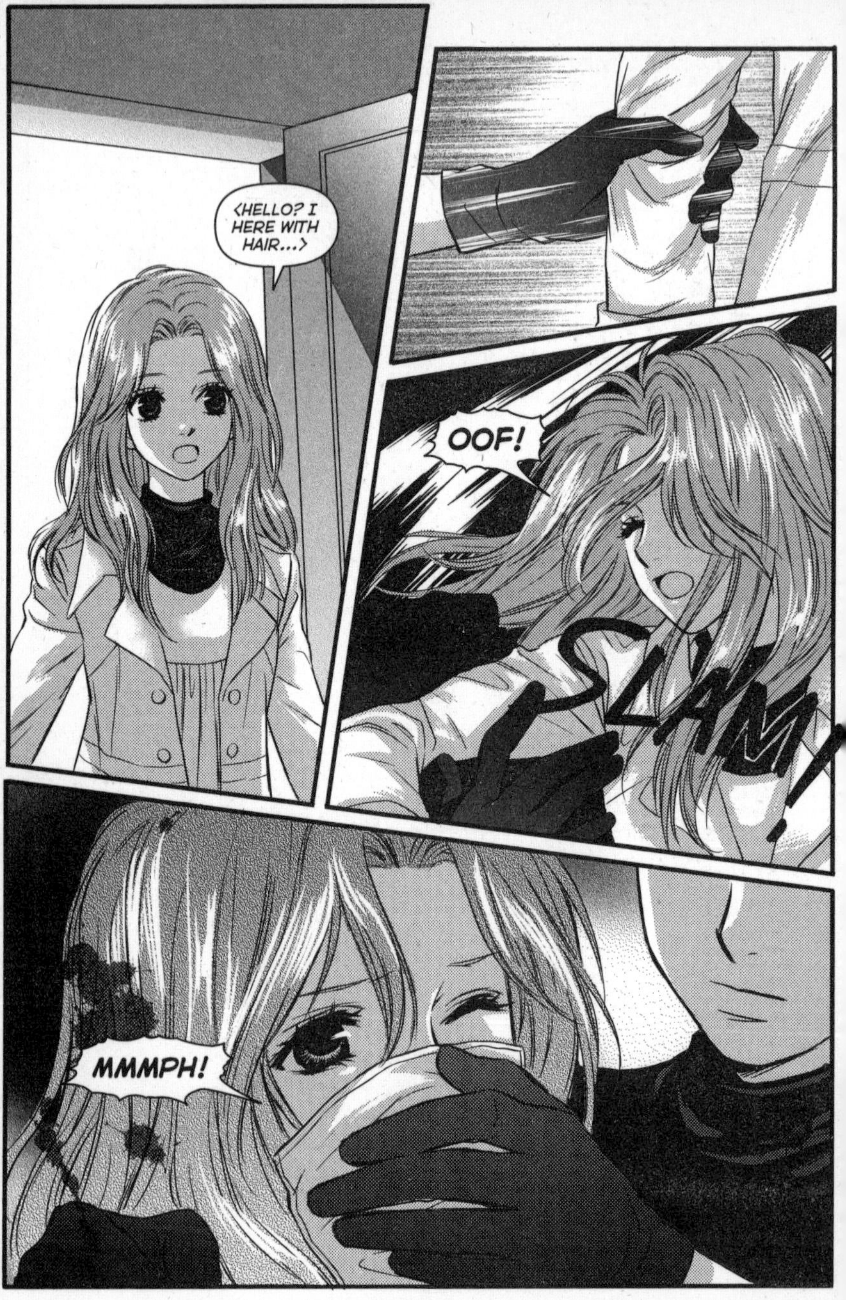
<HELLO? I HERE WITH HAIR...>
OOF!
SLAM!
MMMPH!

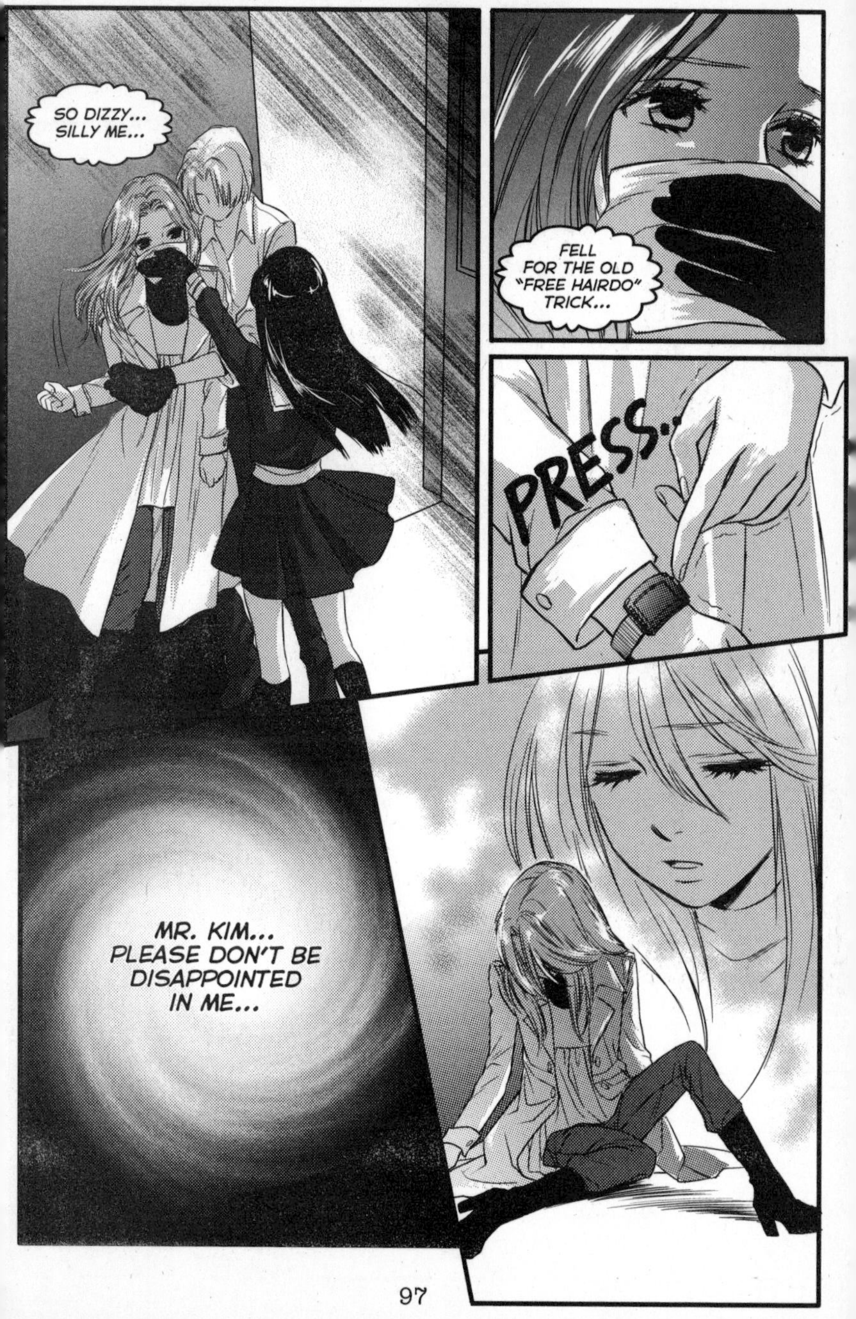
SO DIZZY... SILLY ME...
FELL FOR THE OLD "FREE HAIRDO" TRICK...
PRESS...
MR. KIM... PLEASE DON'T BE DISAPPOINTED IN ME...

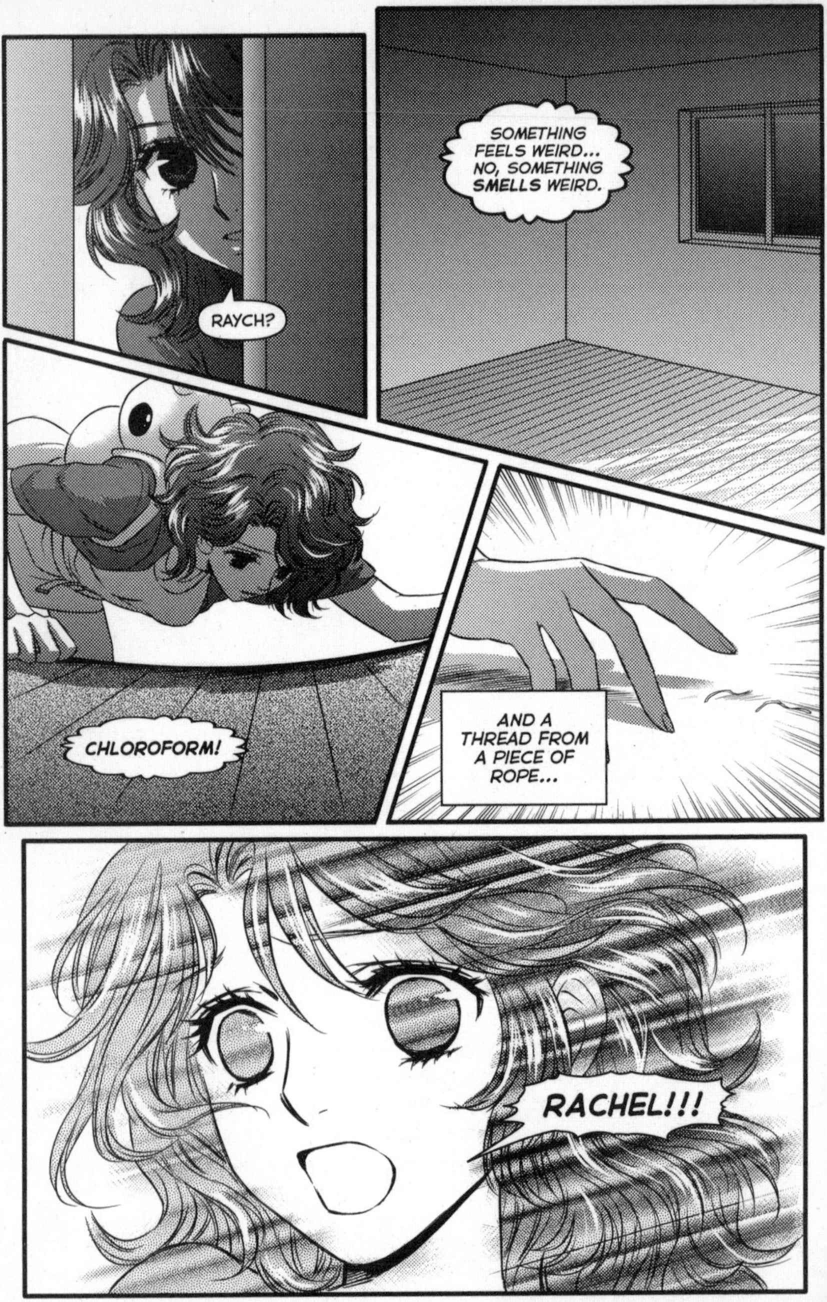
RAYCH?
SOMETHING FEELS WEIRD... NO, SOMETHING SMELLS WEIRD.
CHLOROFORM!
AND A THREAD FROM A PIECE OF ROPE...
RACHEL!!!

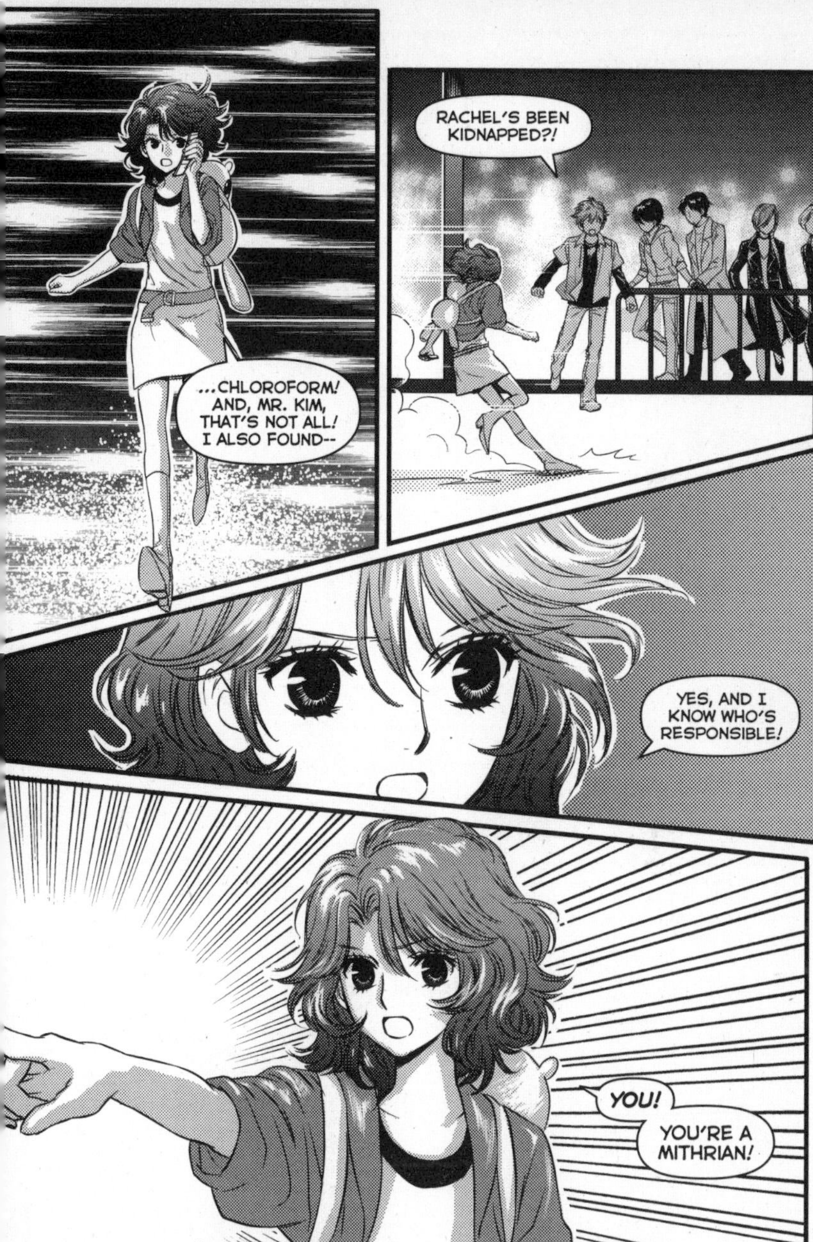
...CHLOROFORM! AND, MR. KIM, THAT'S NOT ALL! I ALSO FOUND--
RACHEL'S BEEN KIDNAPPED?!
YES, AND I KNOW WHO'S RESPONSIBLE!
YOU!
YOU'RE A MITHRIAN!

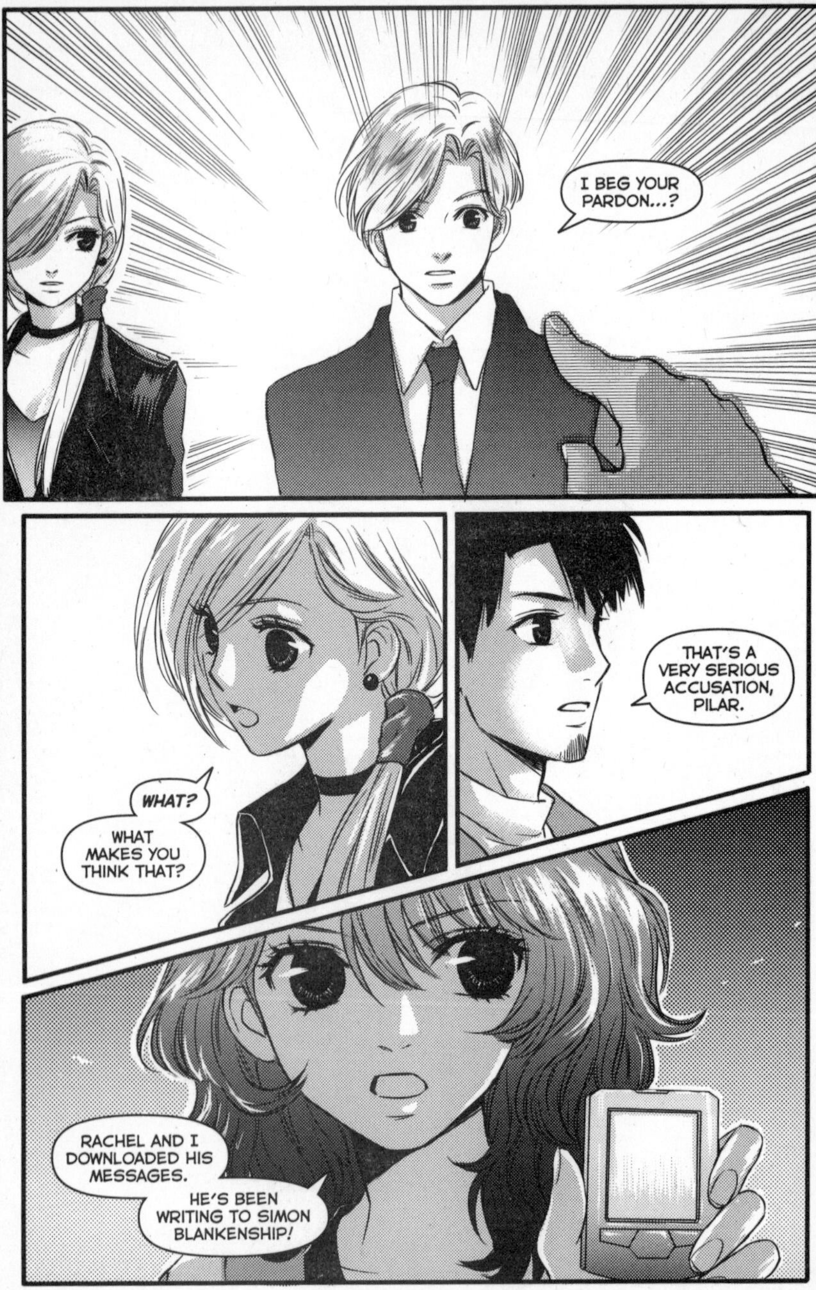
I BEG YOUR PARDON...?
WHAT?
WHAT MAKES YOU THINK THAT?
THAT'S A VERY SERIOUS ACCUSATION, PILAR.
RACHEL AND I DOWNLOADED HIS MESSAGES.
HE'S BEEN WRITING TO SIMON BLANKENSHIP!

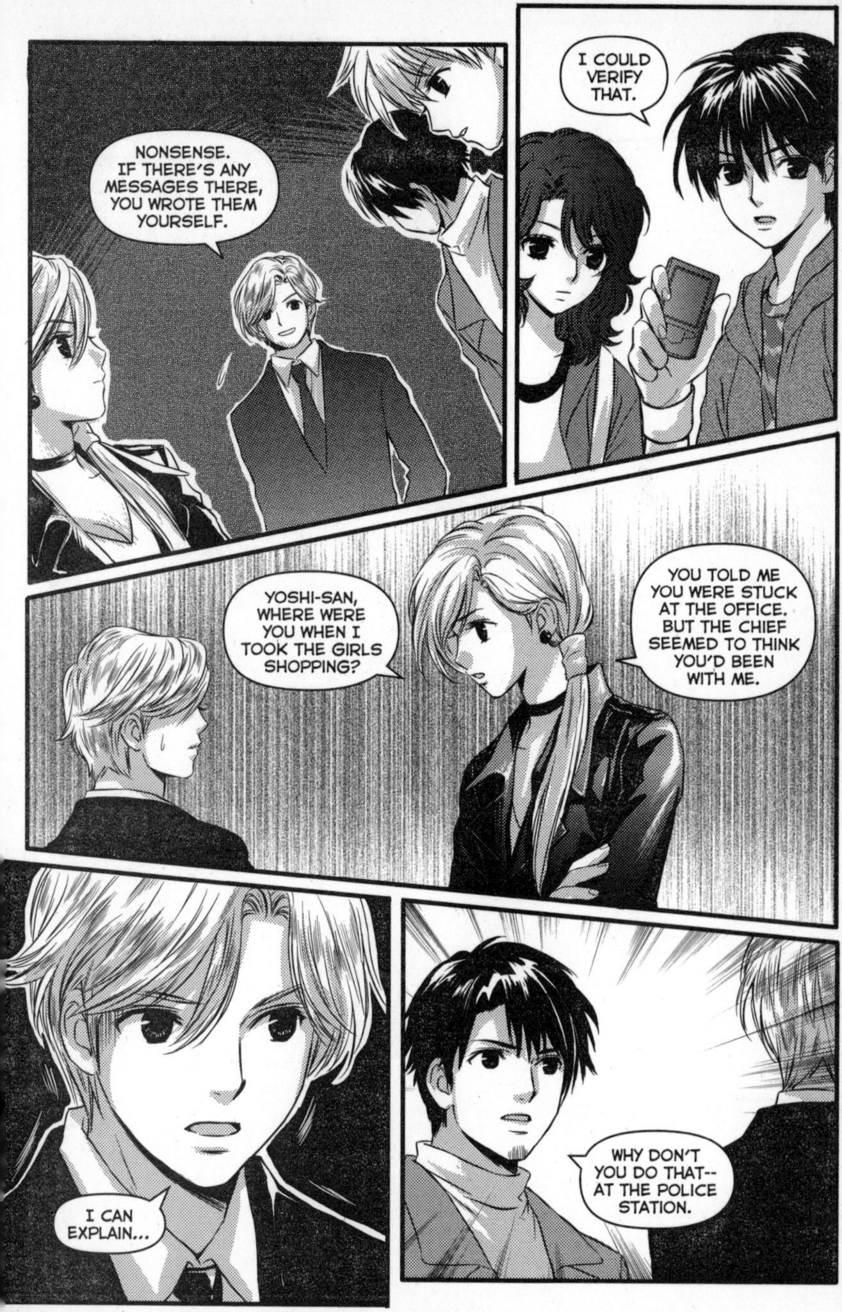
NONSENSE. IF THERE'S ANY MESSAGES THERE, YOU WROTE THEM YOURSELF.
I COULD VERIFY THAT.
YOSHI-SAN, WHERE WERE YOU WHEN I TOOK THE GIRLS SHOPPING?
YOU TOLD ME YOU WERE STUCK AT THE OFFICE. BUT THE CHIEF SEEMED TO THINK YOU'D BEEN WITH ME.
I CAN EXPLAIN...
WHY DON'T YOU DO THAT-- AT THE POLICE STATION.

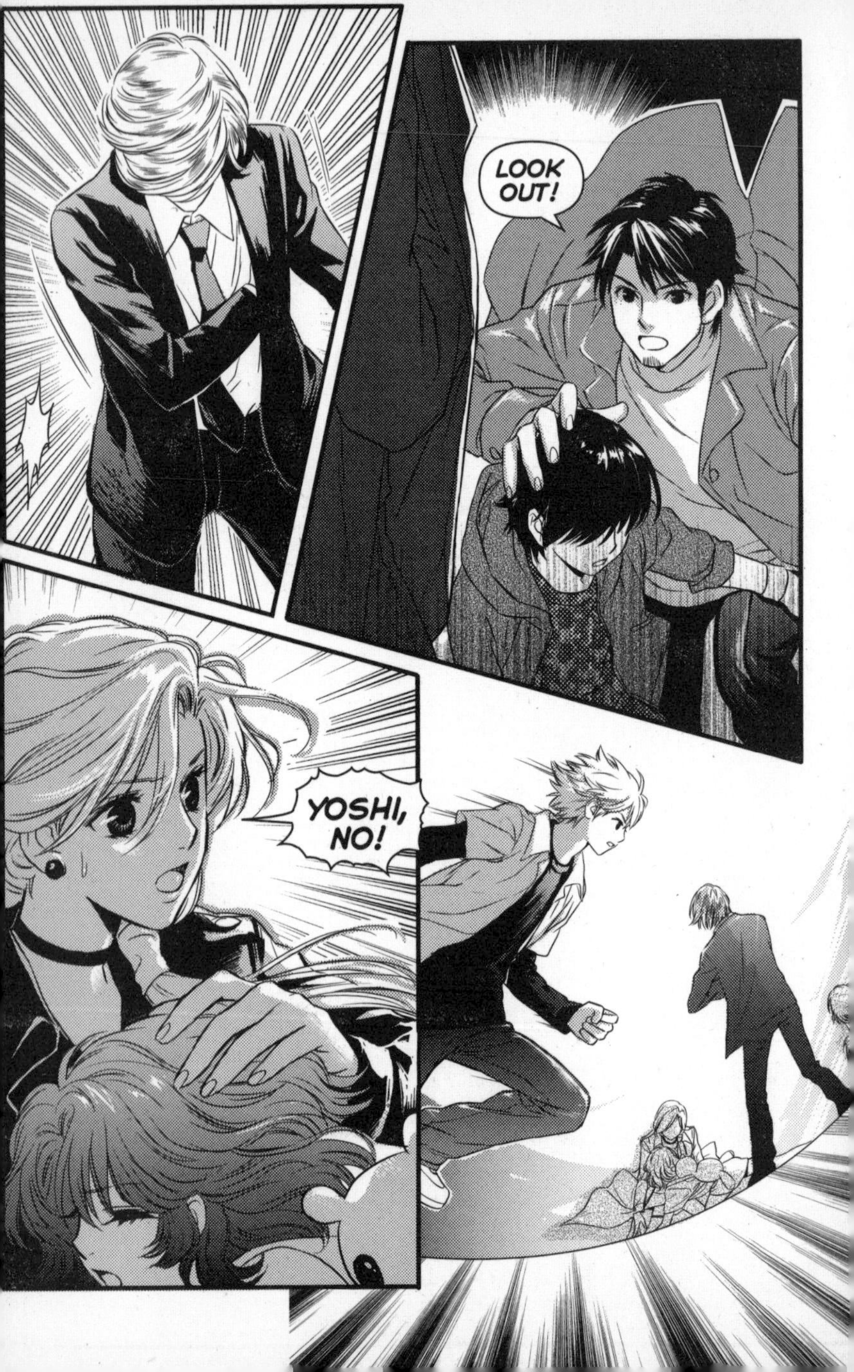
LOOK OUT!
YOSHI, NO!

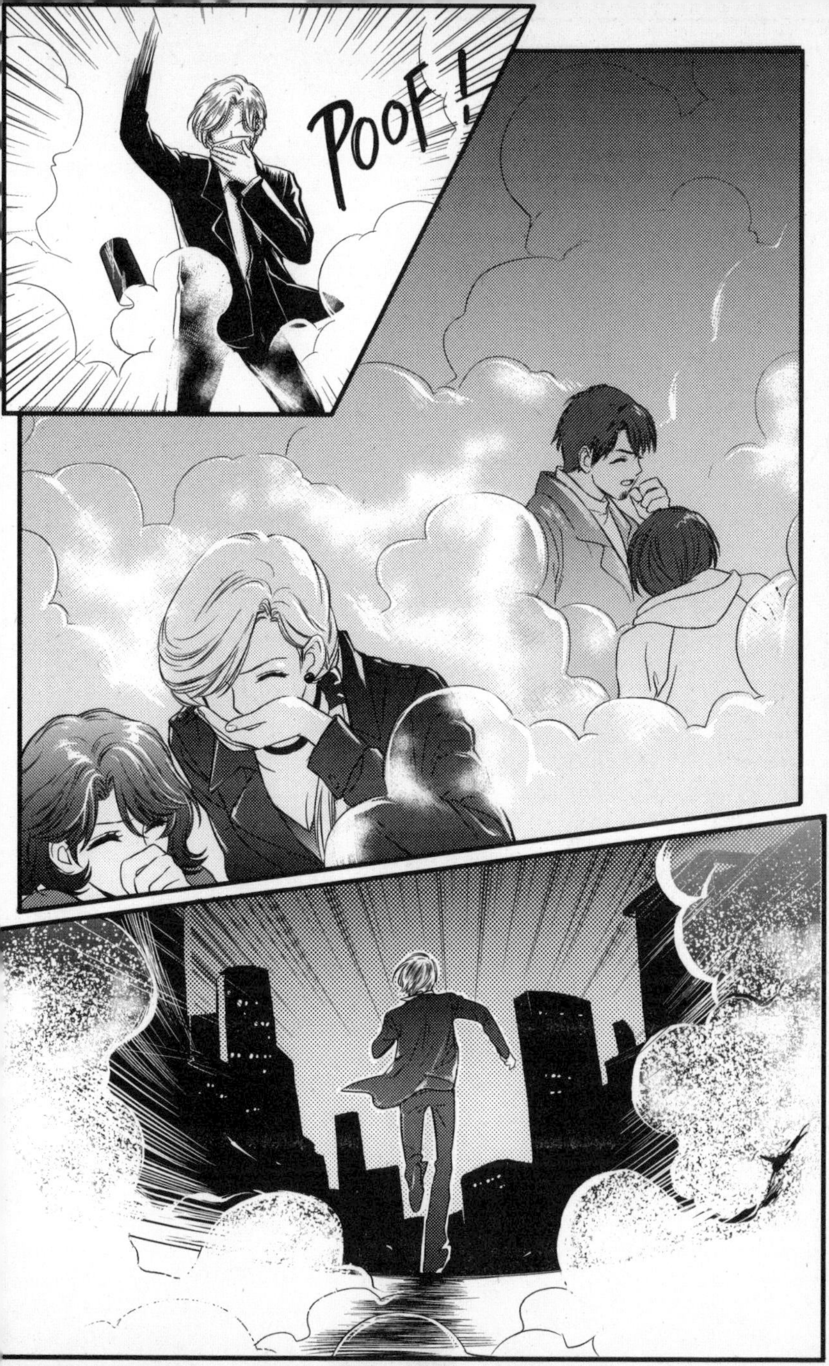
POOF!

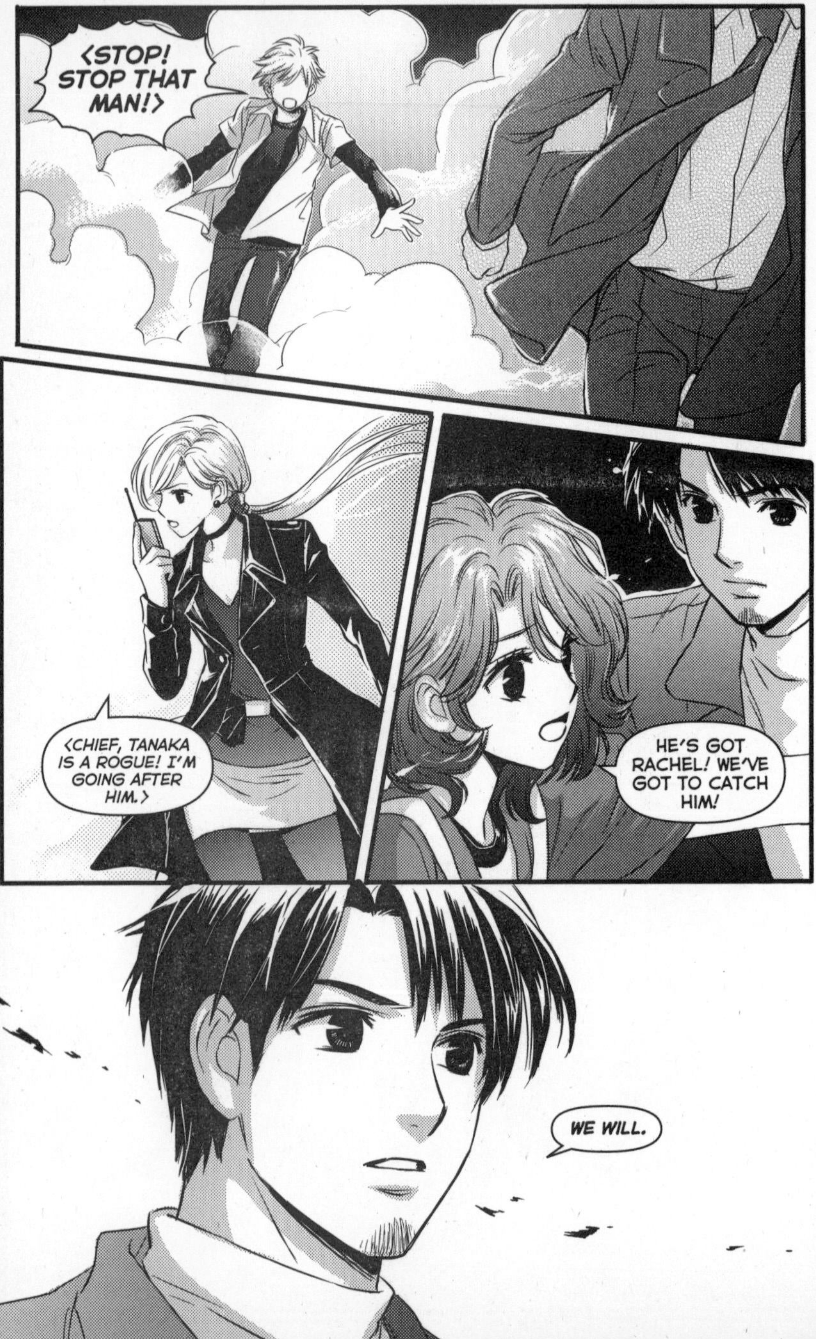
<STOP! STOP THAT MAN!>
<CHIEF, TANAKA IS A ROGUE! I'M GOING AFTER HIM.>
HE'S GOT RACHEL! WE'VE GOT TO CATCH HIM!
WE WILL.

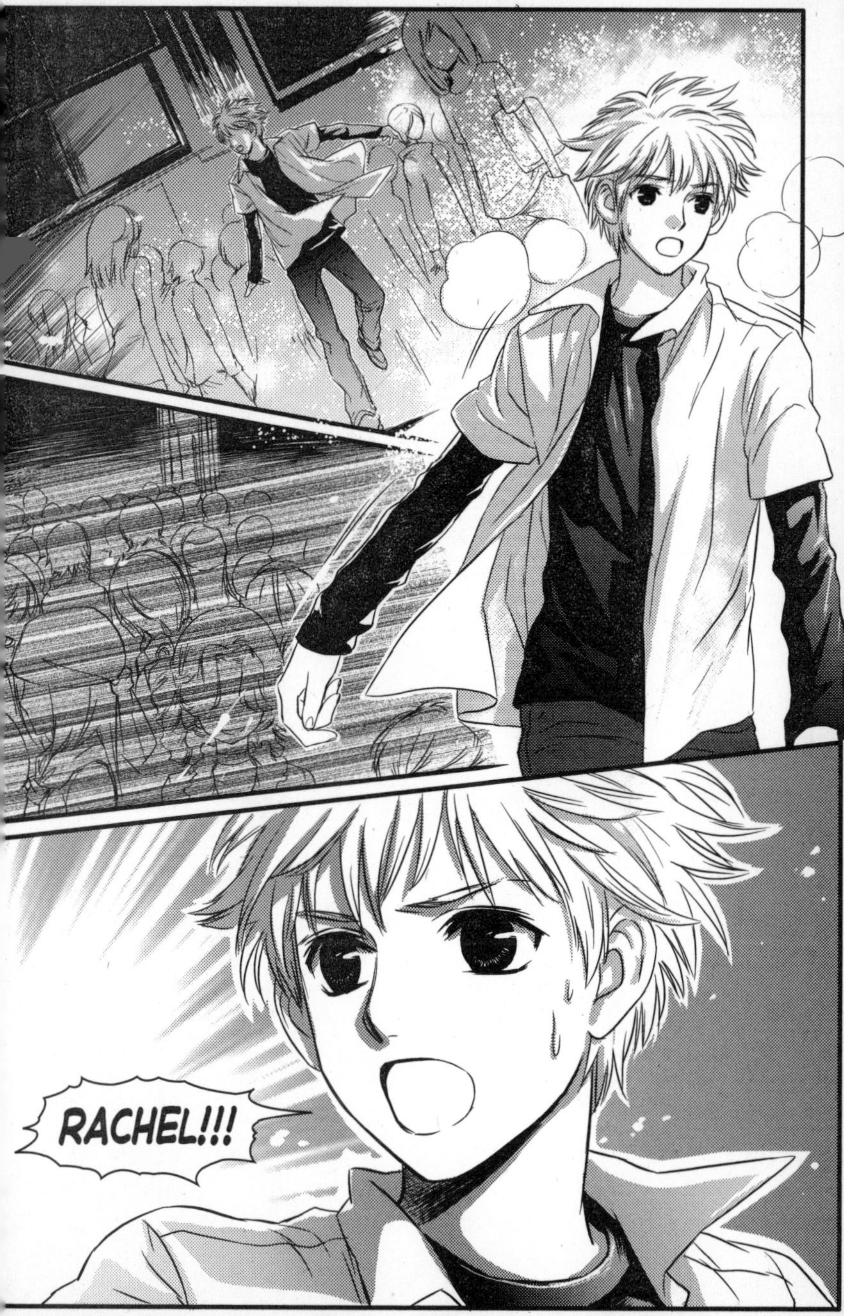
RACHEL!!!

Chapter Five

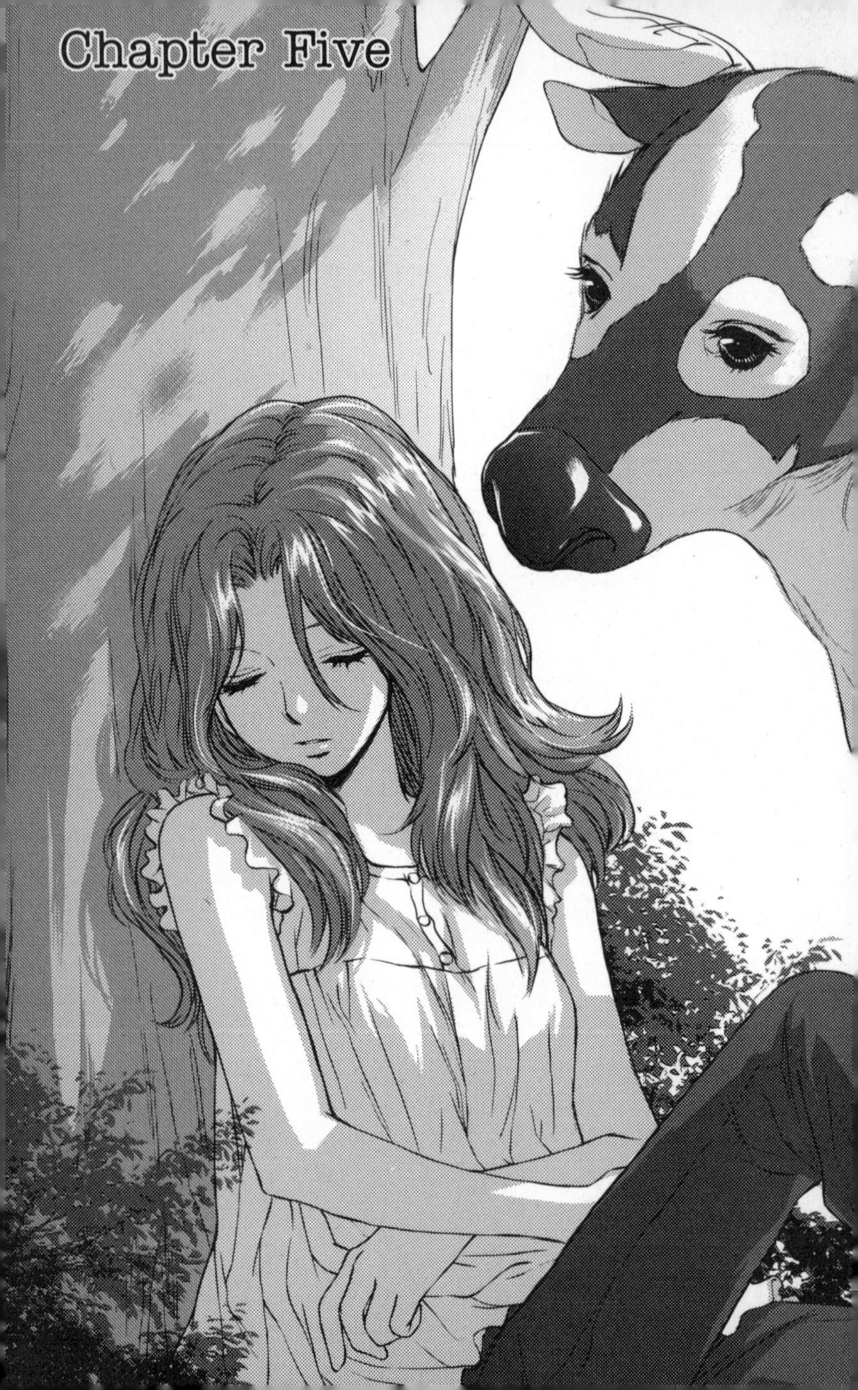

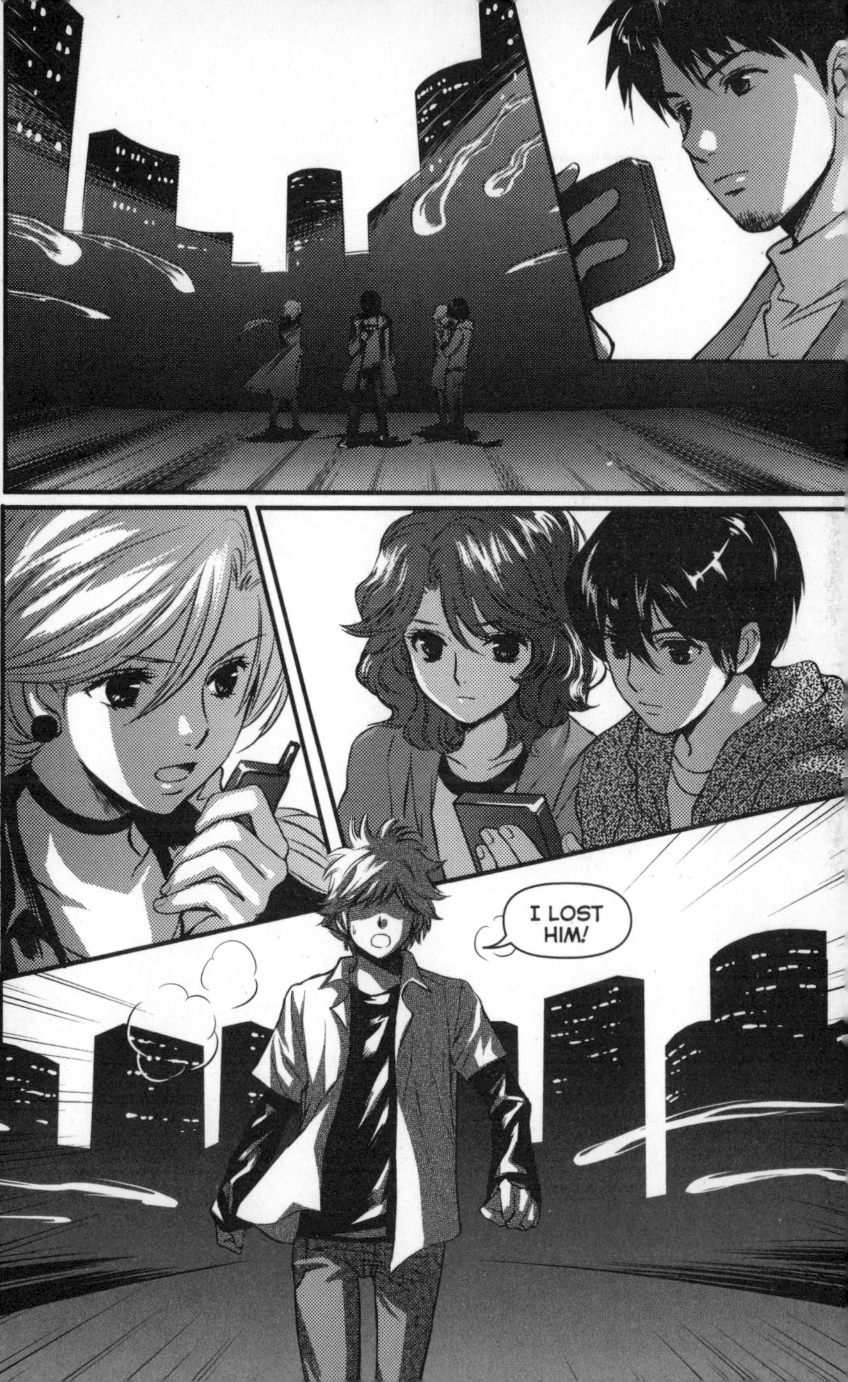
I LOST HIM!

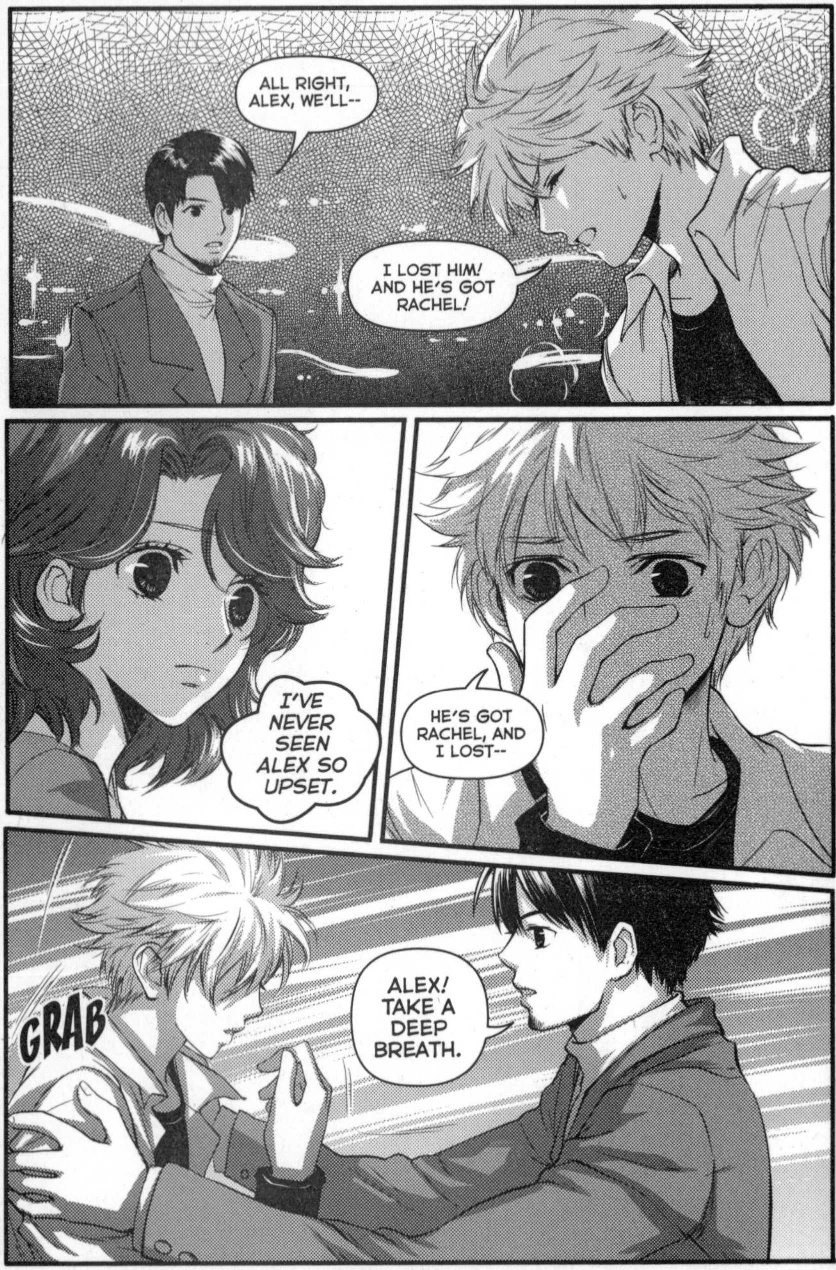
ALL RIGHT, ALEX, WE'LL--
I LOST HIM! AND HE'S GOT RACHEL!
I'VE NEVER SEEN ALEX SO UPSET.
HE'S GOT RACHEL, AND I LOST--
GRAB
ALEX! TAKE A DEEP BREATH.

I SHOULD COMFORT HIM...BUT I CAN'T HELP BUT WONDER...

THAT'S IT...NOW BREATHE OUT.

THEY'RE ALL SO YOUNG...

IN...AND OUT...

IS IT BECAUSE HE FAILED? OR BECAUSE IT'S RACHEL WHO'S IN DANGER?

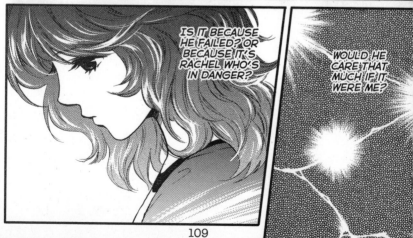

WOULD HE CARE THAT MUCH IF IT WERE ME?

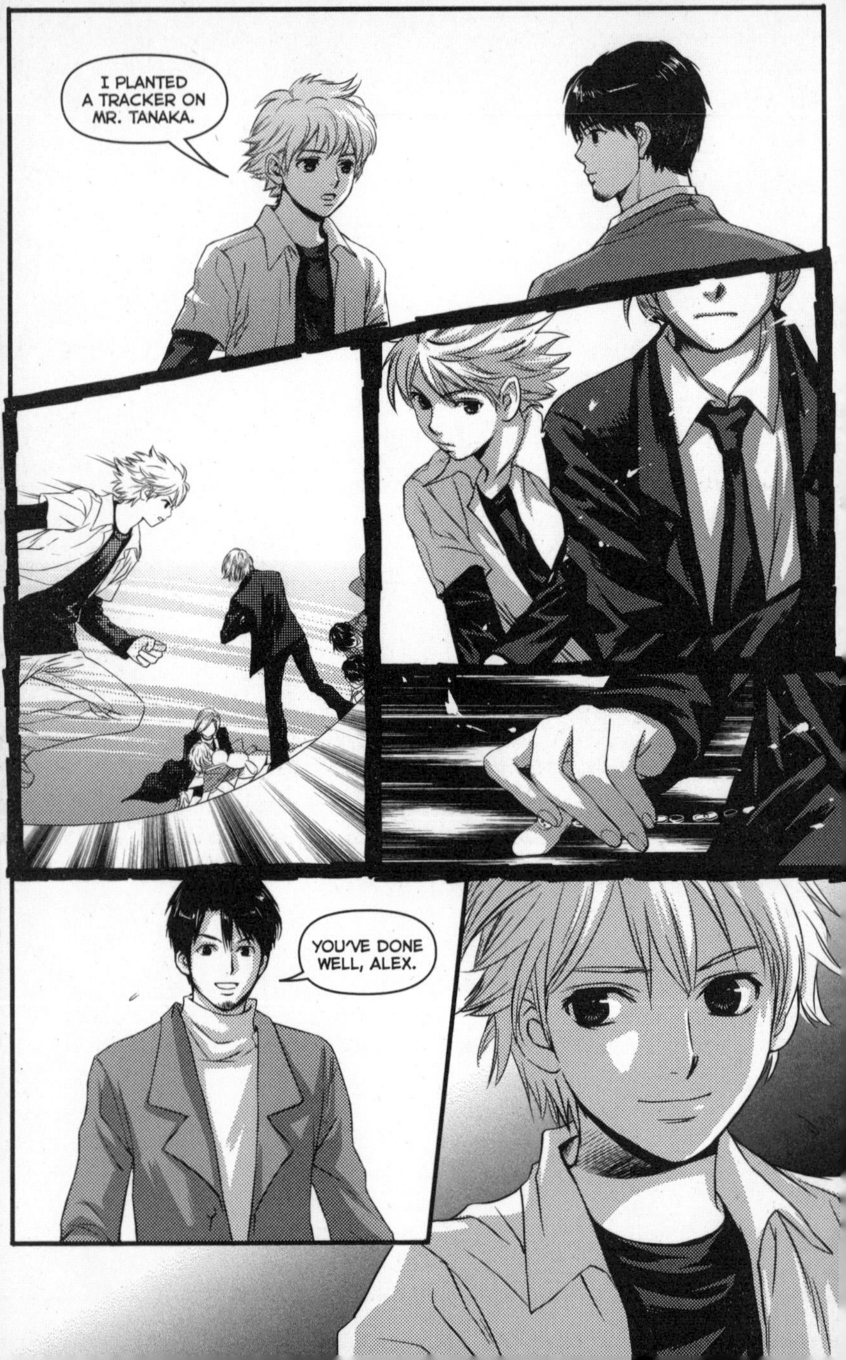
I PLANTED A TRACKER ON MR. TANAKA.
YOU'VE DONE WELL, ALEX.

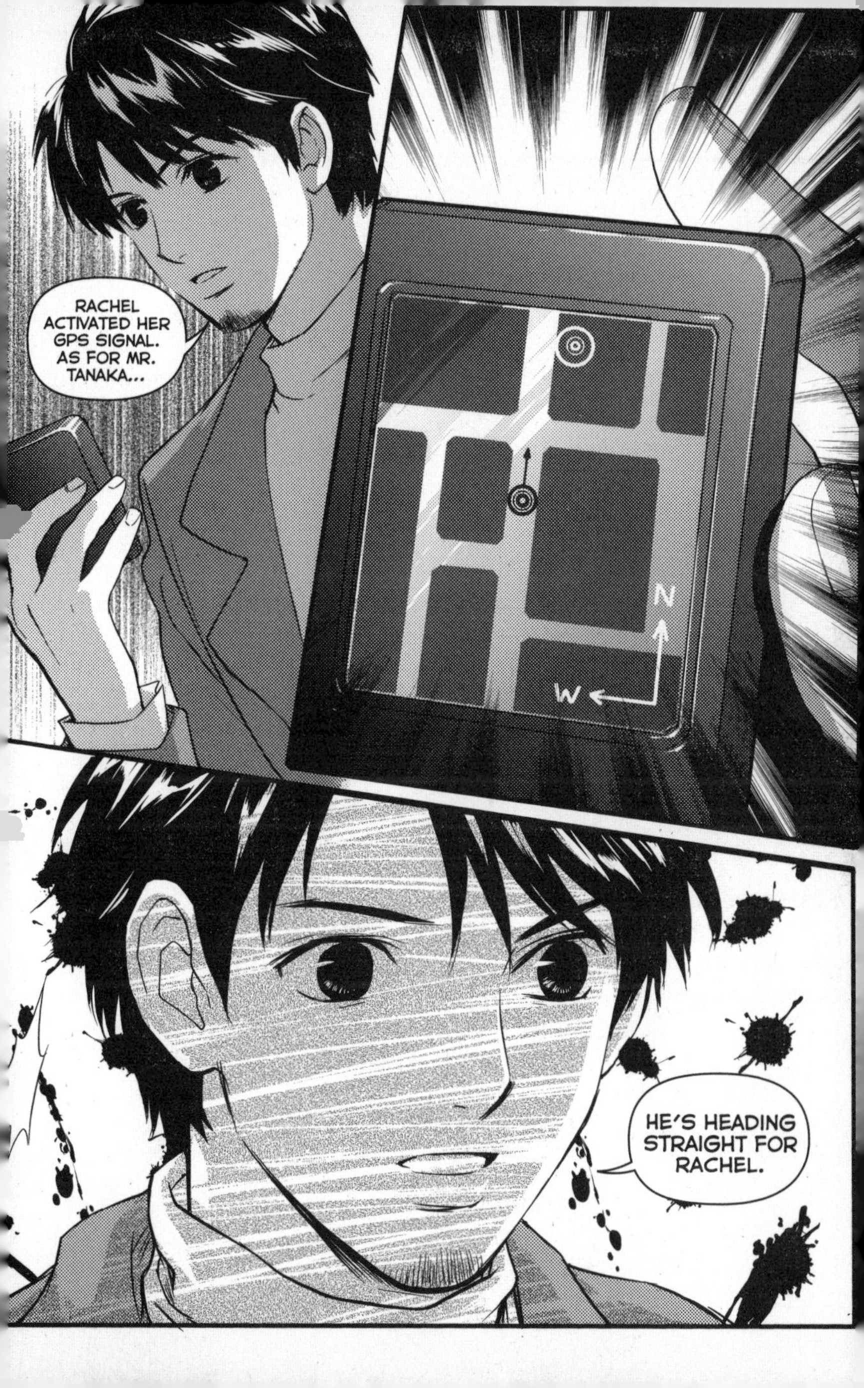
RACHEL ACTIVATED HER GPS SIGNAL. AS FOR MR. TANAKA...
N
W
HE'S HEADING STRAIGHT FOR RACHEL.

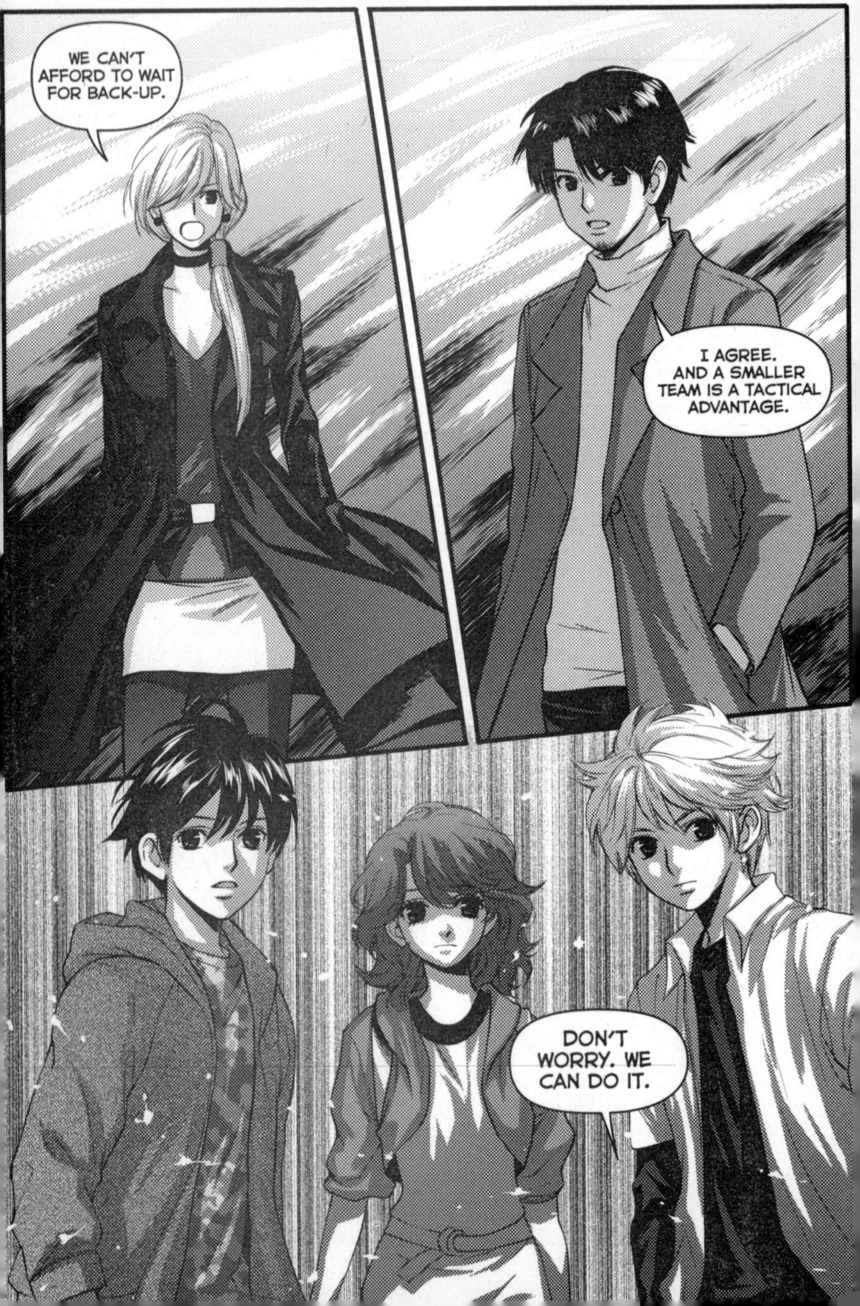
WE CAN'T AFFORD TO WAIT FOR BACK-UP.
I AGREE. AND A SMALLER TEAM IS A TACTICAL ADVANTAGE.
DON'T WORRY. WE CAN DO IT.

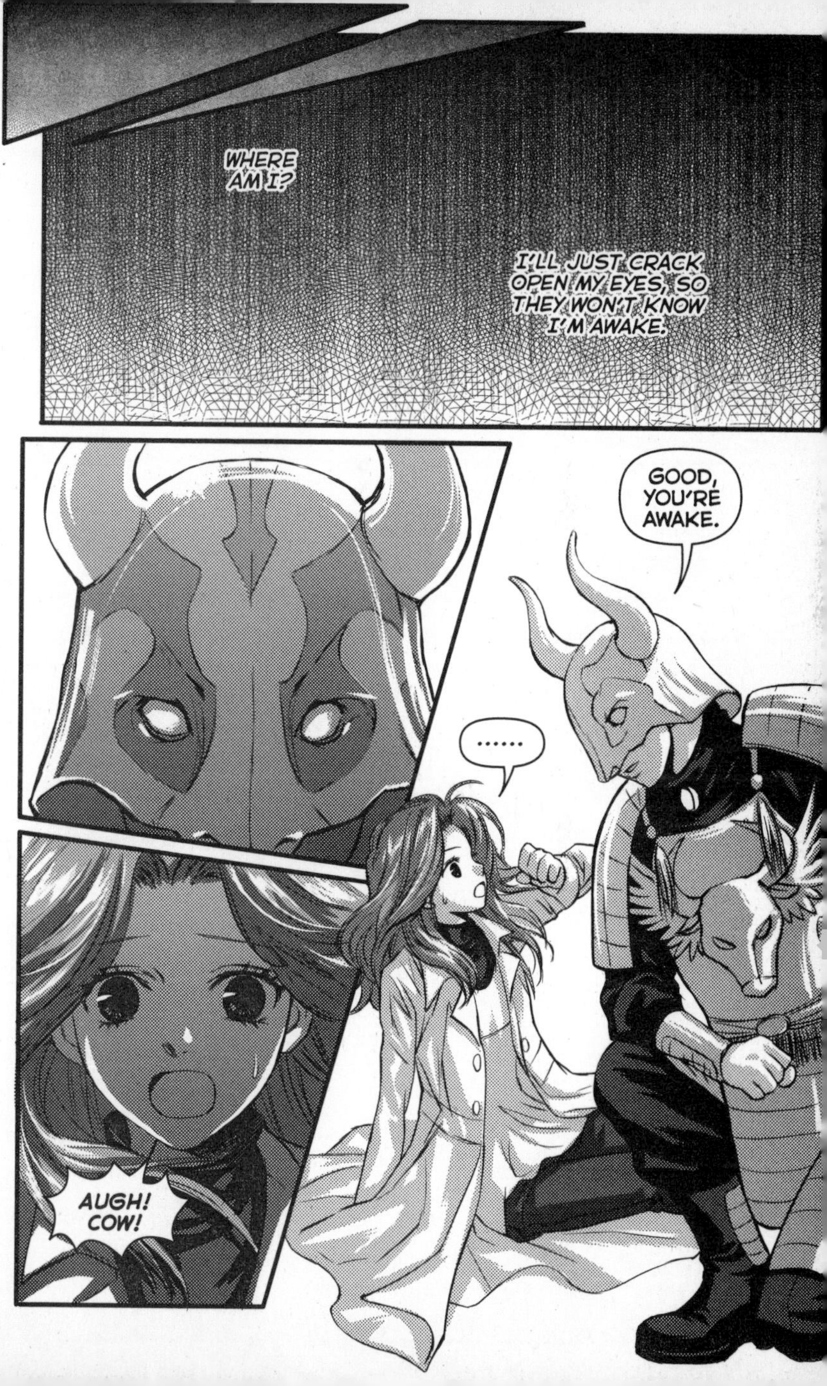
WHERE AM I?
I'LL JUST CRACK OPEN MY EYES, SO THEY WON'T KNOW I'M AWAKE.
GOOD, YOU'RE AWAKE.
......
AUGH! COW!

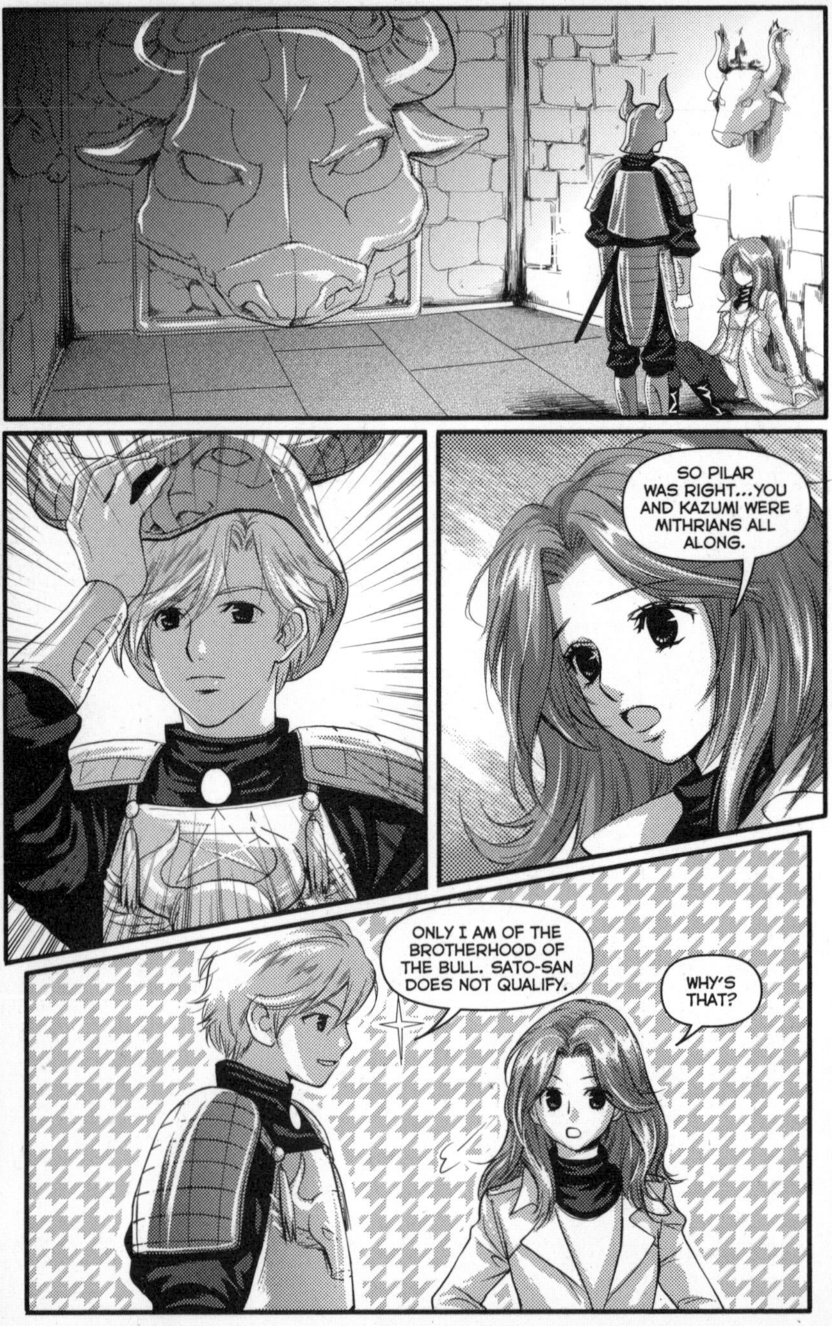
SO PILAR WAS RIGHT...YOU AND KAZUMI WERE MITHRIANS ALL ALONG.
ONLY I AM OF THE BROTHERHOOD OF THE BULL. SATO-SAN DOES NOT QUALIFY.
WHY'S THAT?

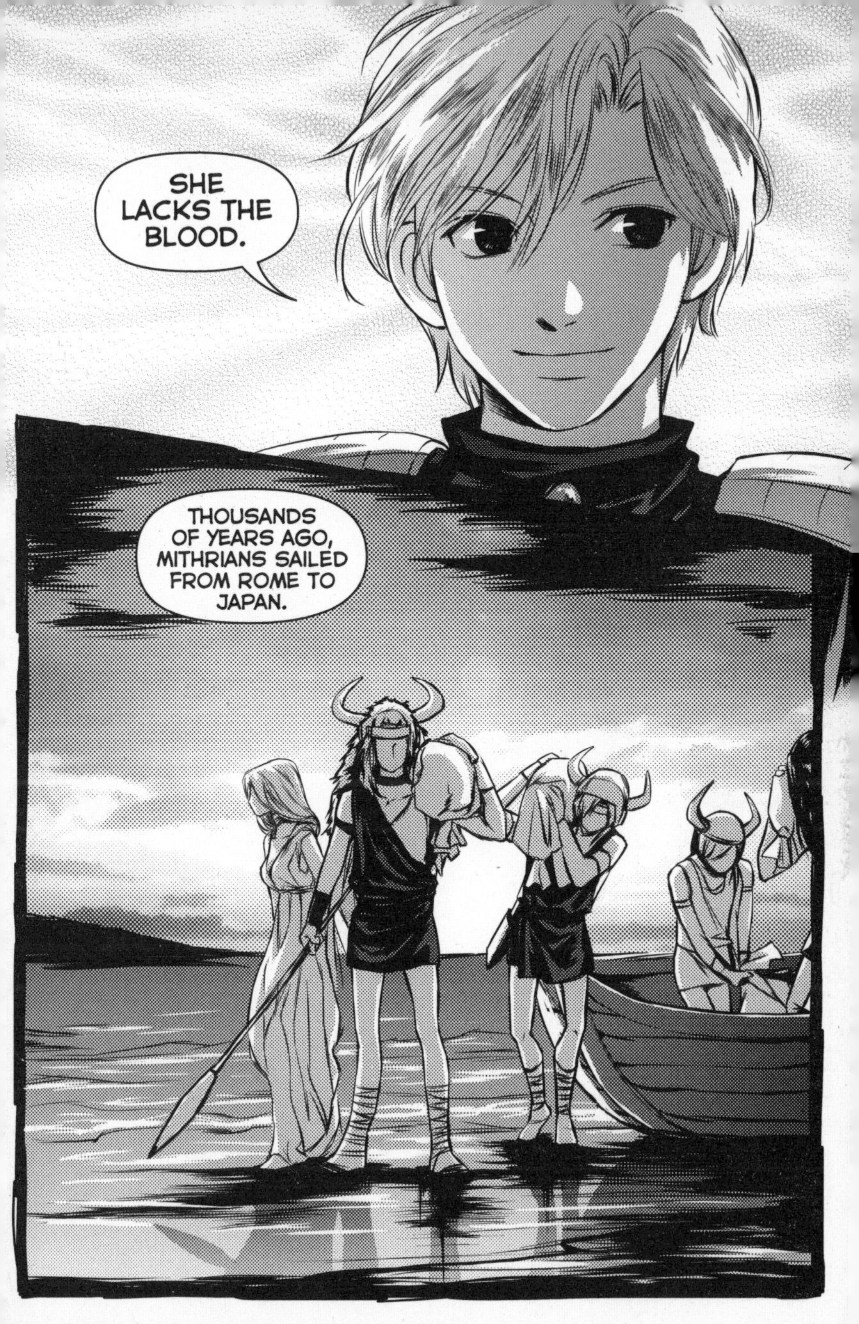
SHE LACKS THE BLOOD.
THOUSANDS OF YEARS AGO, MITHRIANS SAILED FROM ROME TO JAPAN.

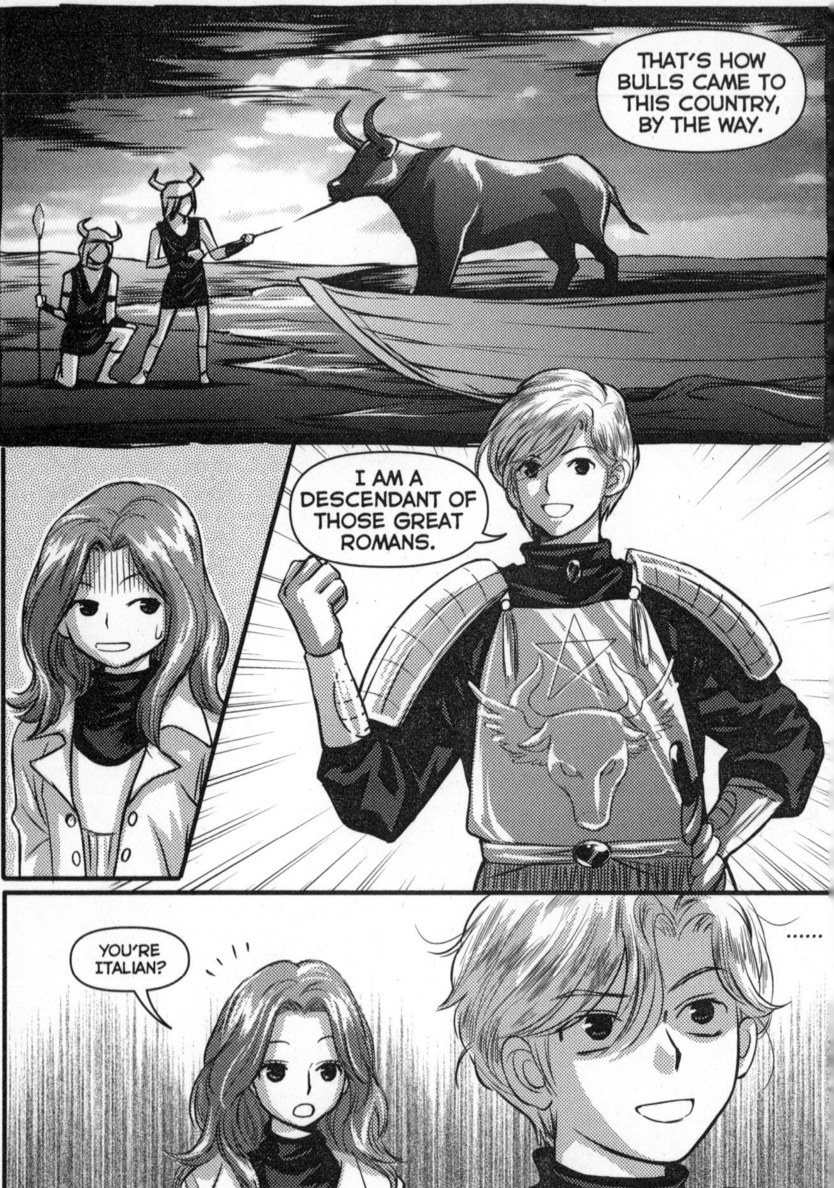
THAT'S HOW BULLS CAME TO THIS COUNTRY, BY THE WAY.
I AM A DESCENDANT OF THOSE GREAT ROMANS.
YOU'RE ITALIAN?
......

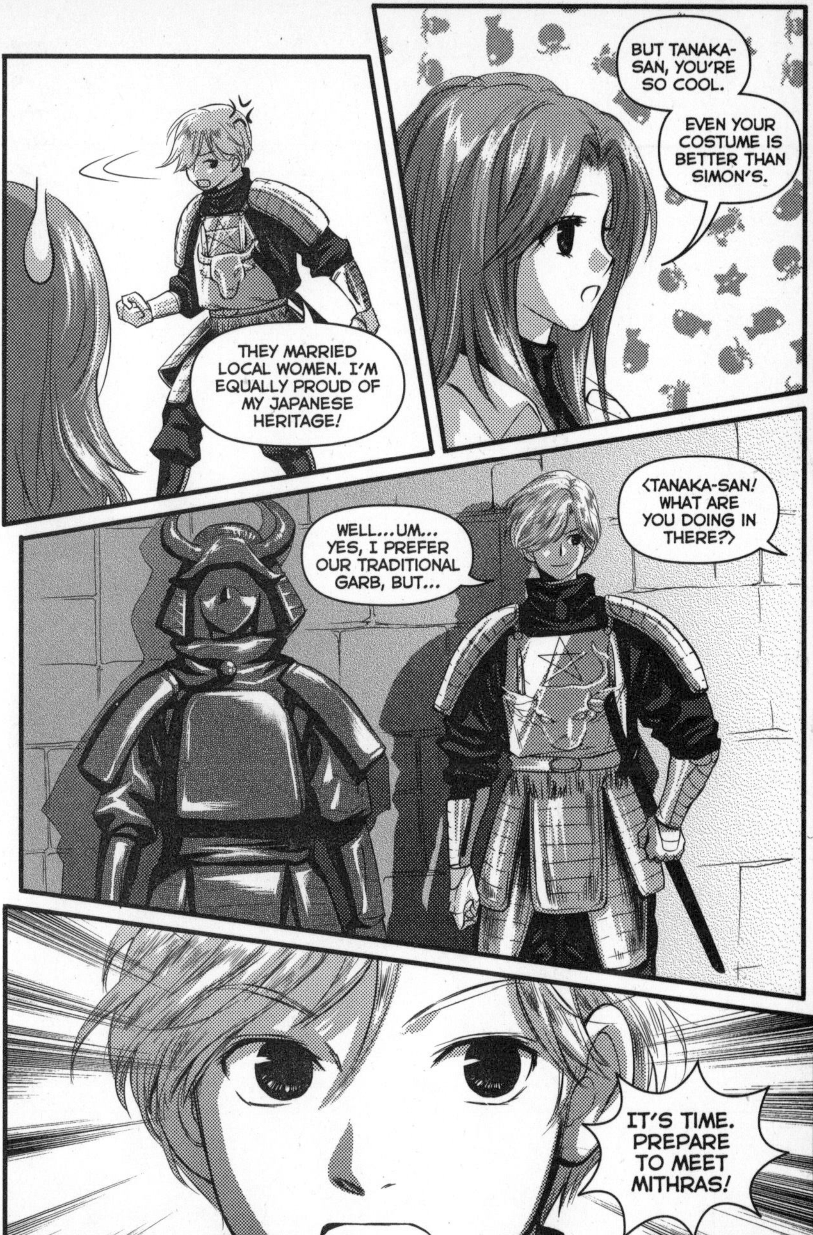
THEY MARRIED LOCAL WOMEN. I'M EQUALLY PROUD OF MY JAPANESE HERITAGE!
BUT TANAKA-SAN, YOU'RE SO COOL.
EVEN YOUR COSTUME IS BETTER THAN SIMON'S.
WELL...UM... YES, I PREFER OUR TRADITIONAL GARB, BUT...
<TANAKA-SAN! WHAT ARE YOU DOING IN THERE?>
IT'S TIME. PREPARE TO MEET MITHRAS!

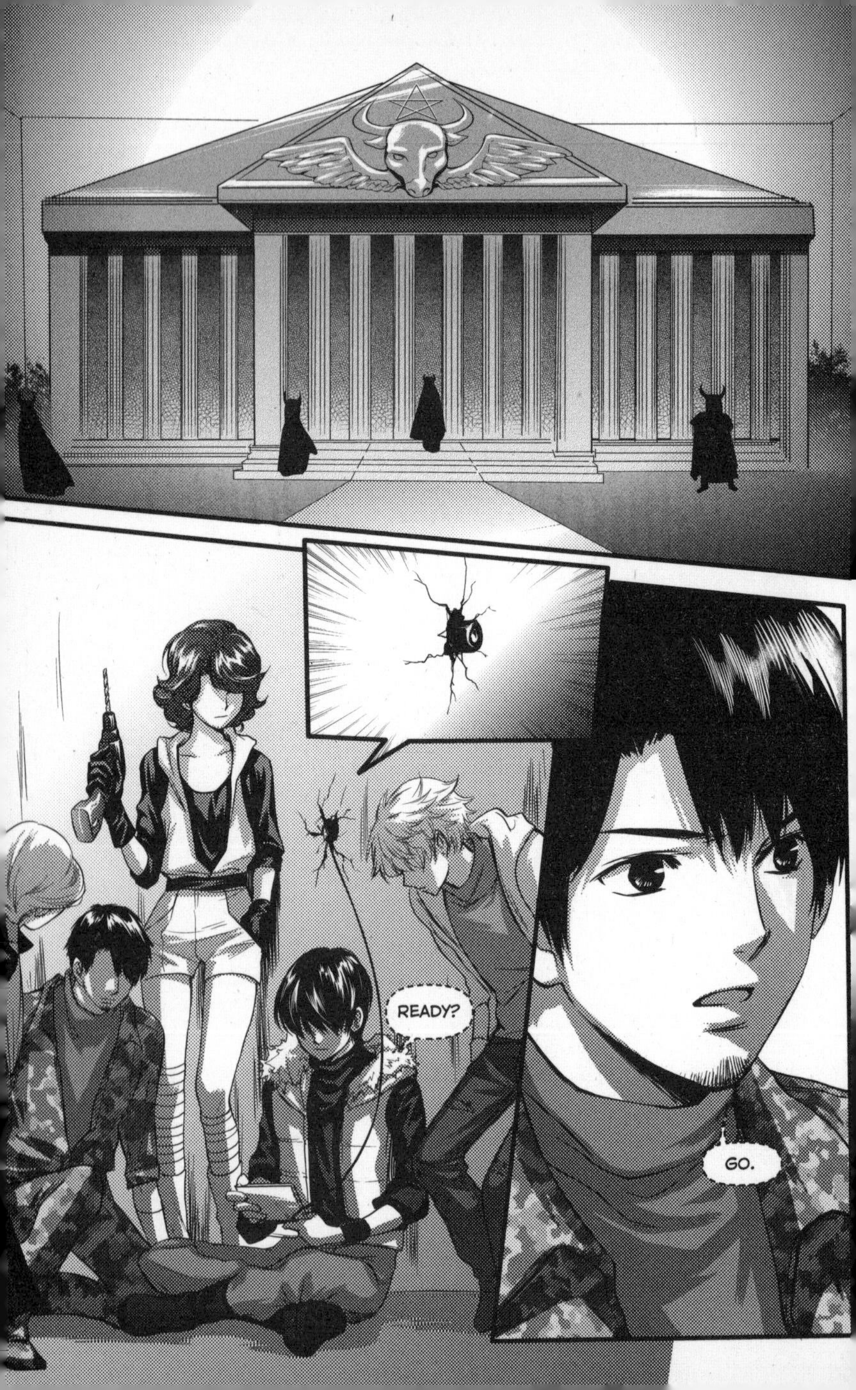
READY?
GO.

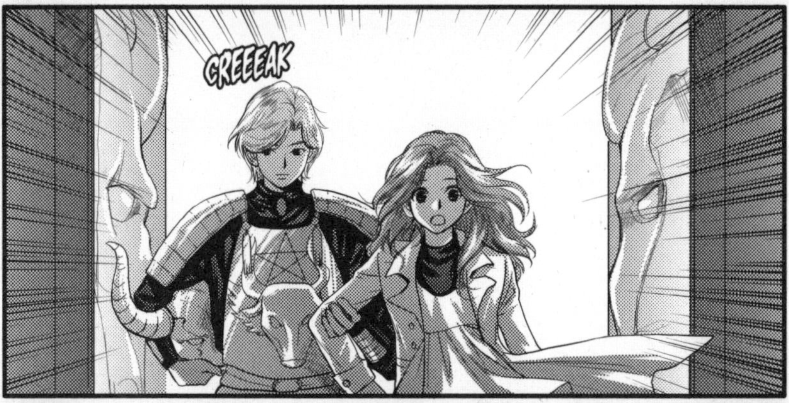
CREEEAK

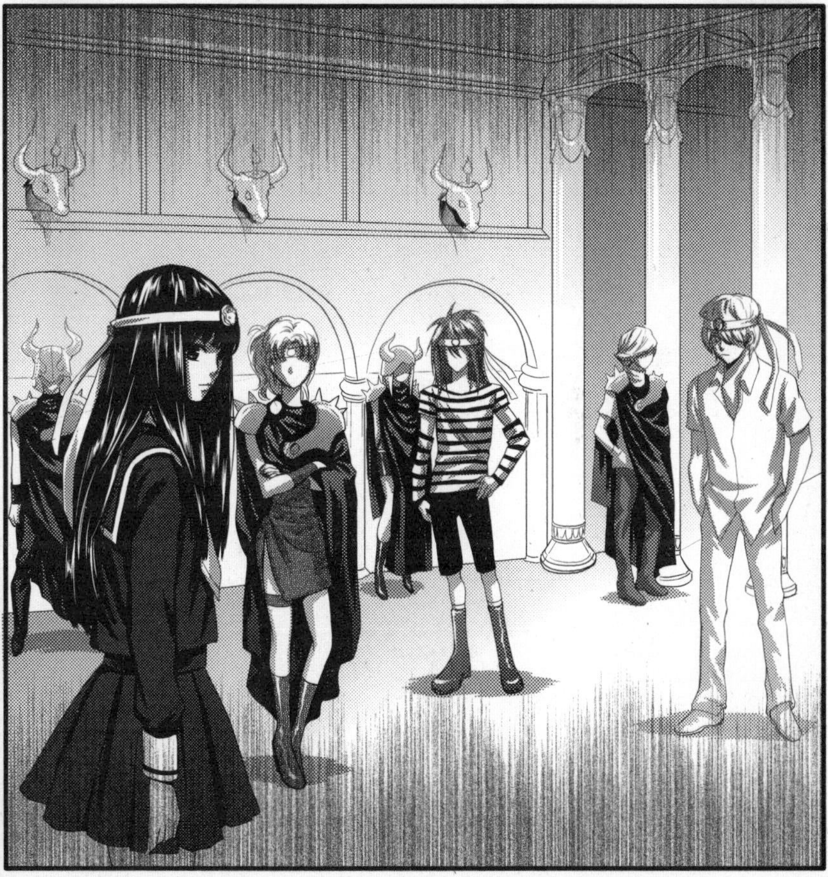

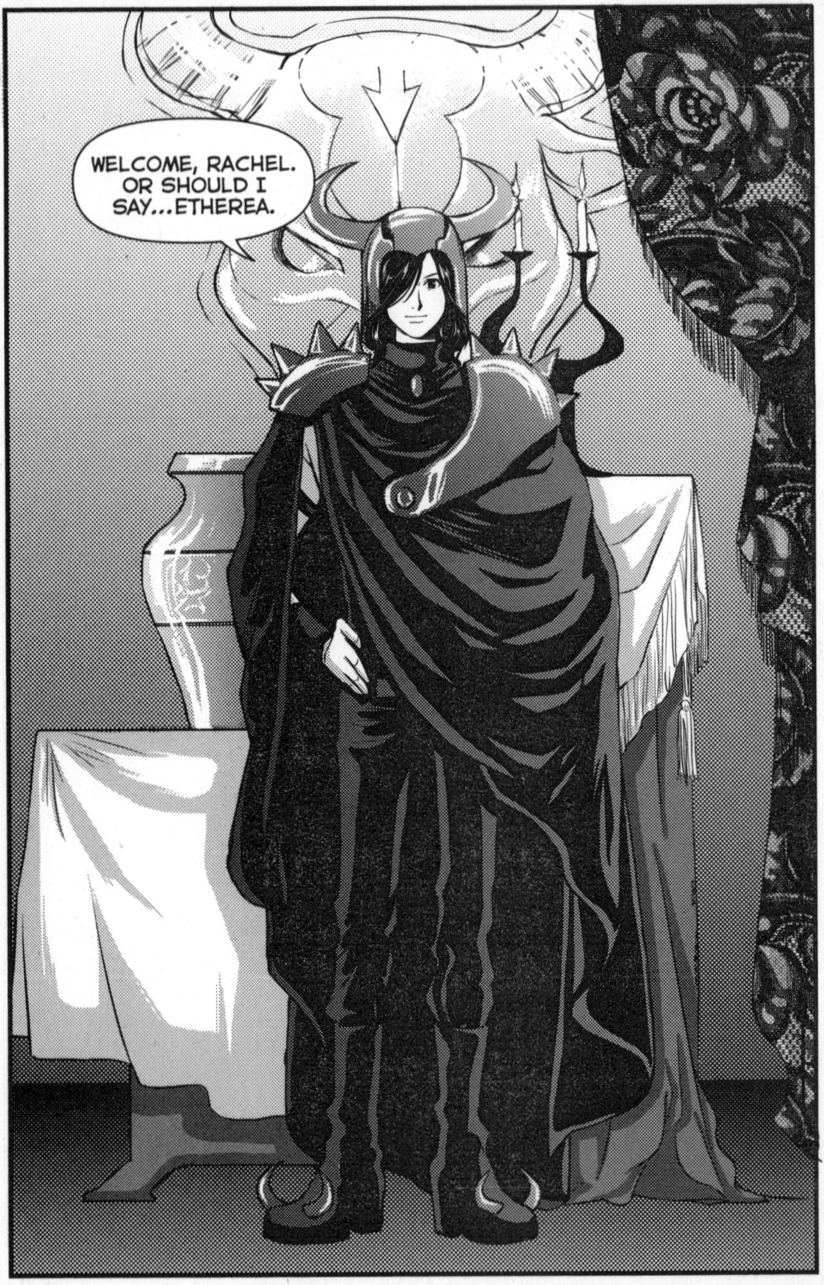
WELCOME, RACHEL. OR SHOULD I SAY...ETHEREA.

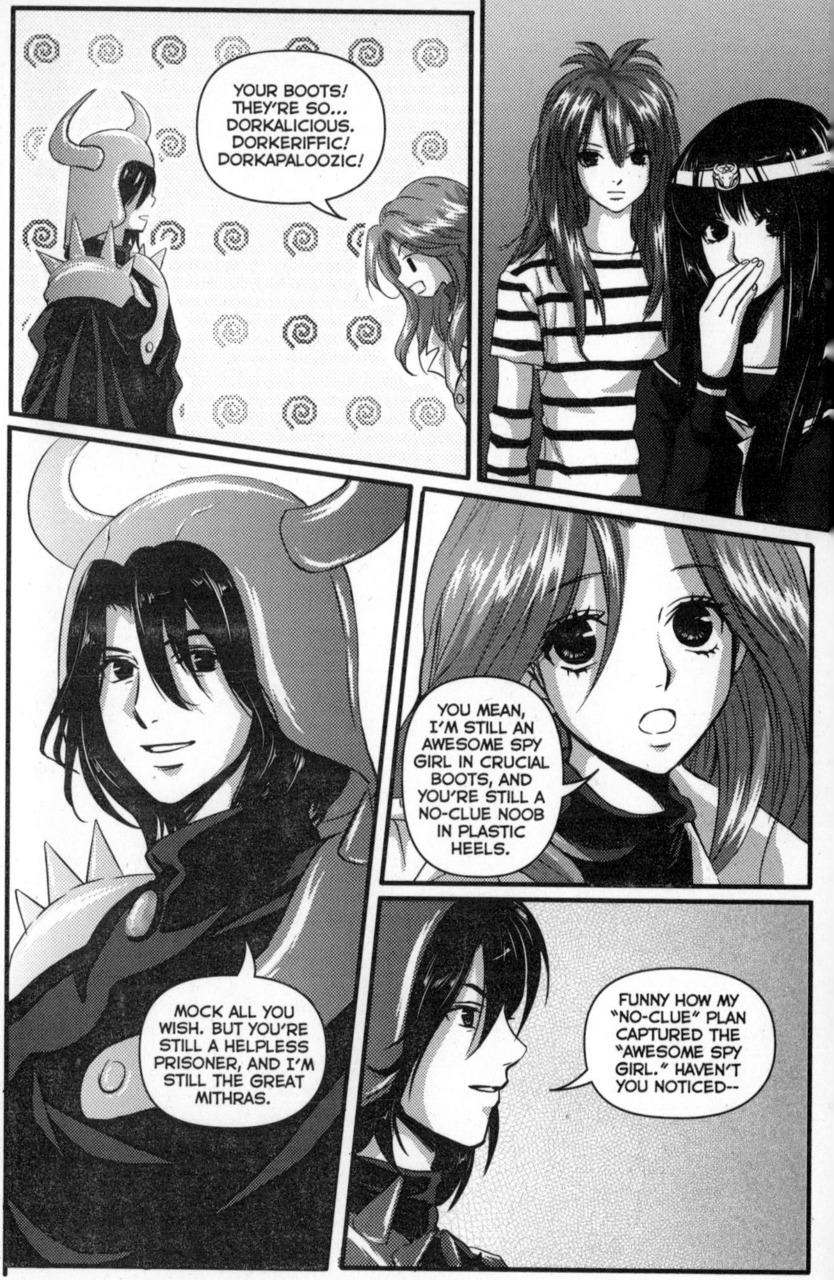
YOUR BOOTS! THEY'RE SO... DORKALICIOUS. DORKERIFFIC! DORKAPALOOZIC!
MOCK ALL YOU WISH. BUT YOU'RE STILL A HELPLESS PRISONER, AND I'M STILL THE GREAT MITHRAS.
YOU MEAN, I'M STILL AN AWESOME SPY GIRL IN CRUCIAL BOOTS, AND YOU'RE STILL A NO-CLUE NOOB IN PLASTIC HEELS.
FUNNY HOW MY "NO-CLUE" PLAN CAPTURED THE "AWESOME SPY GIRL." HAVEN'T YOU NOTICED--

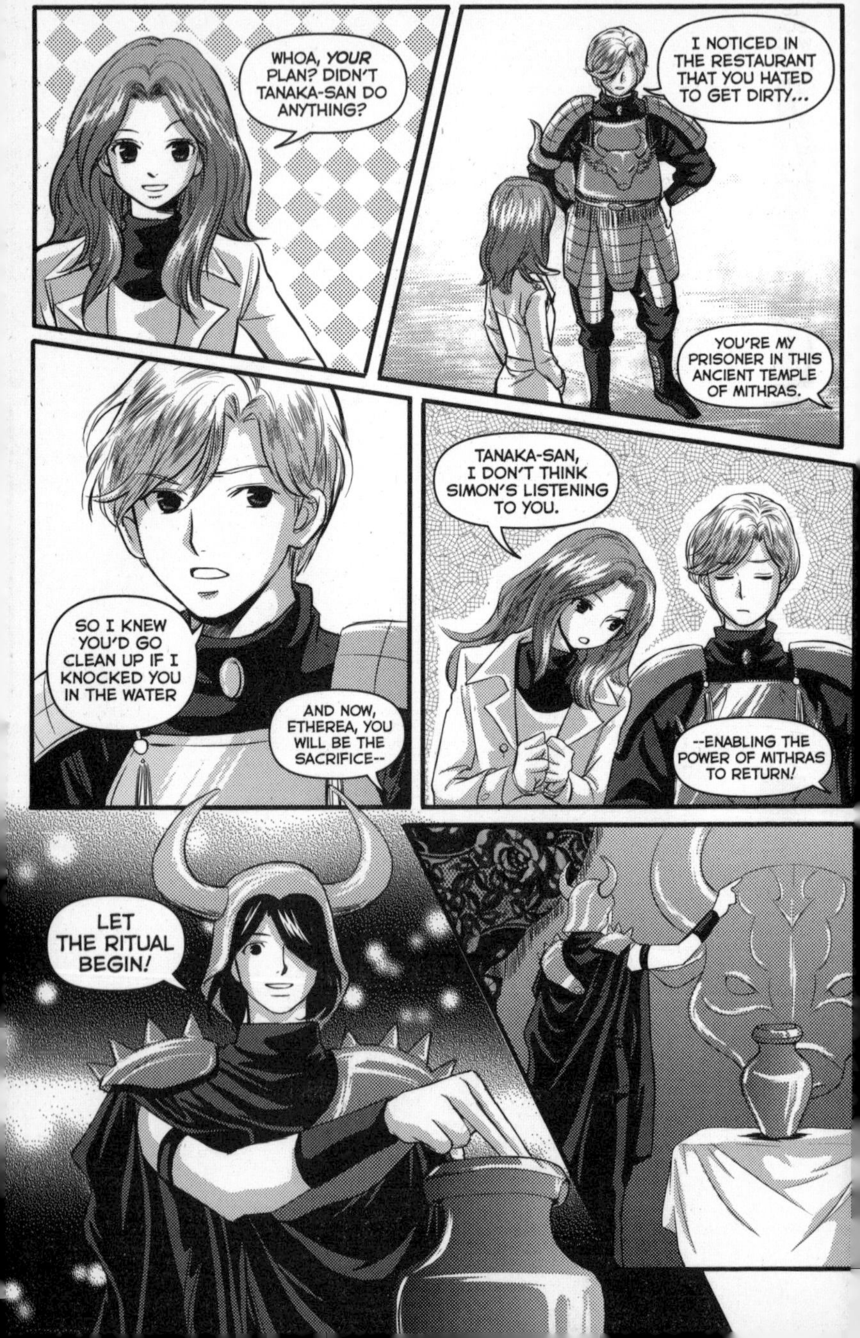
WHOA, *YOUR* PLAN? DIDN'T TANAKA-SAN DO ANYTHING?
I NOTICED IN THE RESTAURANT THAT YOU HATED TO GET DIRTY...
YOU'RE MY PRISONER IN THIS ANCIENT TEMPLE OF MITHRAS.
SO I KNEW YOU'D GO CLEAN UP IF I KNOCKED YOU IN THE WATER
AND NOW, ETHEREA, YOU WILL BE THE SACRIFICE--
TANAKA-SAN, I DON'T THINK SIMON'S LISTENING TO YOU.
--ENABLING THE POWER OF MITHRAS TO RETURN!
LET THE RITUAL BEGIN!

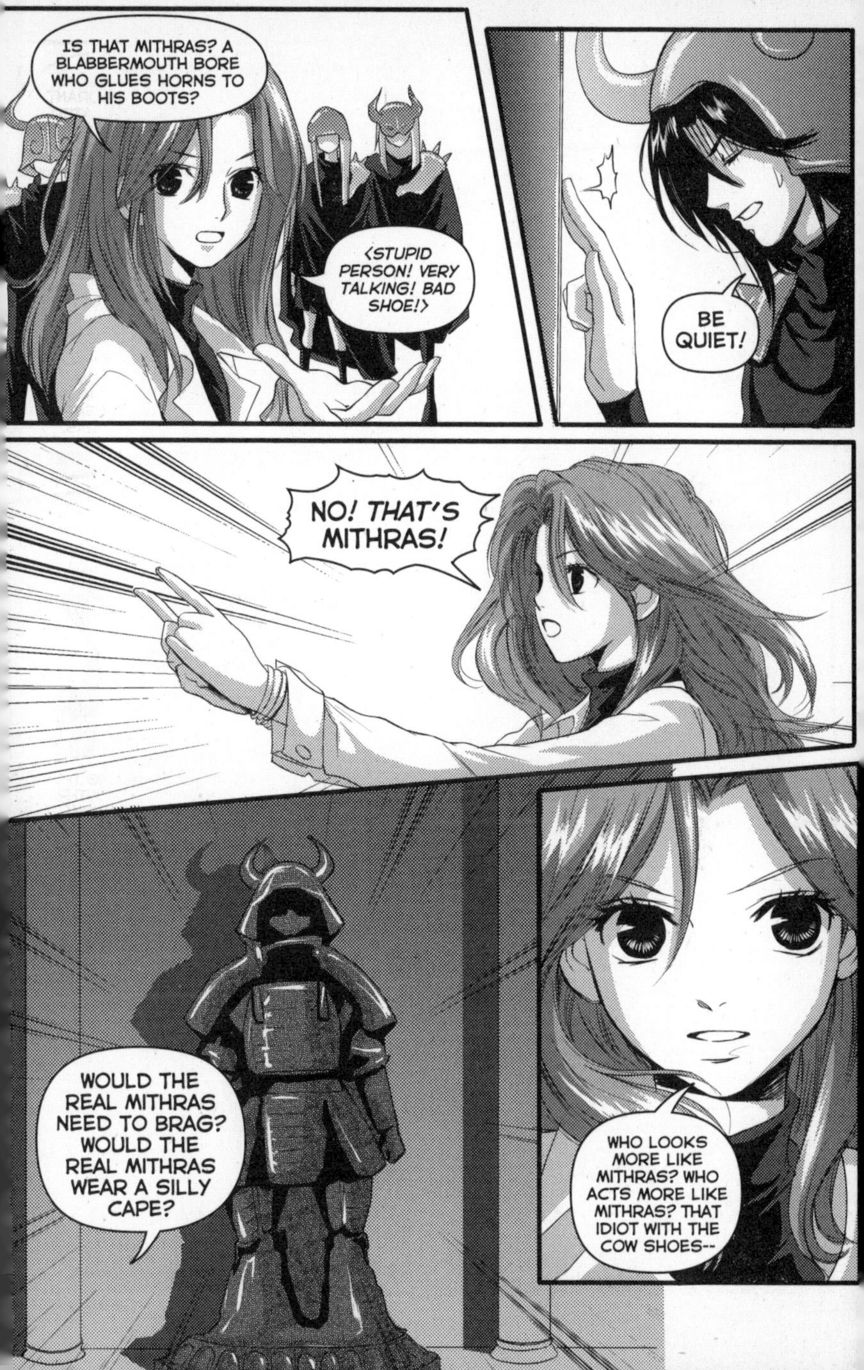
IS THAT MITHRAS? A BLABBERMOUTH BORE WHO GLUES HORNS TO HIS BOOTS?
<STUPID PERSON! VERY TALKING! BAD SHOE!>
BE QUIET!
NO! *THAT'S* MITHRAS!
WOULD THE REAL MITHRAS NEED TO BRAG? WOULD THE REAL MITHRAS WEAR A SILLY CAPE?
WHO LOOKS MORE LIKE MITHRAS? WHO ACTS MORE LIKE MITHRAS? THAT IDIOT WITH THE COW SHOES--

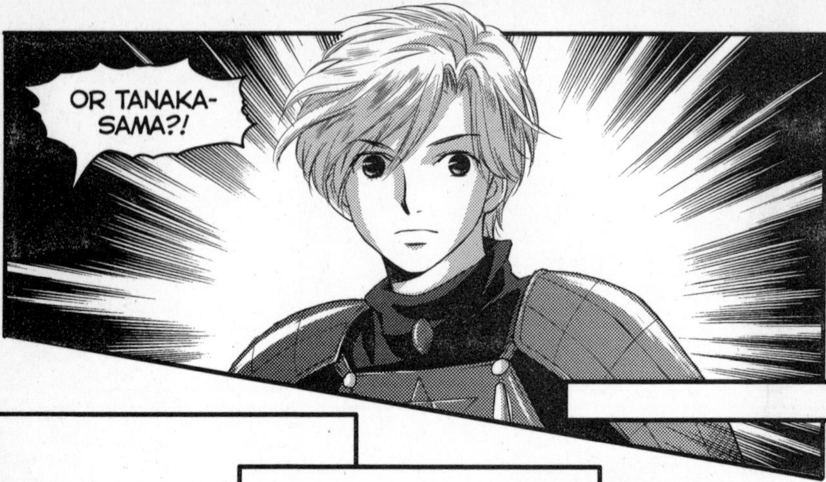
OR TANAKA-SAMA?!

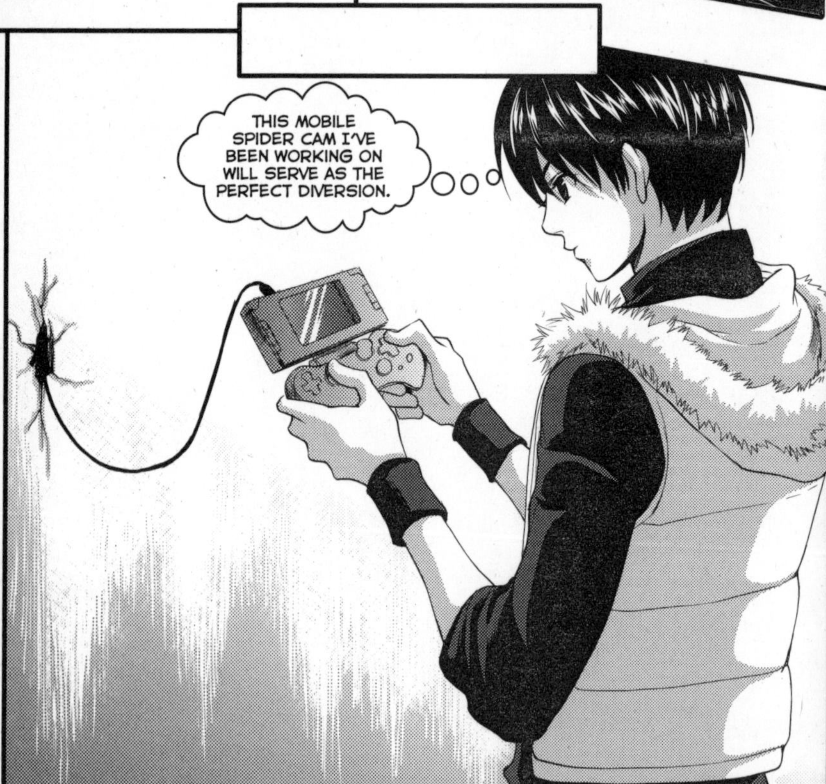
THIS MOBILE SPIDER CAM I'VE BEEN WORKING ON WILL SERVE AS THE PERFECT DIVERSION.

Sama: Lord

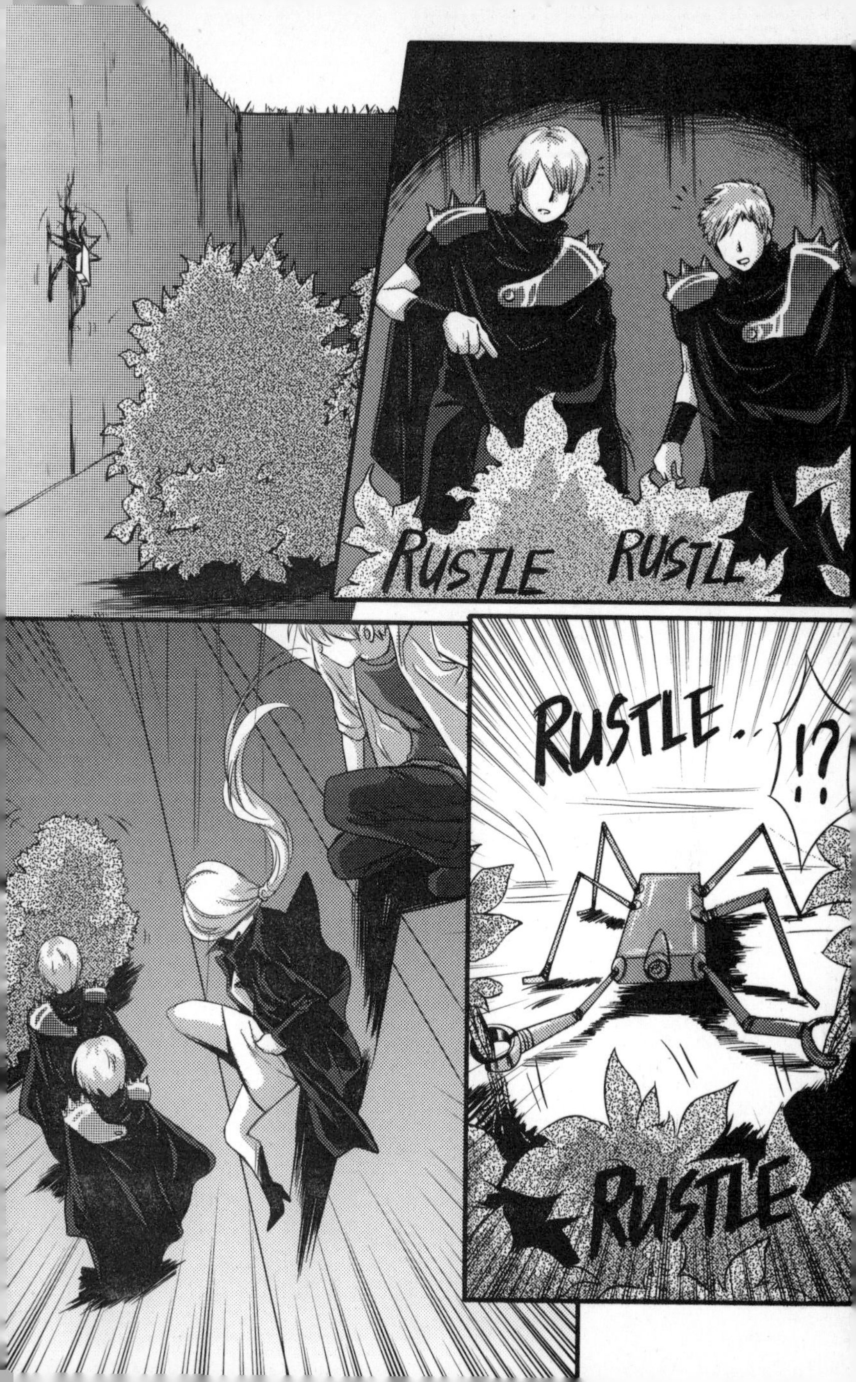
RUSTLE RUSTLE
RUSTLE..
!?
RUSTLE

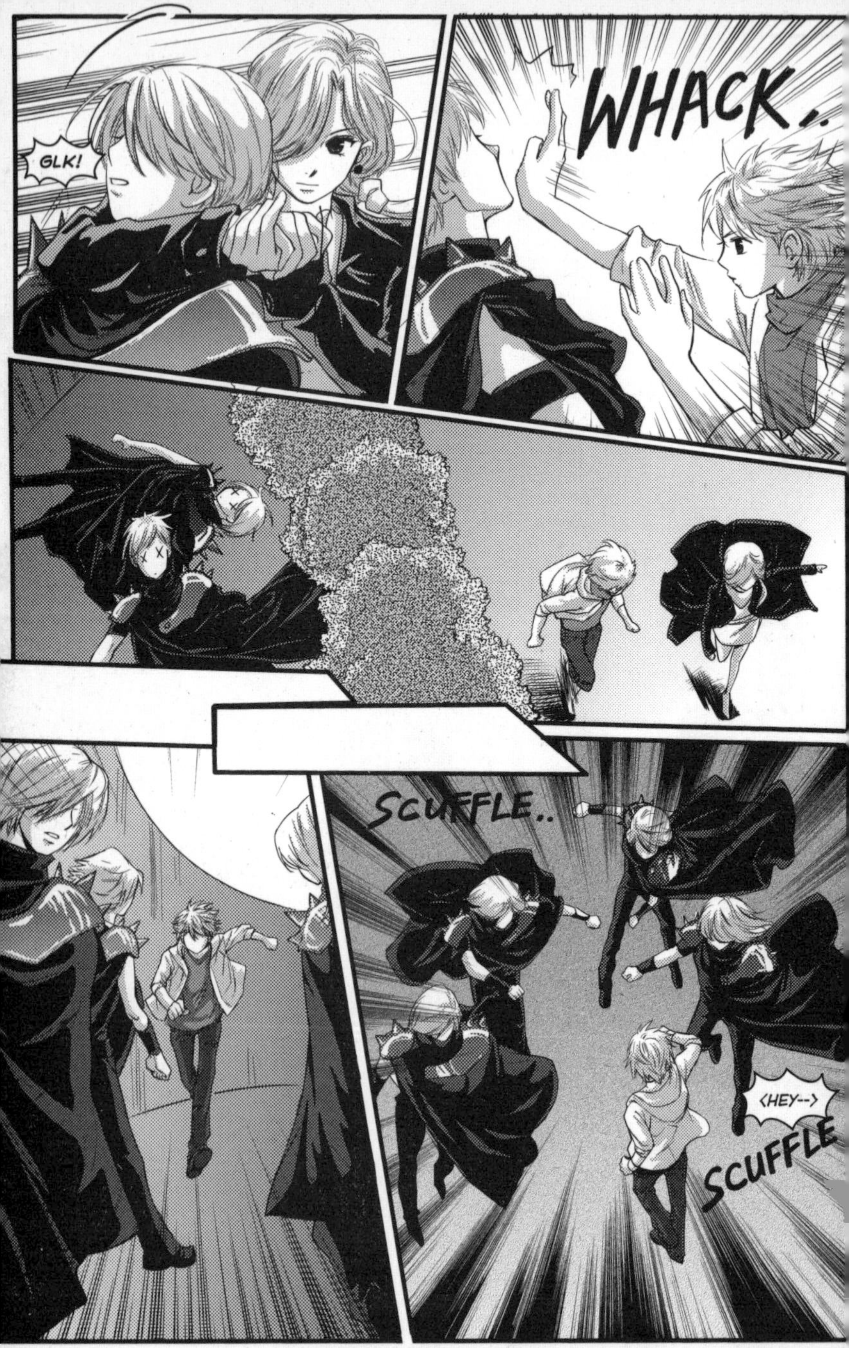
GLK!
WHACK..
SCUFFLE..
<HEY-->
SCUFFLE

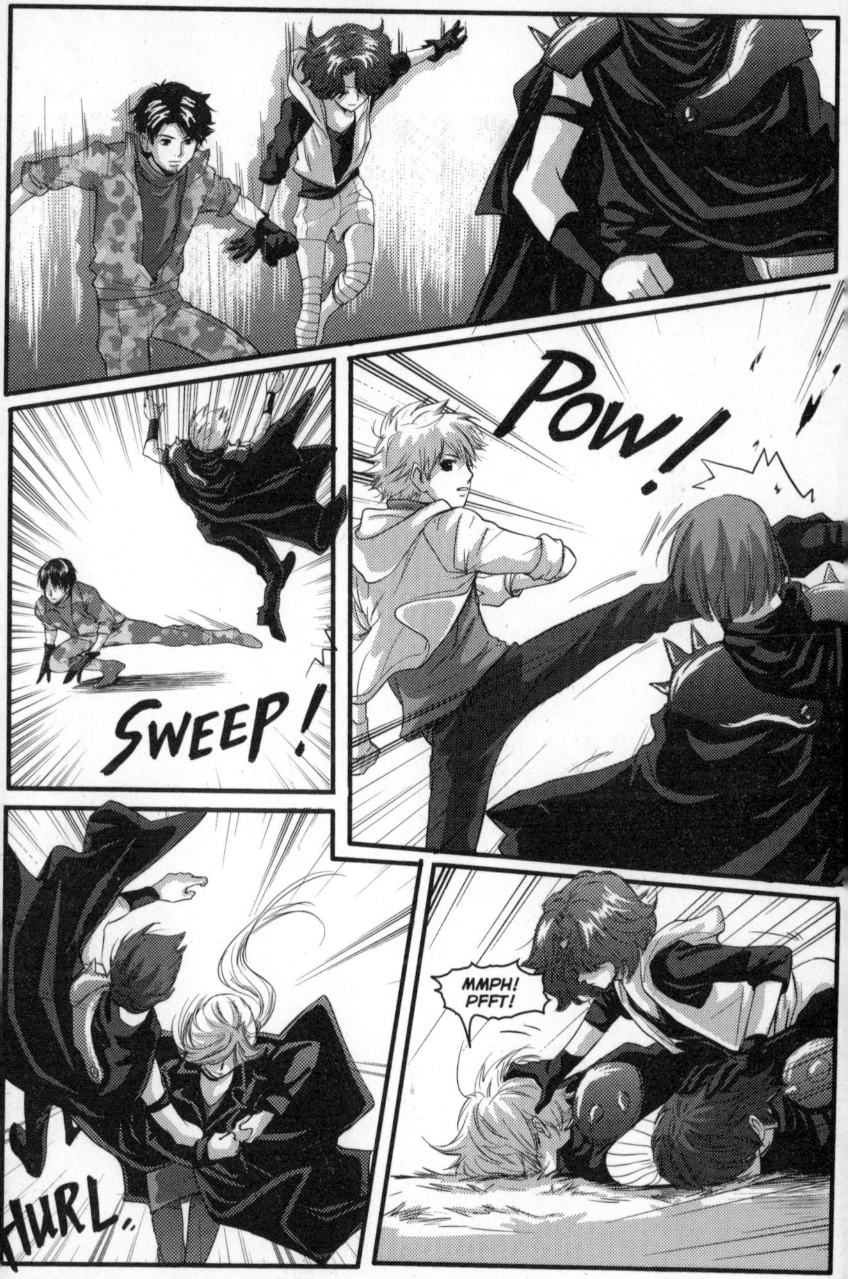
SWEEP!
POW!
HURL
MMPH! PFFT!

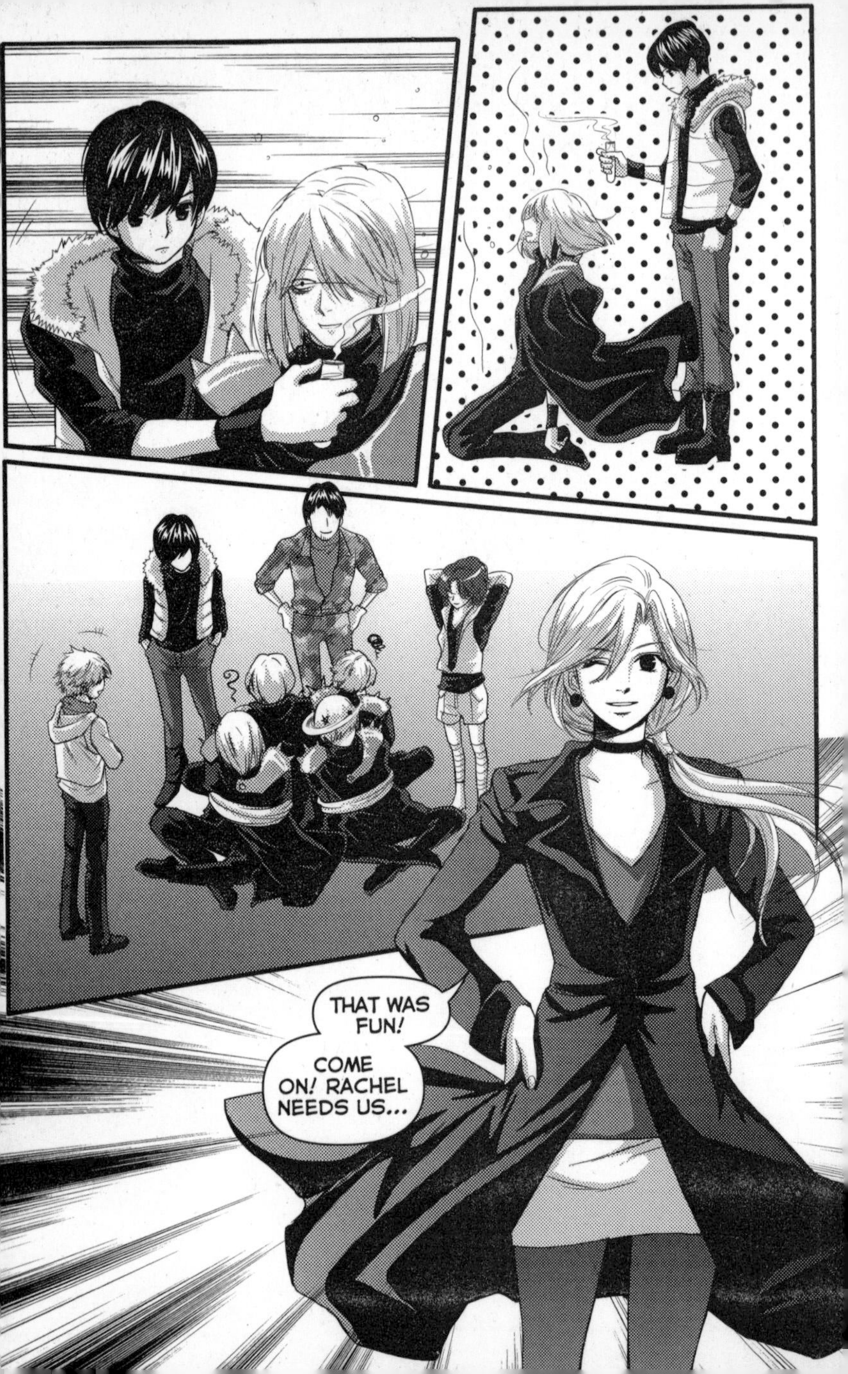
THAT WAS FUN!
COME ON! RACHEL NEEDS US...

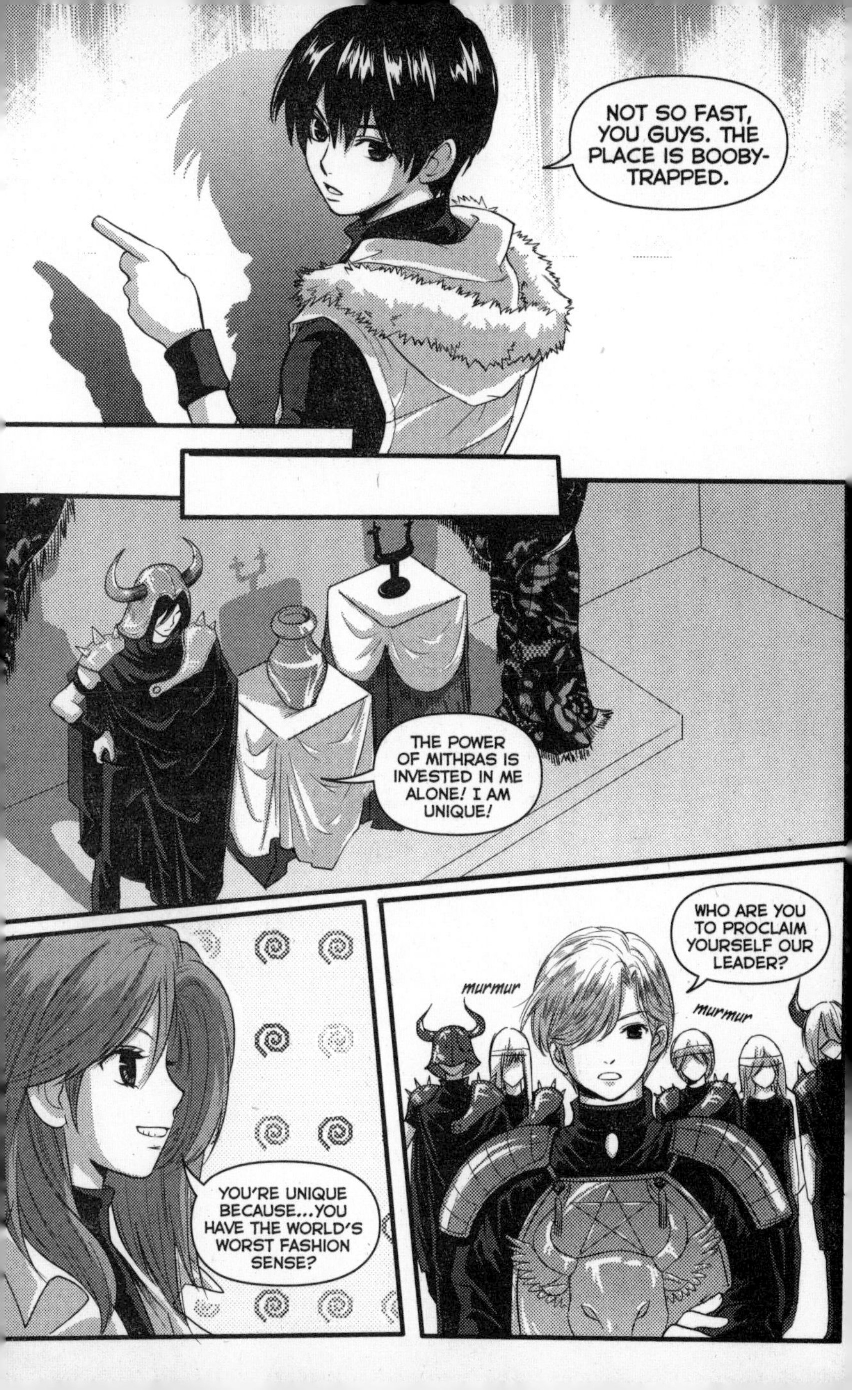
NOT SO FAST, YOU GUYS. THE PLACE IS BOOBY-TRAPPED.
THE POWER OF MITHRAS IS INVESTED IN ME ALONE! I AM UNIQUE!
YOU'RE UNIQUE BECAUSE...YOU HAVE THE WORLD'S WORST FASHION SENSE?
WHO ARE YOU TO PROCLAIM YOURSELF OUR LEADER?
murmur
murmur

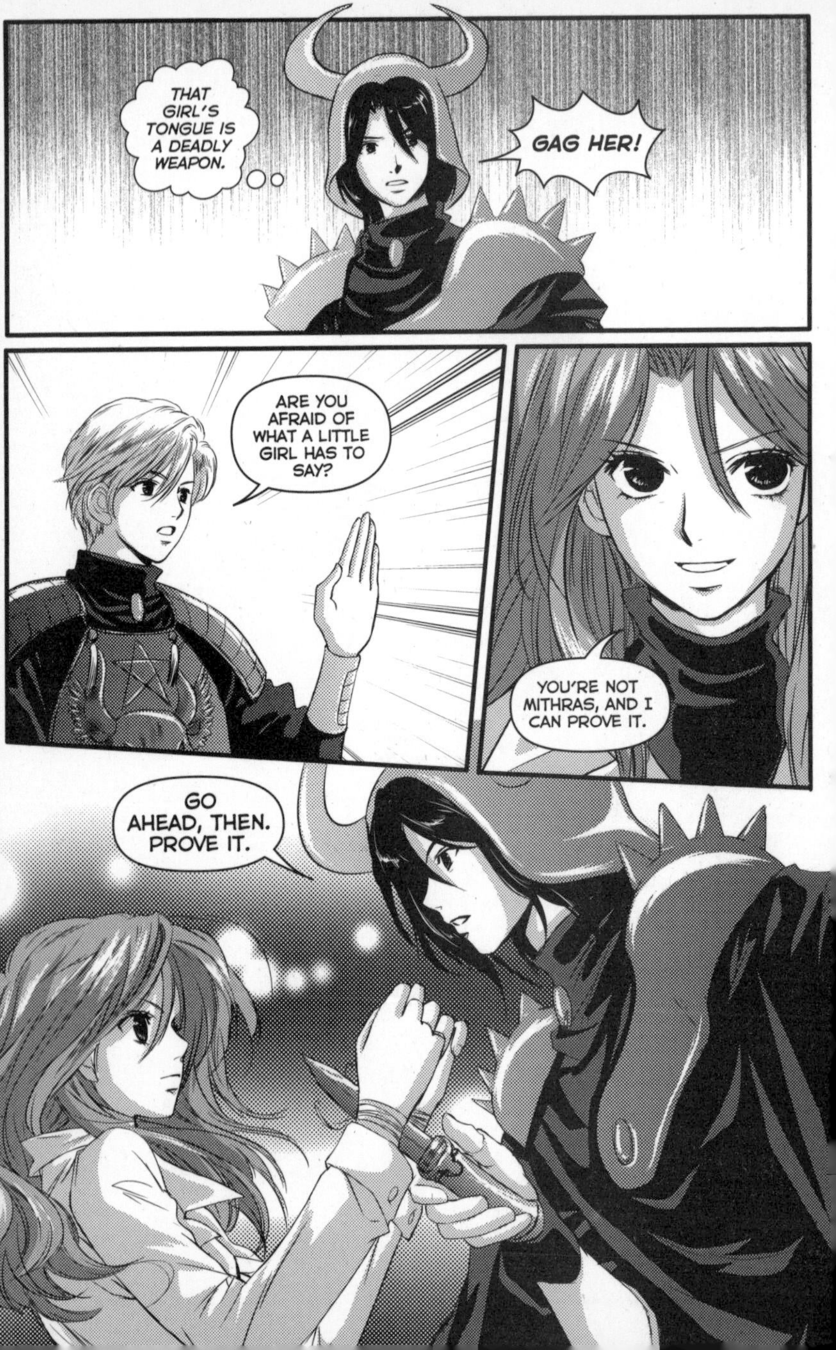
THAT GIRL'S TONGUE IS A DEADLY WEAPON.
GAG HER!
ARE YOU AFRAID OF WHAT A LITTLE GIRL HAS TO SAY?
YOU'RE NOT MITHRAS, AND I CAN PROVE IT.
GO AHEAD, THEN. PROVE IT.

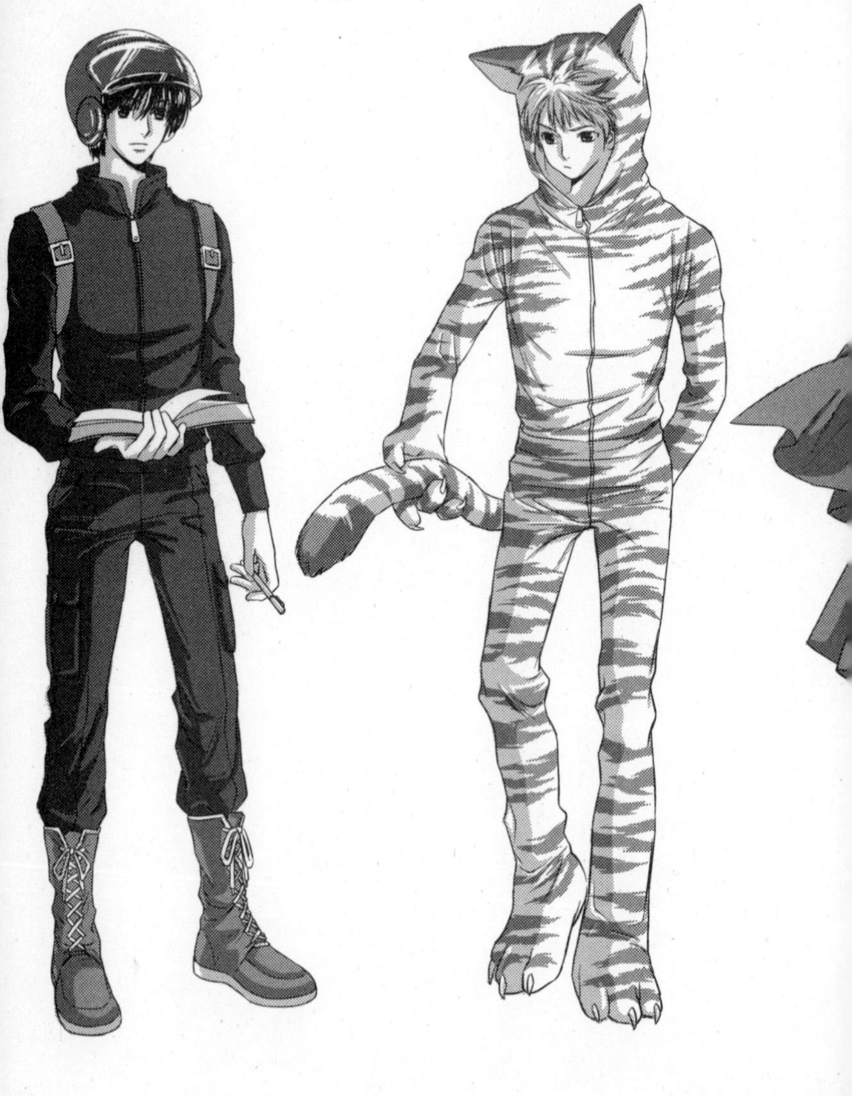

Chapter Six

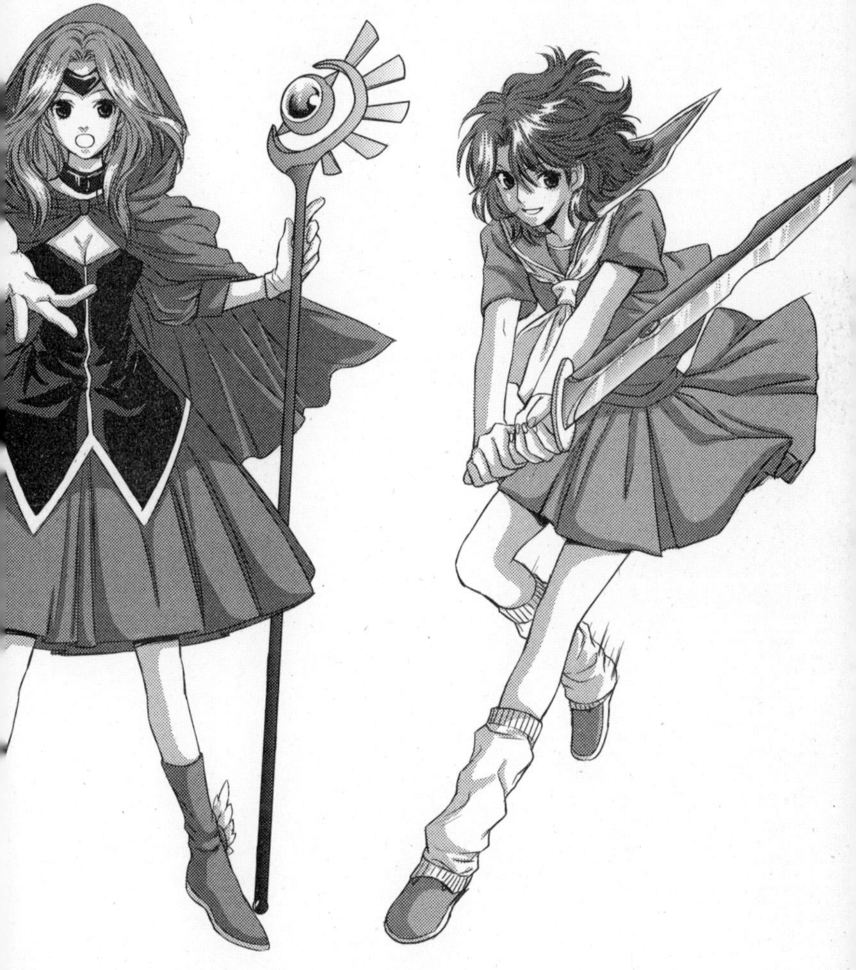

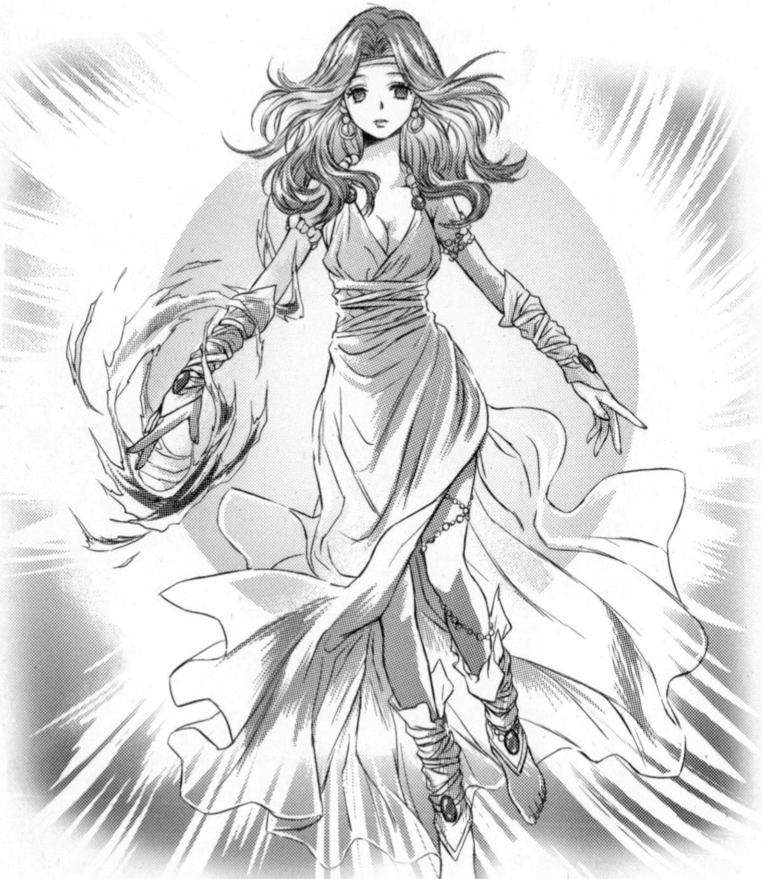

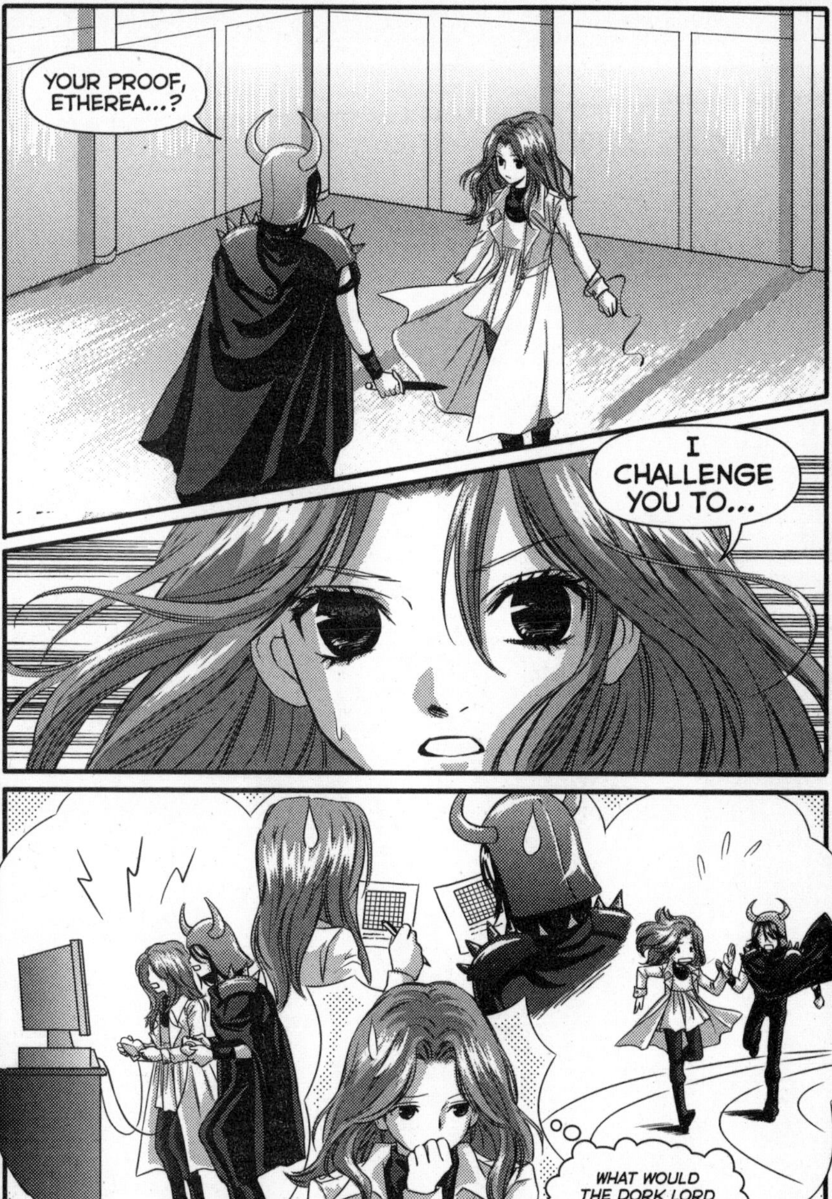
YOUR PROOF, ETHEREA...?
I CHALLENGE YOU TO...
WHAT WOULD THE DORK LORD GO FOR...?

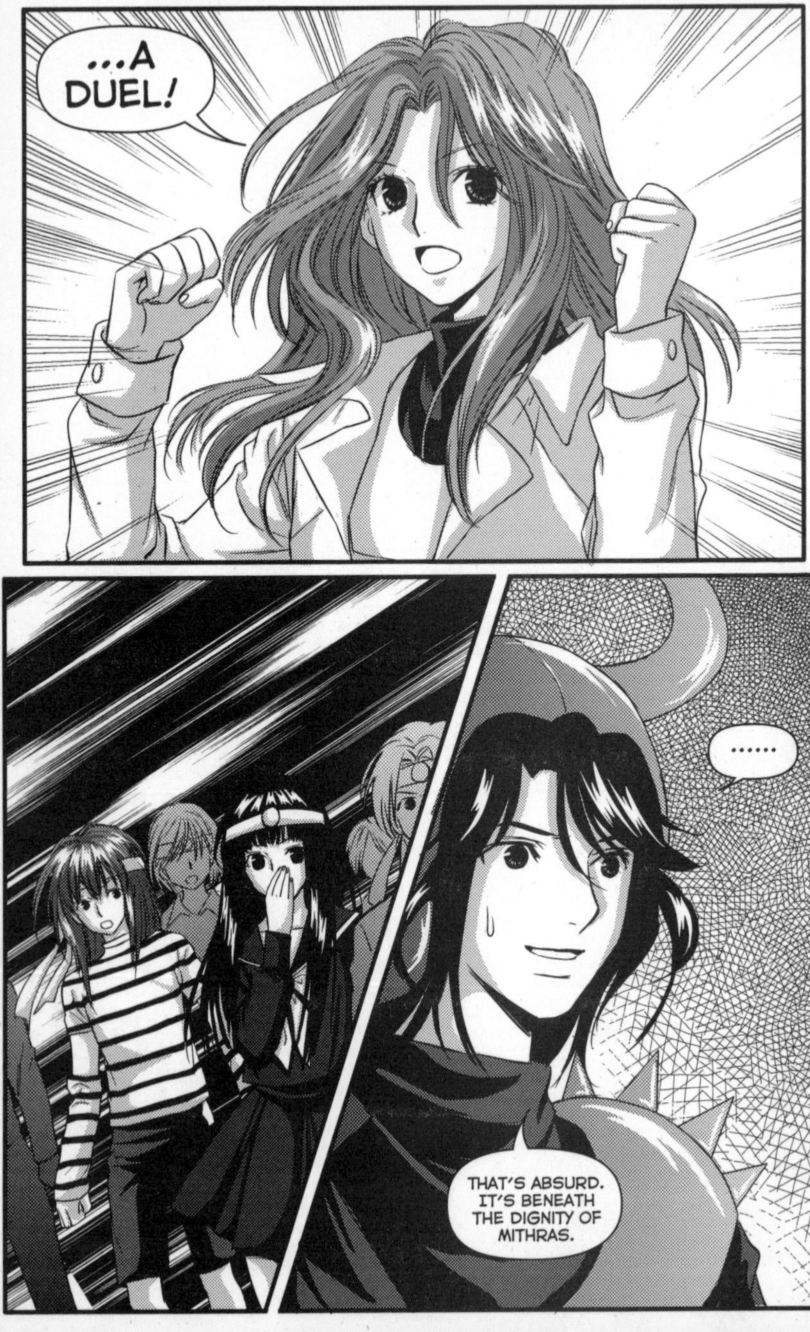
...A DUEL!
......
THAT'S ABSURD. IT'S BENEATH THE DIGNITY OF MITHRAS.

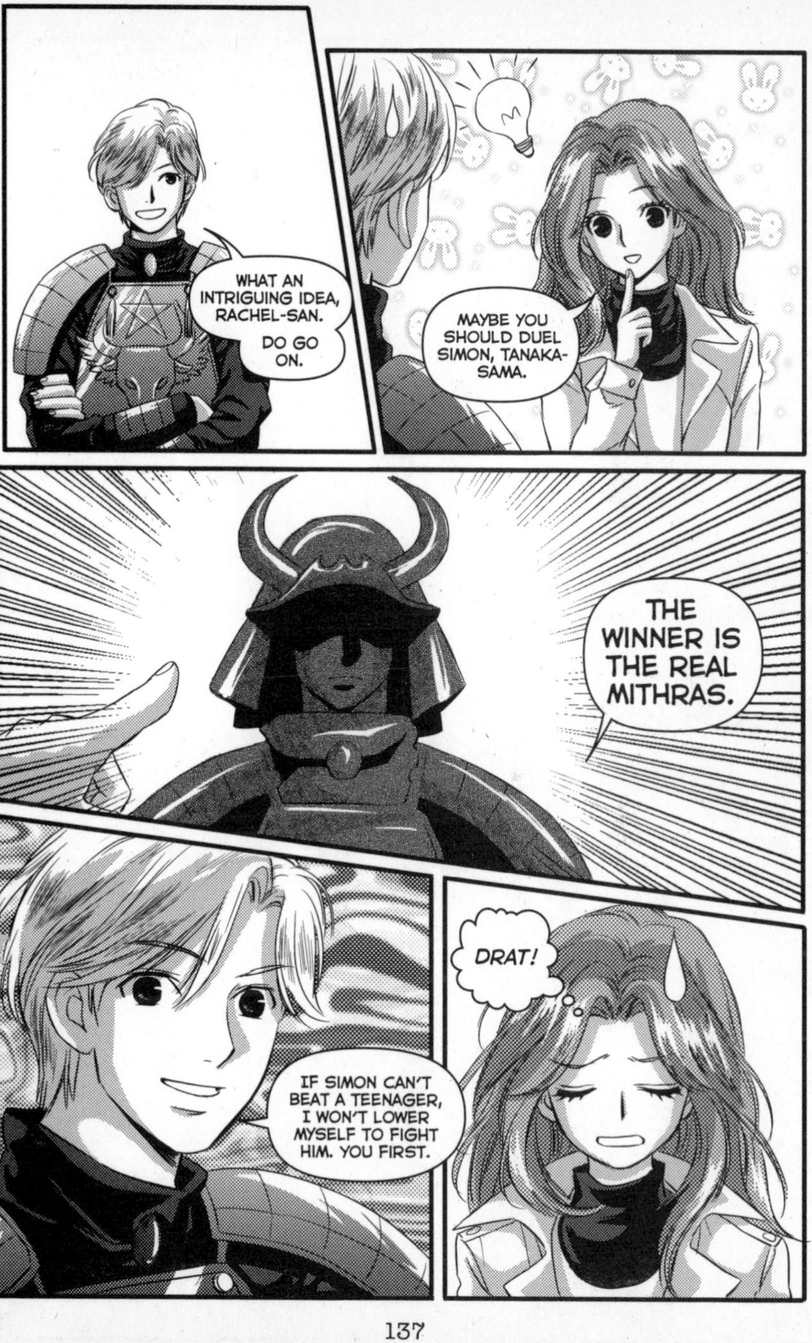
WHAT AN INTRIGUING IDEA, RACHEL-SAN.
DO GO ON.
MAYBE YOU SHOULD DUEL SIMON, TANAKA-SAMA.
THE WINNER IS THE REAL MITHRAS.
IF SIMON CAN'T BEAT A TEENAGER, I WON'T LOWER MYSELF TO FIGHT HIM. YOU FIRST.
DRAT!

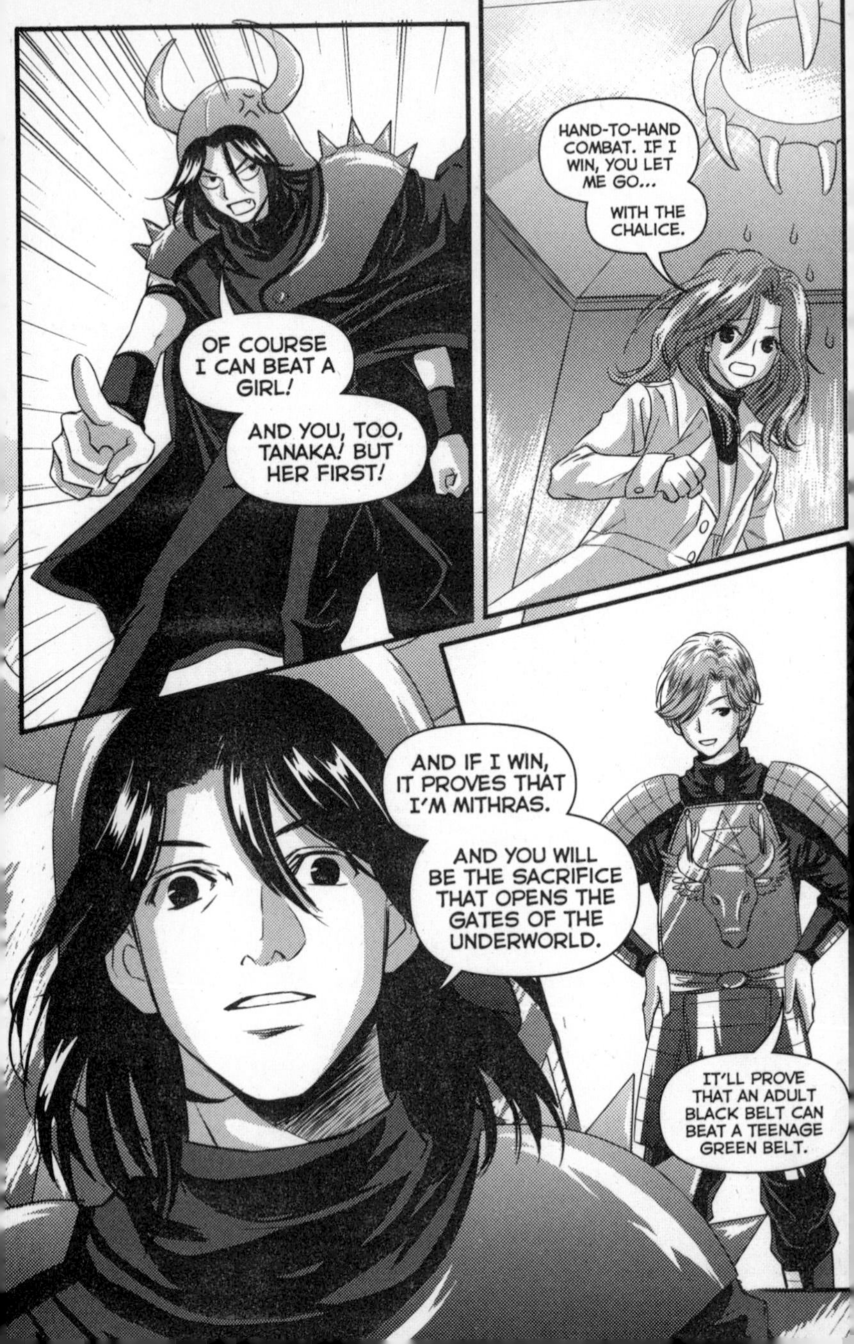
OF COURSE I CAN BEAT A GIRL!
AND YOU, TOO, TANAKA! BUT HER FIRST!
HAND-TO-HAND COMBAT. IF I WIN, YOU LET ME GO...
WITH THE CHALICE.
AND IF I WIN, IT PROVES THAT I'M MITHRAS.
AND YOU WILL BE THE SACRIFICE THAT OPENS THE GATES OF THE UNDERWORLD.
IT'LL PROVE THAT AN ADULT BLACK BELT CAN BEAT A TEENAGE GREEN BELT.

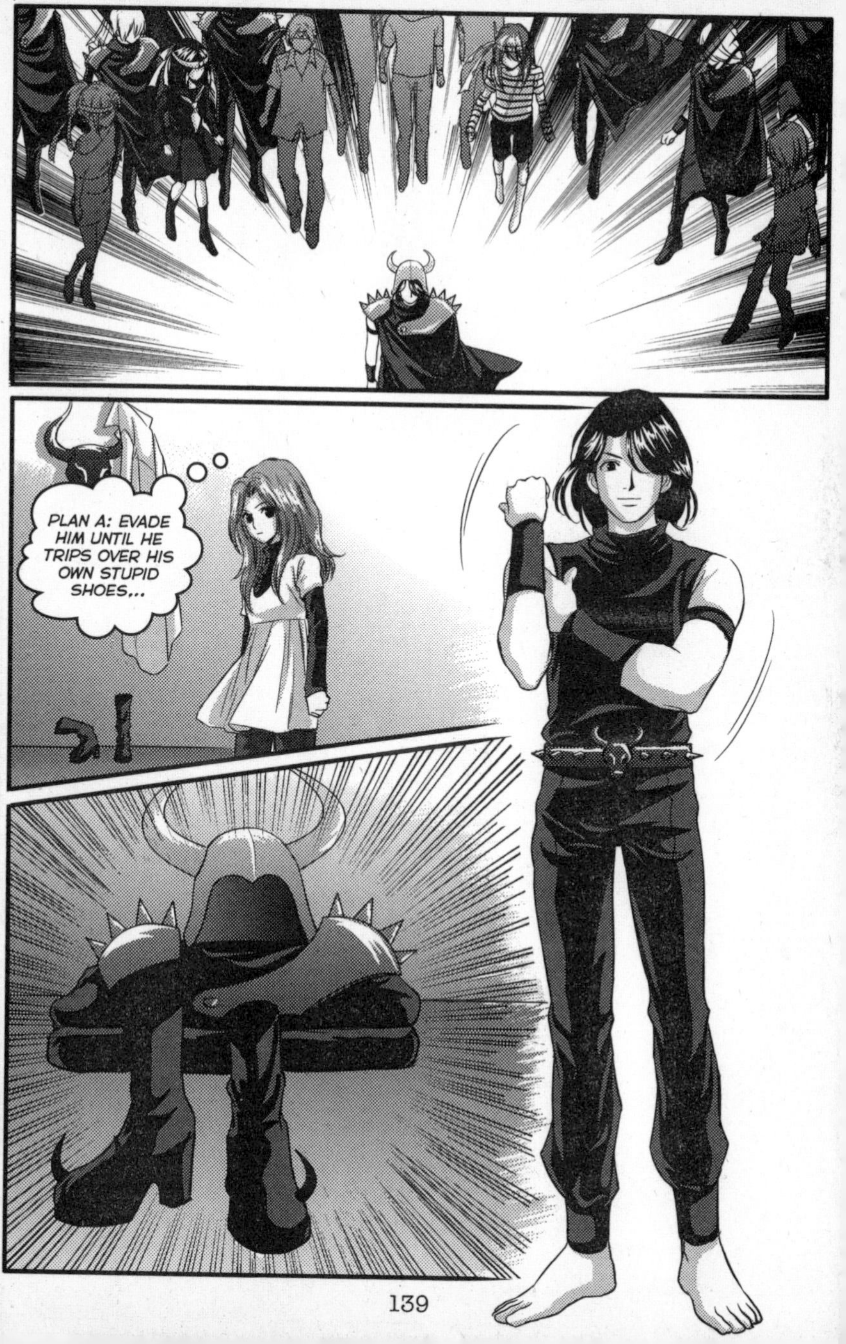
PLAN A: EVADE HIM UNTIL HE TRIPS OVER HIS OWN STUPID SHOES...

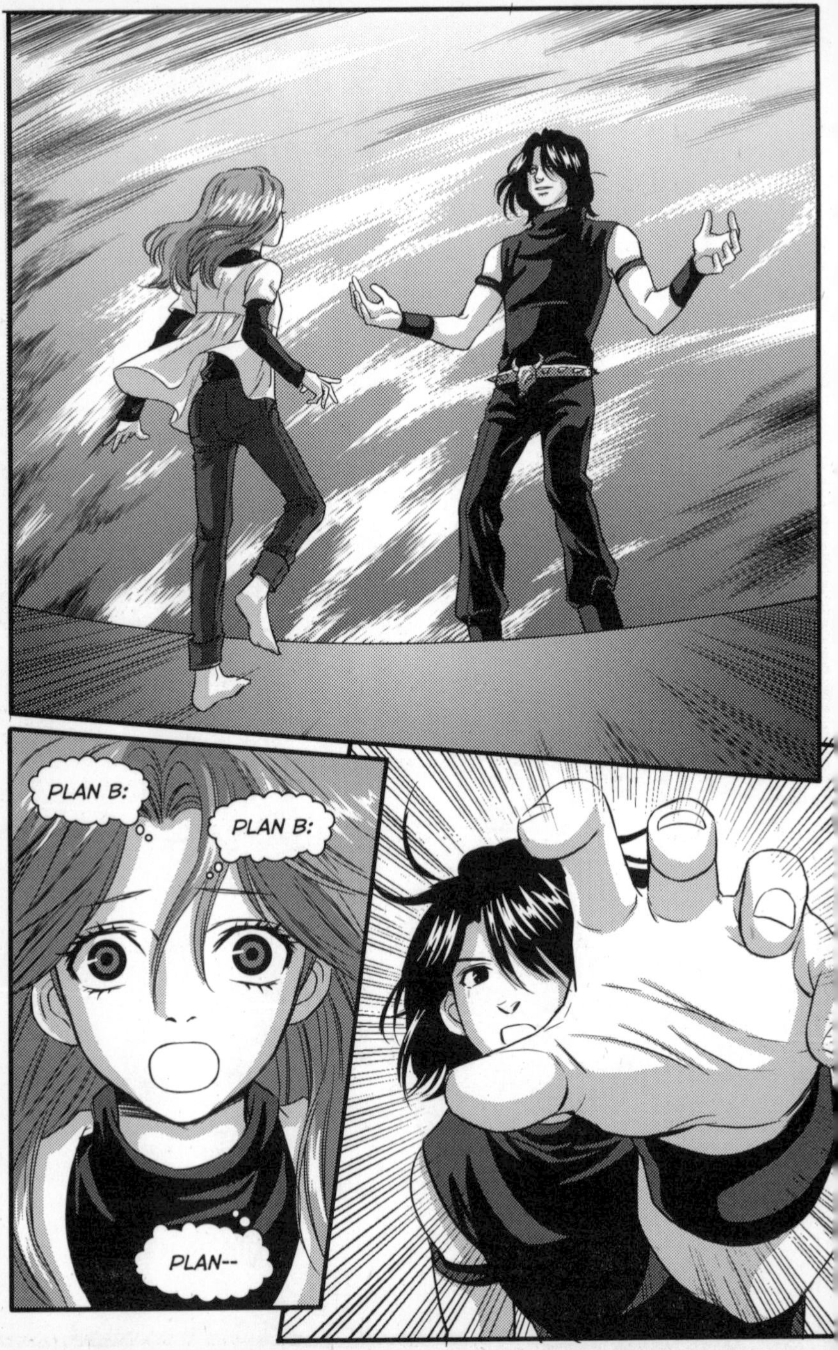
PLAN B:
PLAN B:
PLAN--

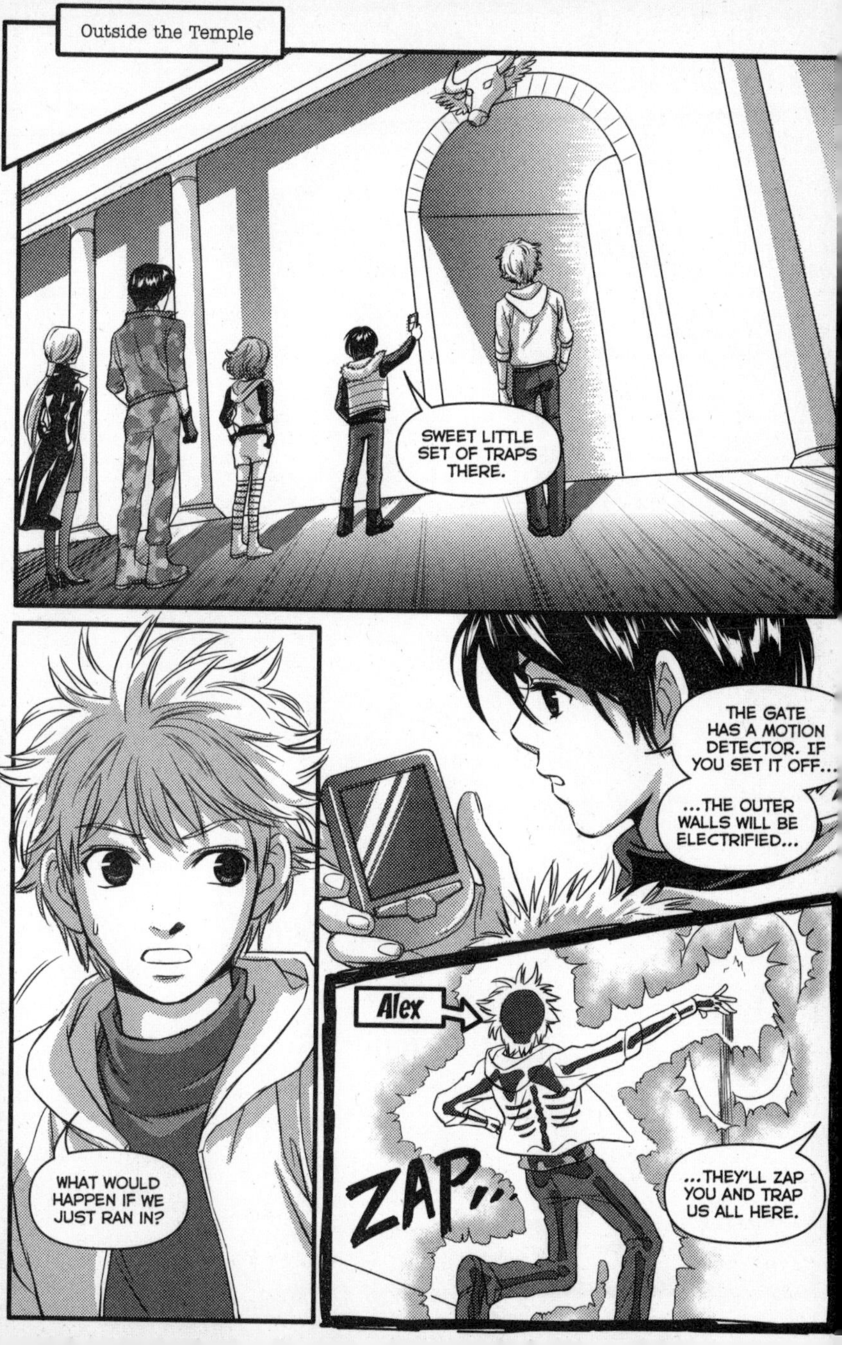
Outside the Temple
SWEET LITTLE SET OF TRAPS THERE.
WHAT WOULD HAPPEN IF WE JUST RAN IN?
THE GATE HAS A MOTION DETECTOR. IF YOU SET IT OFF...
...THE OUTER WALLS WILL BE ELECTRIFIED...
Alex
ZAP
...THEY'LL ZAP YOU AND TRAP US ALL HERE.

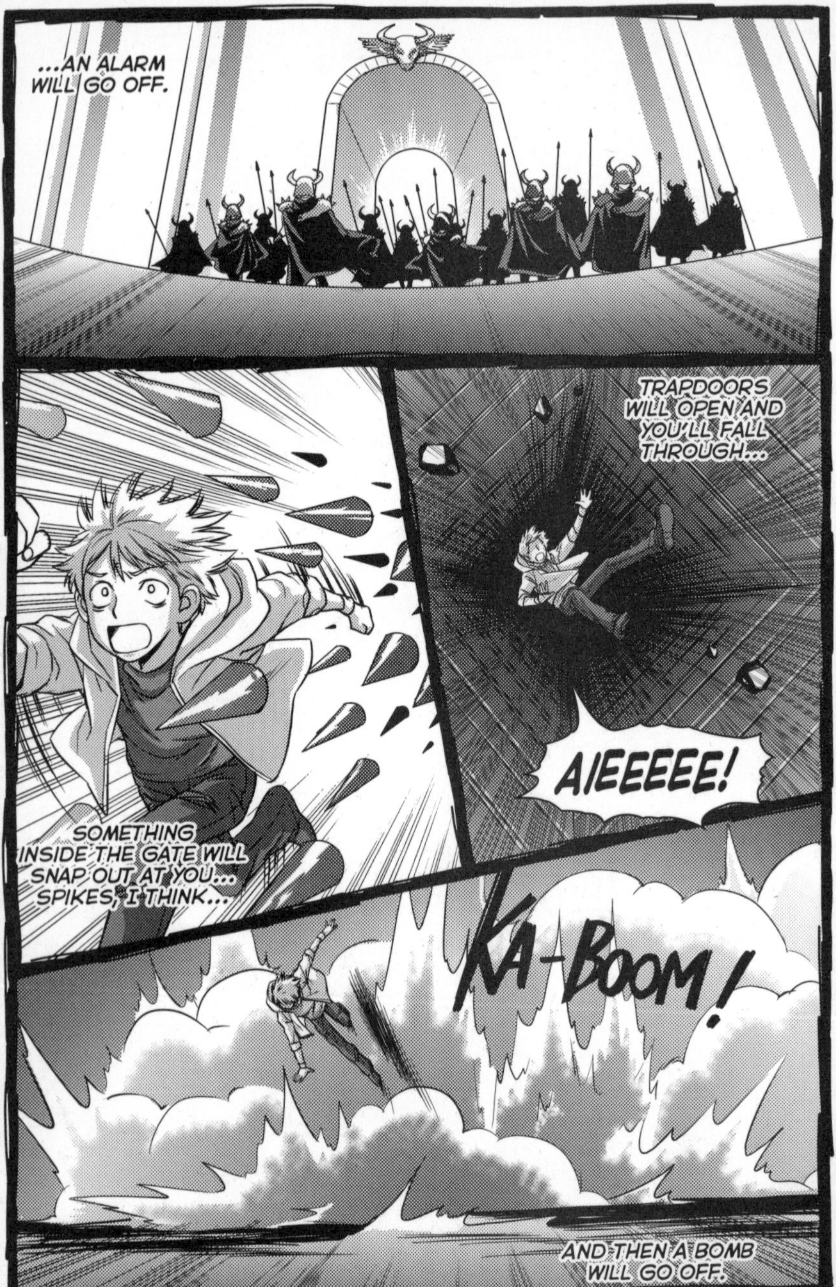
...AN ALARM WILL GO OFF.
TRAPDOORS WILL OPEN AND YOU'LL FALL THROUGH...
AIEEEEE!
SOMETHING INSIDE THE GATE WILL SNAP OUT AT YOU... SPIKES, I THINK...
KA-BOOM!
AND THEN A BOMB WILL GO OFF.

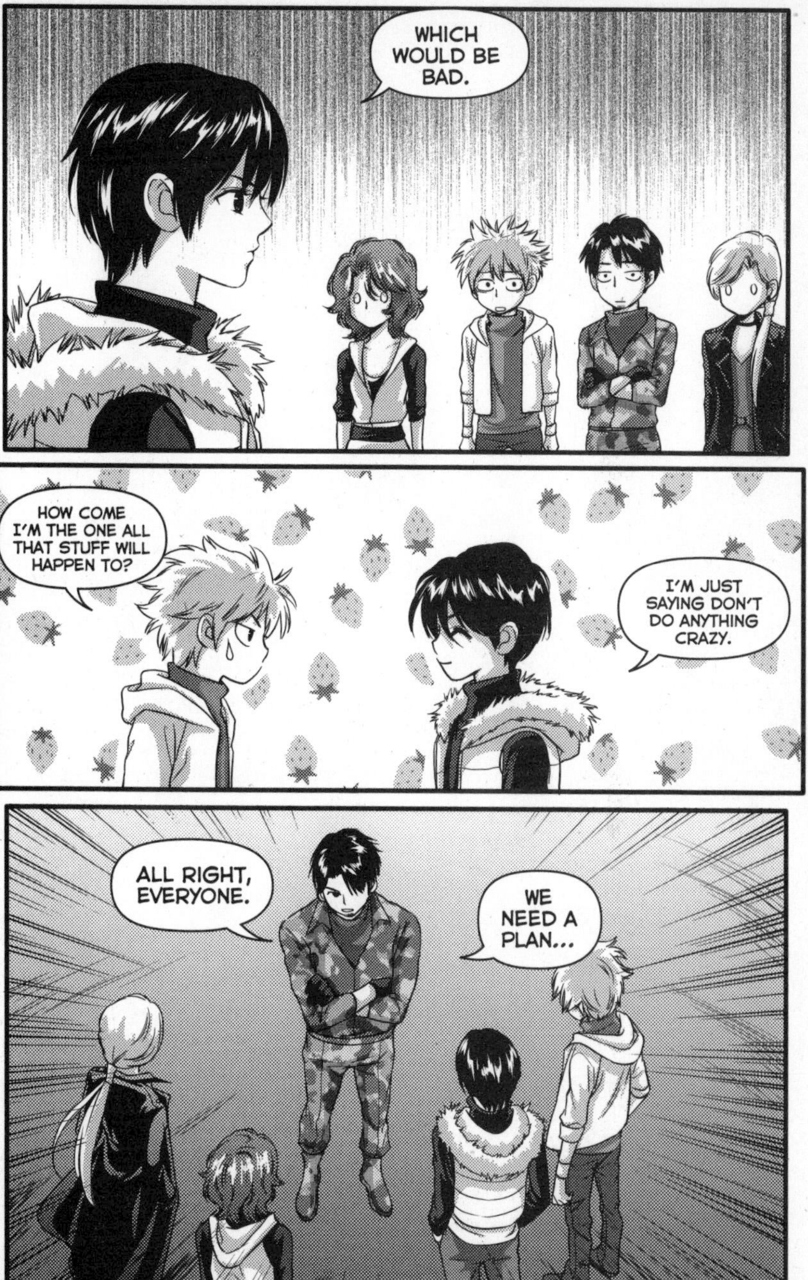
WHICH WOULD BE BAD.
HOW COME I'M THE ONE ALL THAT STUFF WILL HAPPEN TO?
I'M JUST SAYING DON'T DO ANYTHING CRAZY.
ALL RIGHT, EVERYONE.
WE NEED A PLAN...

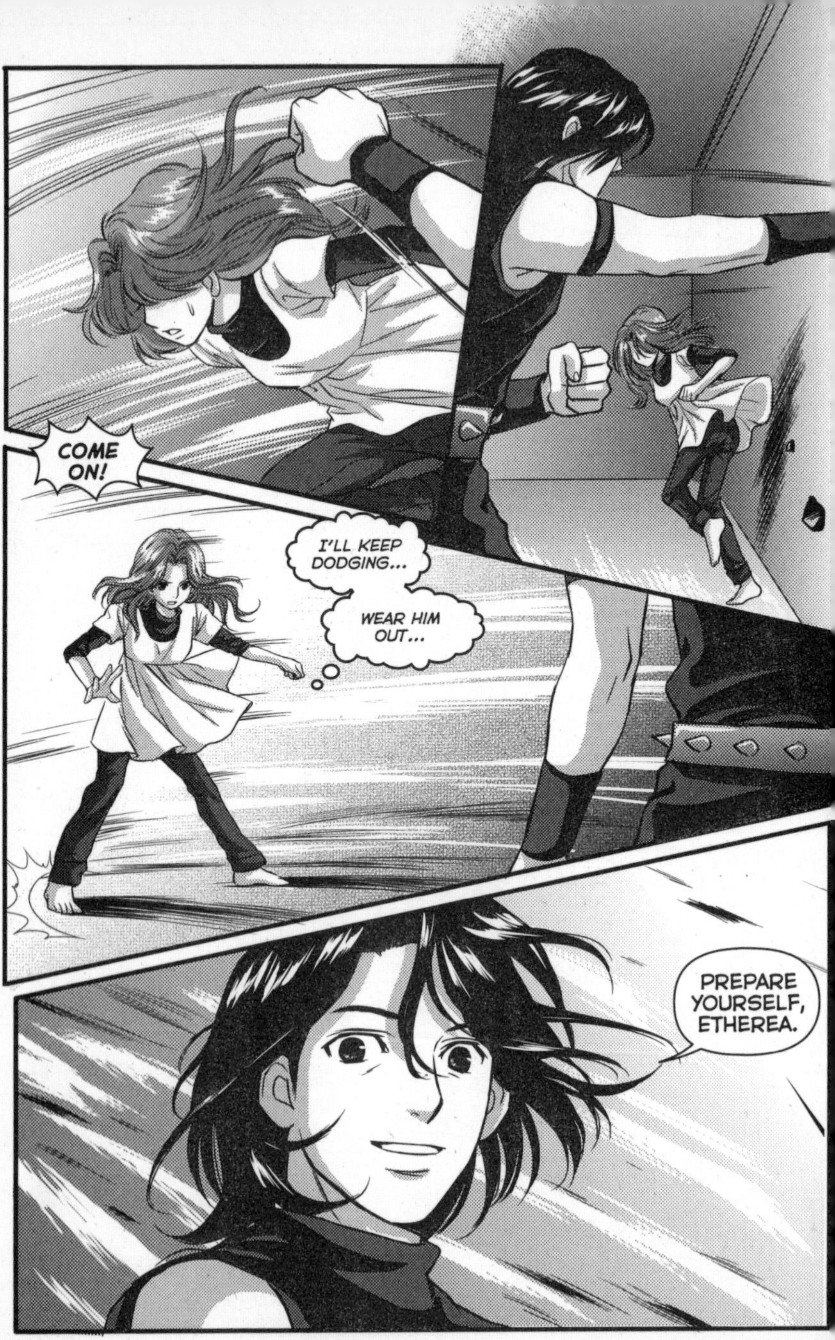
COME ON!
I'LL KEEP DODGING...
WEAR HIM OUT...
PREPARE YOURSELF, ETHEREA.

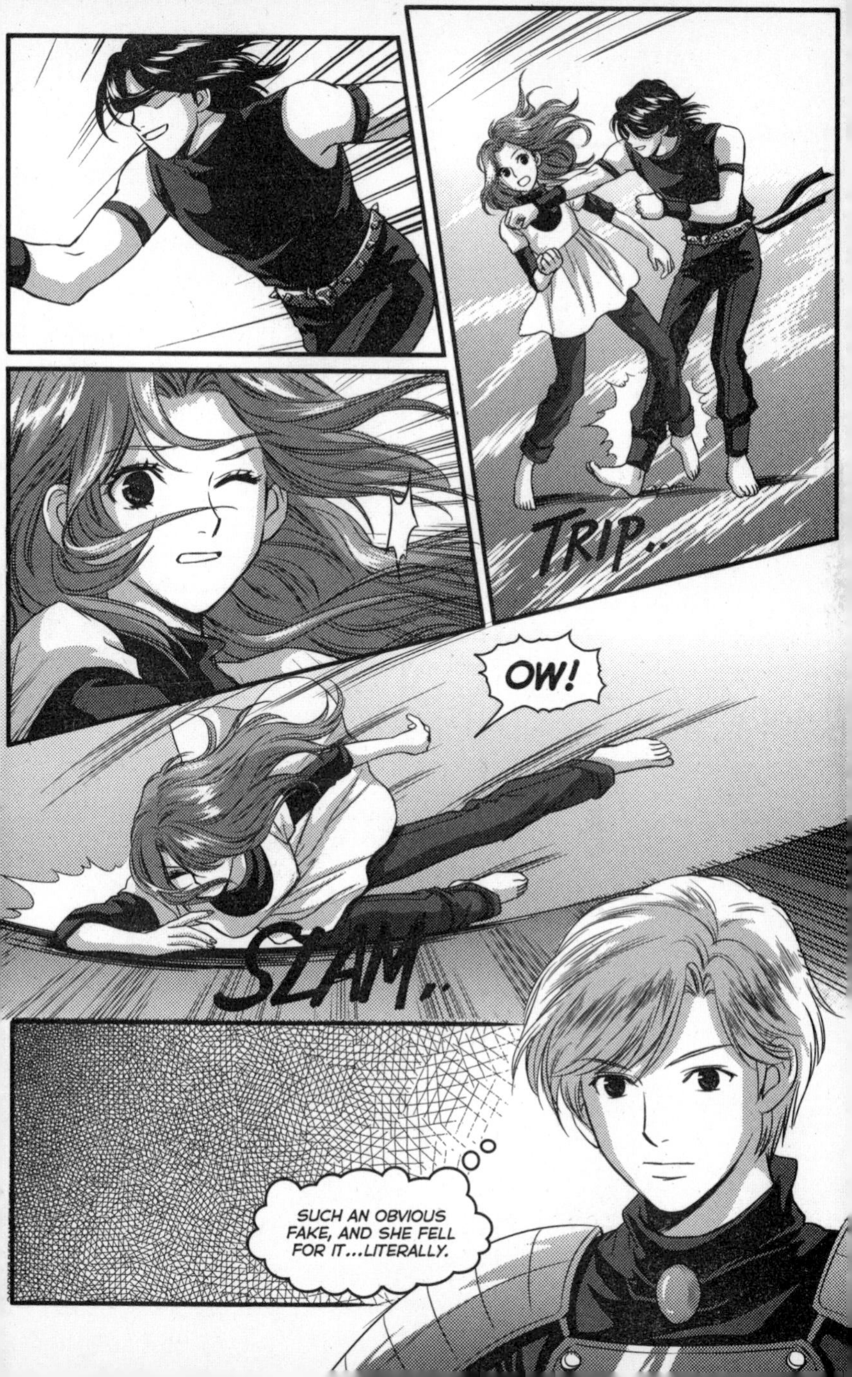
TRIP..
OW!
SLAM..
SUCH AN OBVIOUS FAKE, AND SHE FELL FOR IT...LITERALLY.

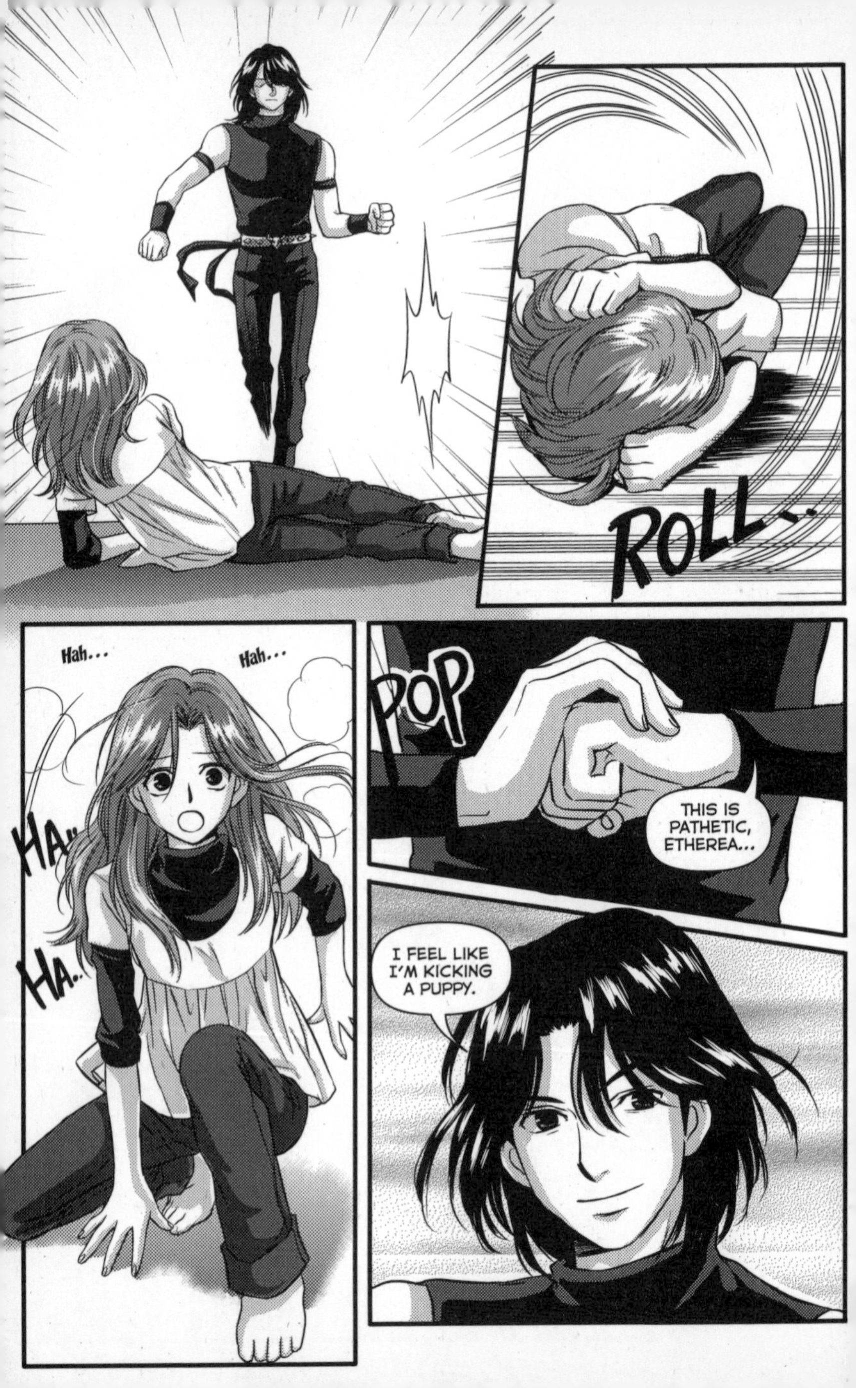
ROLL...
Hah...
Hah...
HA...
HA...
POP
THIS IS PATHETIC, ETHEREA...
I FEEL LIKE I'M KICKING A PUPPY.

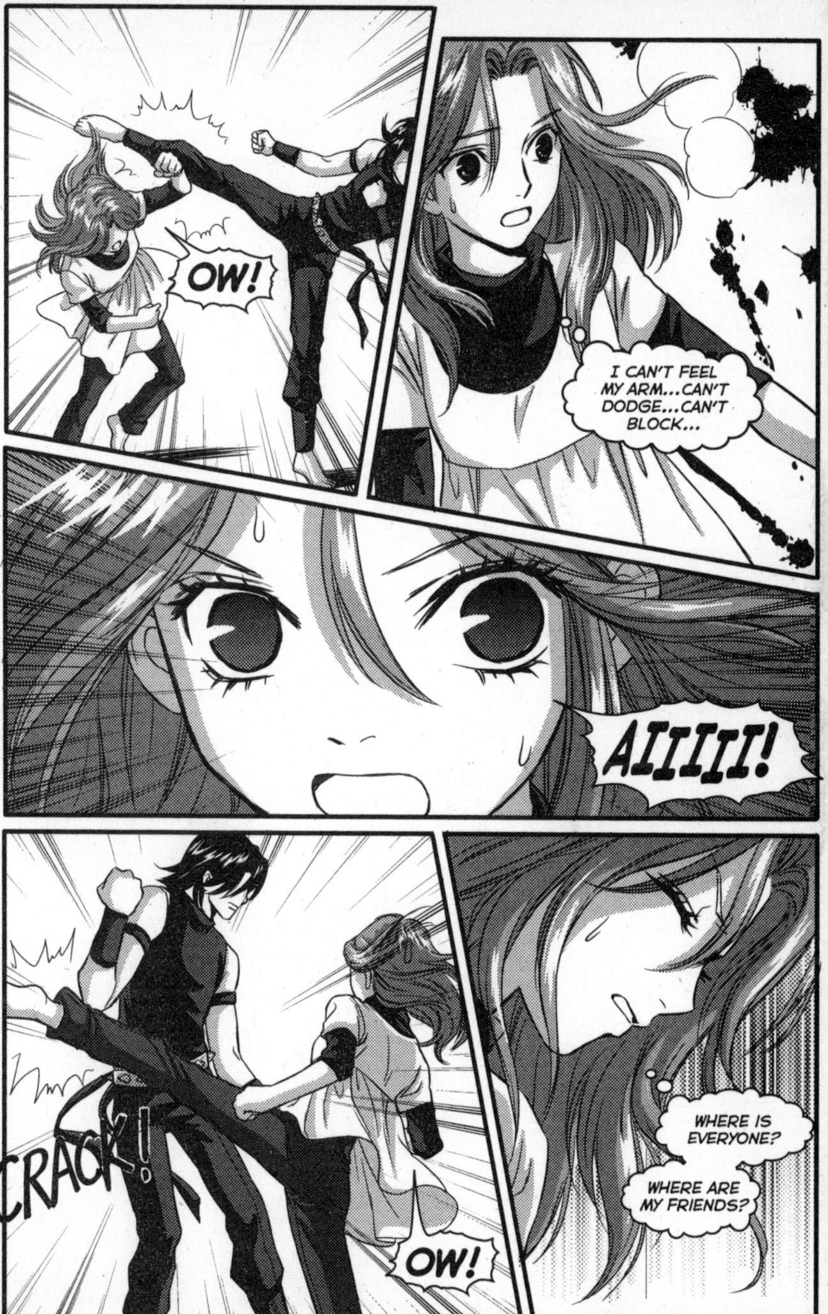
OW!
I CAN'T FEEL MY ARM...CAN'T DODGE...CAN'T BLOCK...
AIIIII!
CRACK!
OW!
WHERE IS EVERYONE?
WHERE ARE MY FRIENDS?

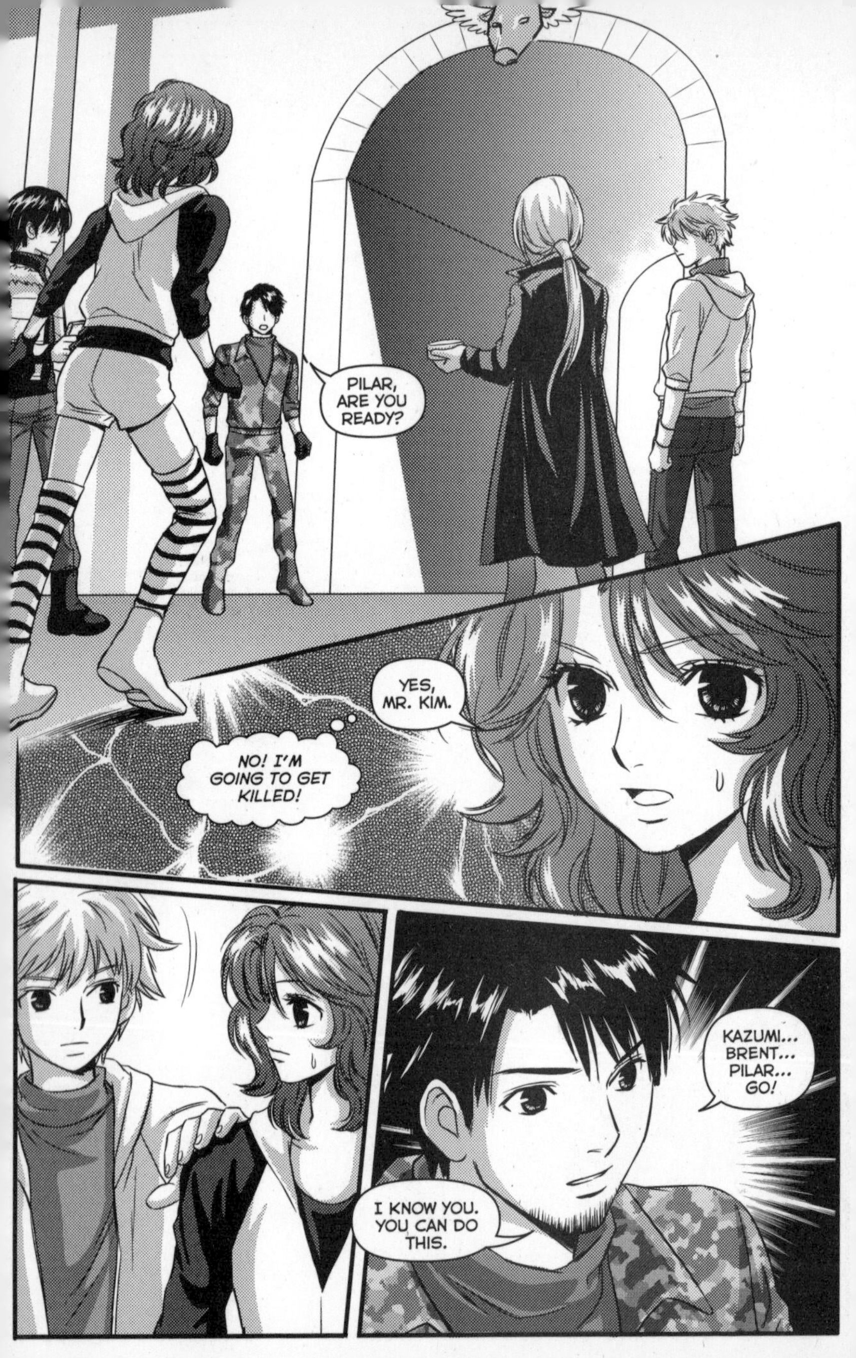
PILAR, ARE YOU READY?
YES, MR. KIM.
NO! I'M GOING TO GET KILLED!
KAZUMI... BRENT... PILAR... GO!
I KNOW YOU. YOU CAN DO THIS.

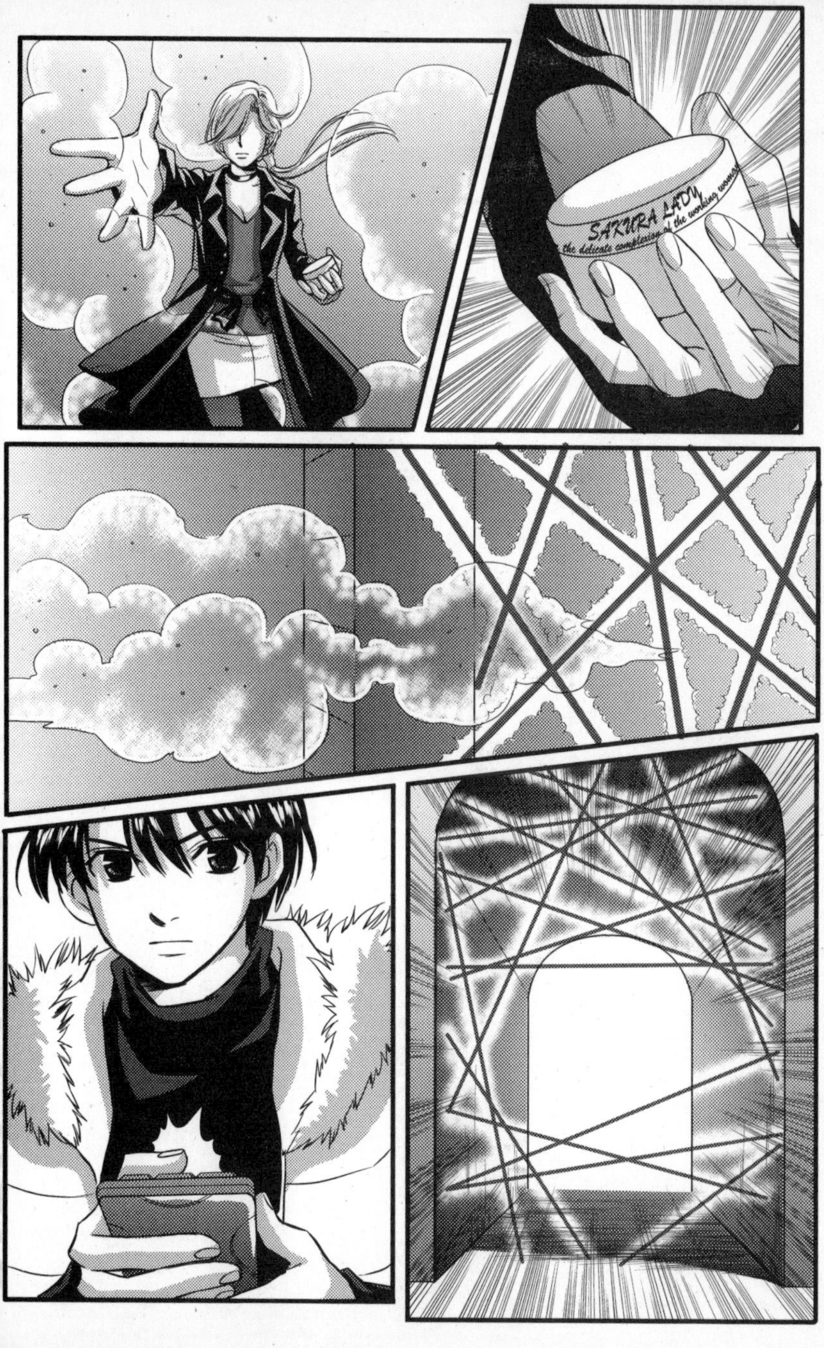
SAKURA LADY
the delicate complexion of the working woma

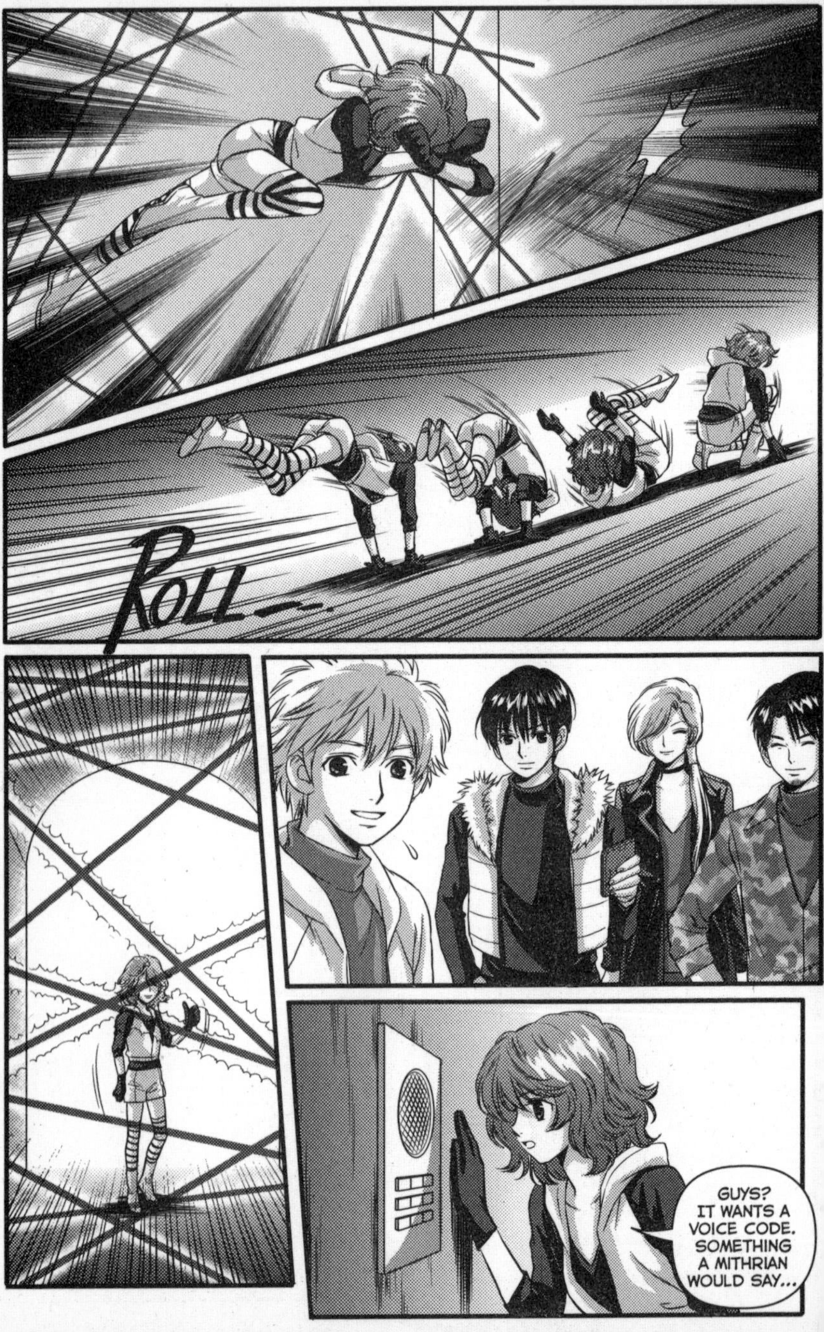
ROLL
GUYS? IT WANTS A VOICE CODE. SOMETHING A MITHRIAN WOULD SAY...

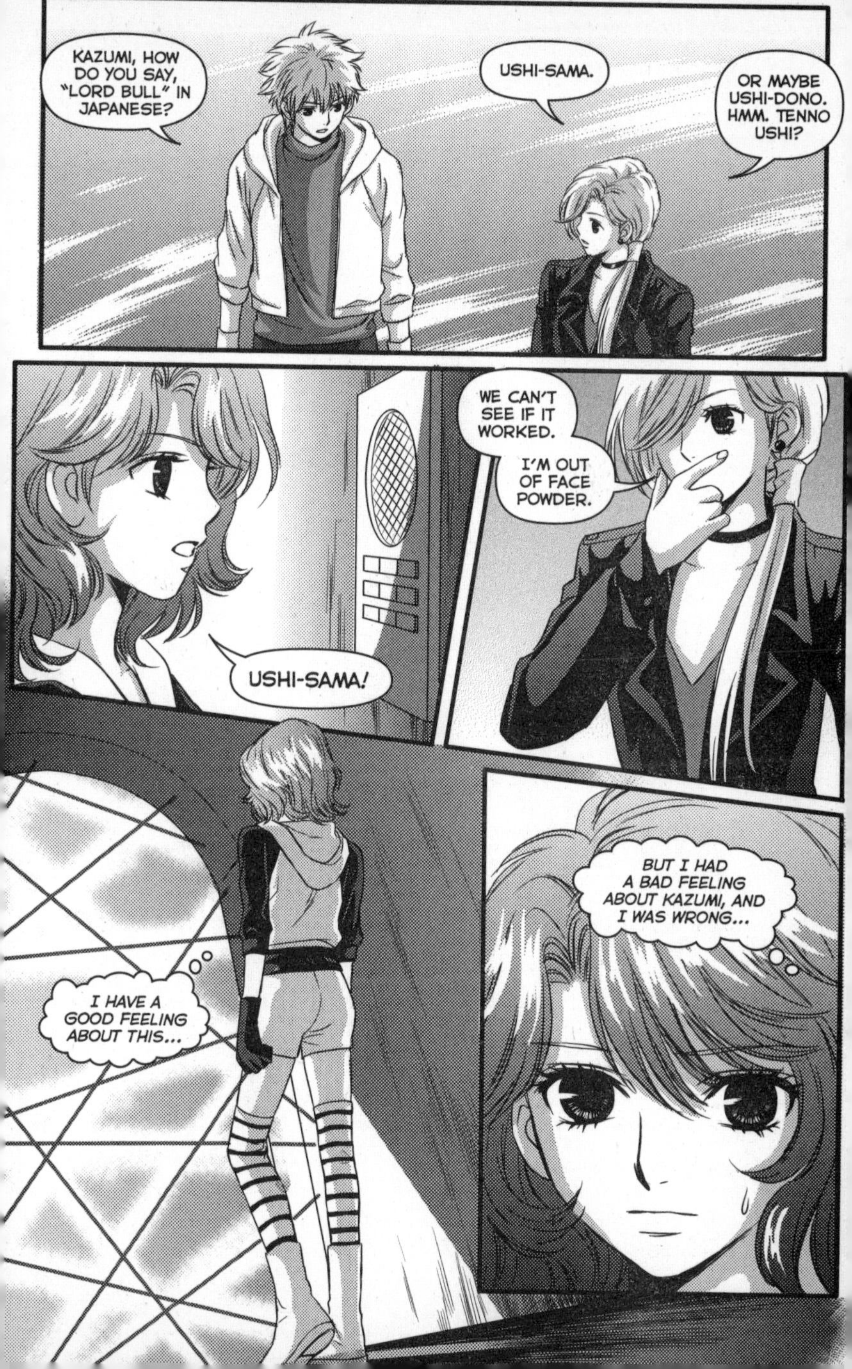
KAZUMI, HOW DO YOU SAY, "LORD BULL" IN JAPANESE?
USHI-SAMA.
OR MAYBE USHI-DONO. HMM. TENNO USHI?
USHI-SAMA!
WE CAN'T SEE IF IT WORKED.
I'M OUT OF FACE POWDER.
I HAVE A GOOD FEELING ABOUT THIS...
BUT I HAD A BAD FEELING ABOUT KAZUMI, AND I WAS WRONG...

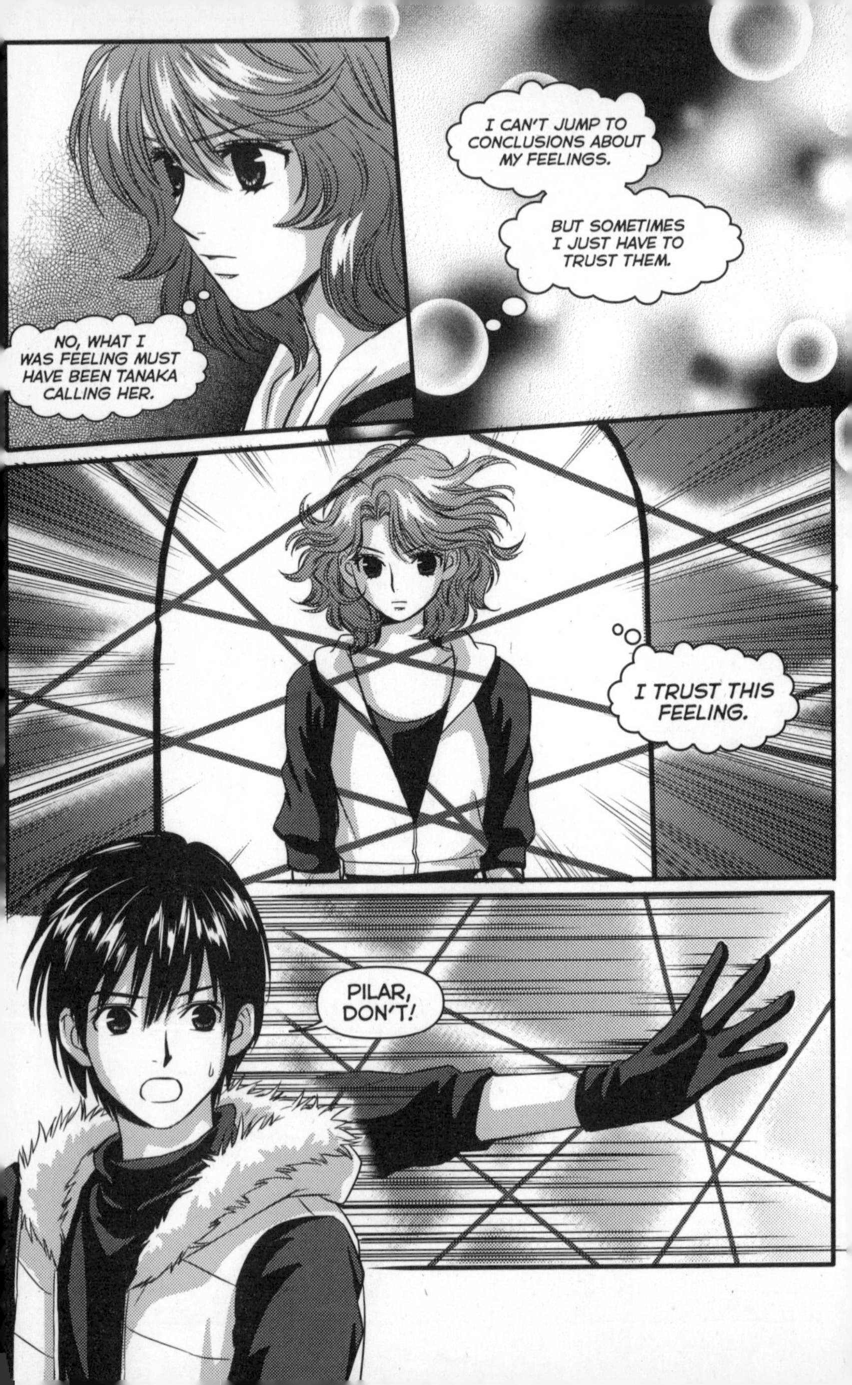
I CAN'T JUMP TO CONCLUSIONS ABOUT MY FEELINGS.
BUT SOMETIMES I JUST HAVE TO TRUST THEM.
NO, WHAT I WAS FEELING MUST HAVE BEEN TANAKA CALLING HER.
I TRUST THIS FEELING.
PILAR, DON'T!

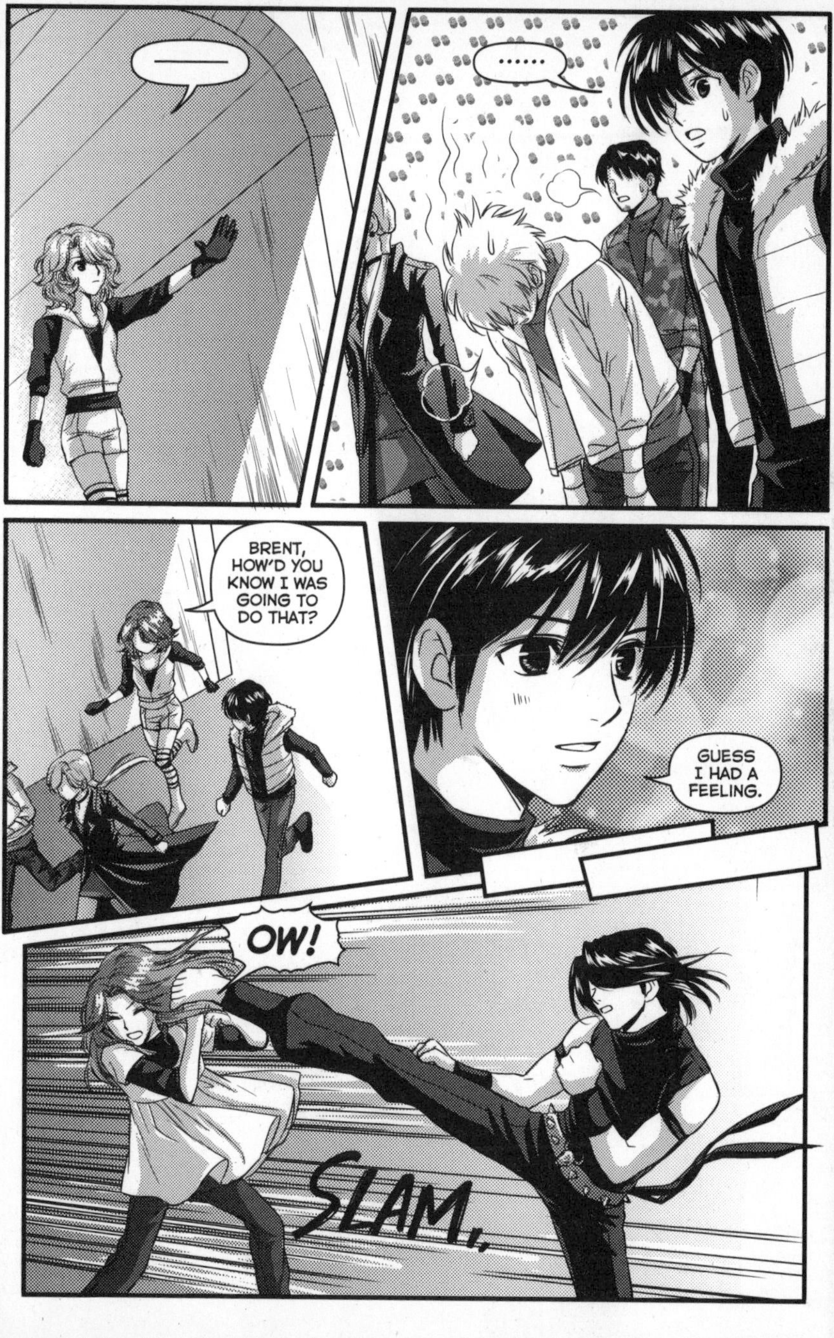
—
......
BRENT, HOW'D YOU KNOW I WAS GOING TO DO THAT?
GUESS I HAD A FEELING.
OW!
SLAM.

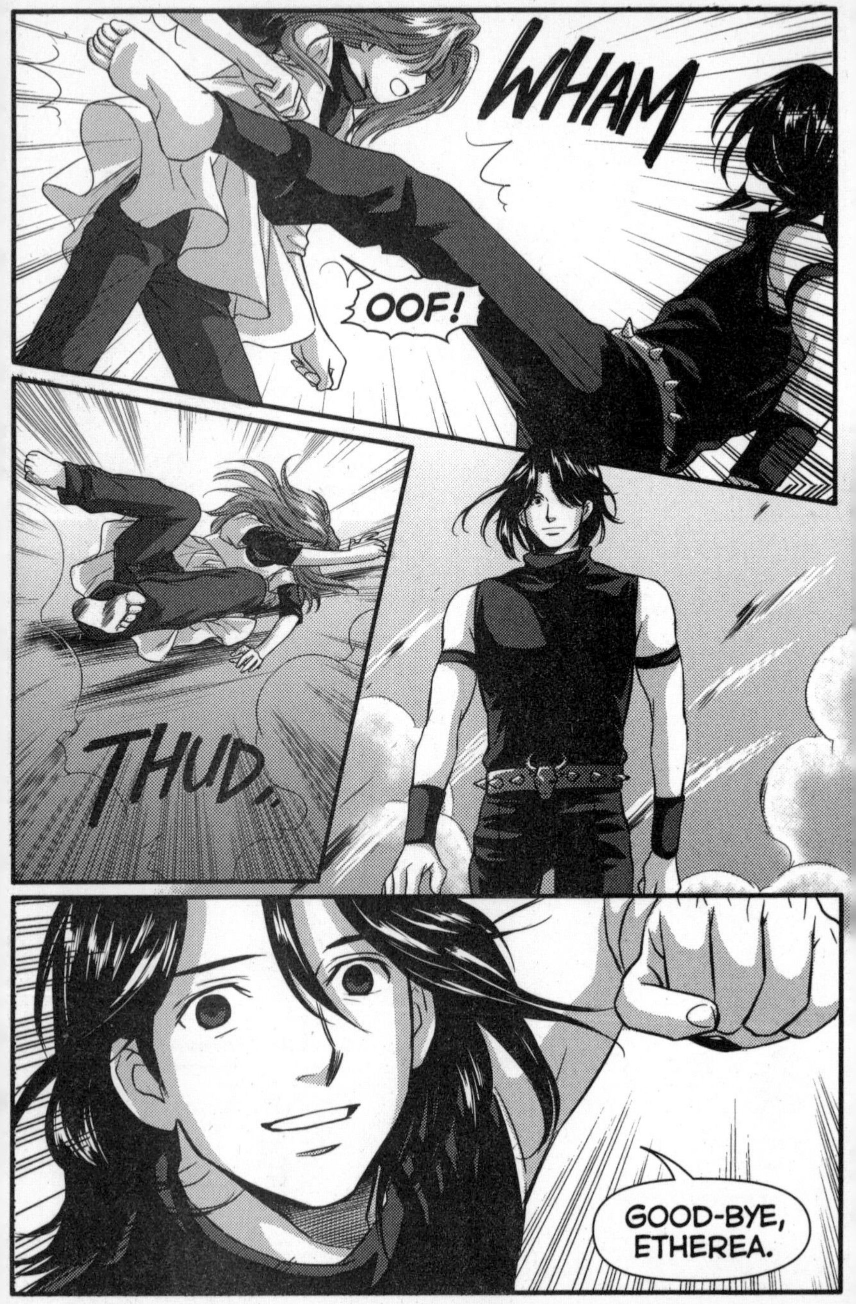
WHAM
OOF!
THUD
GOOD-BYE, ETHEREA.

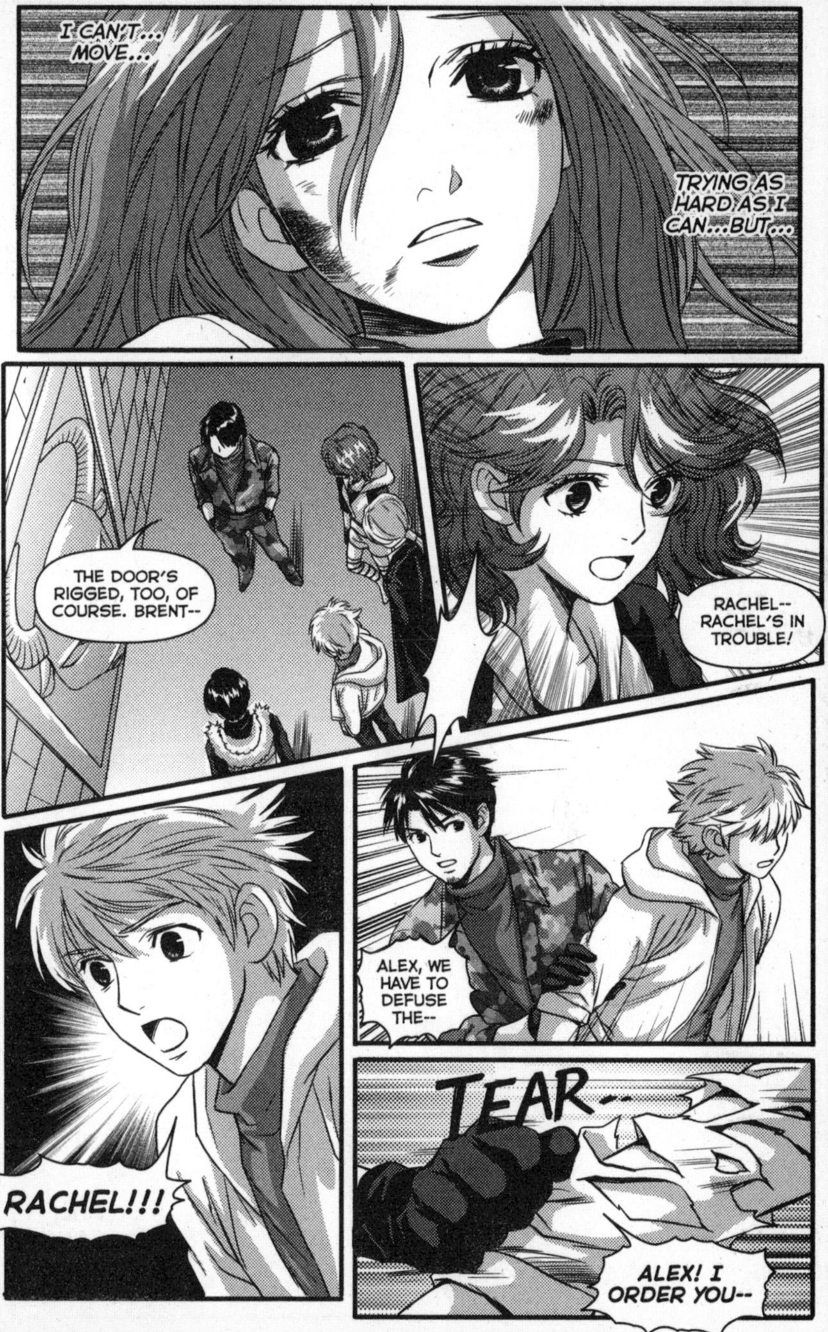
I CAN'T... MOVE...
TRYING AS HARD AS I CAN...BUT...
THE DOOR'S RIGGED, TOO, OF COURSE. BRENT--
RACHEL-- RACHEL'S IN TROUBLE!
RACHEL!!!
ALEX, WE HAVE TO DEFUSE THE--
TEAR...
ALEX! I ORDER YOU--

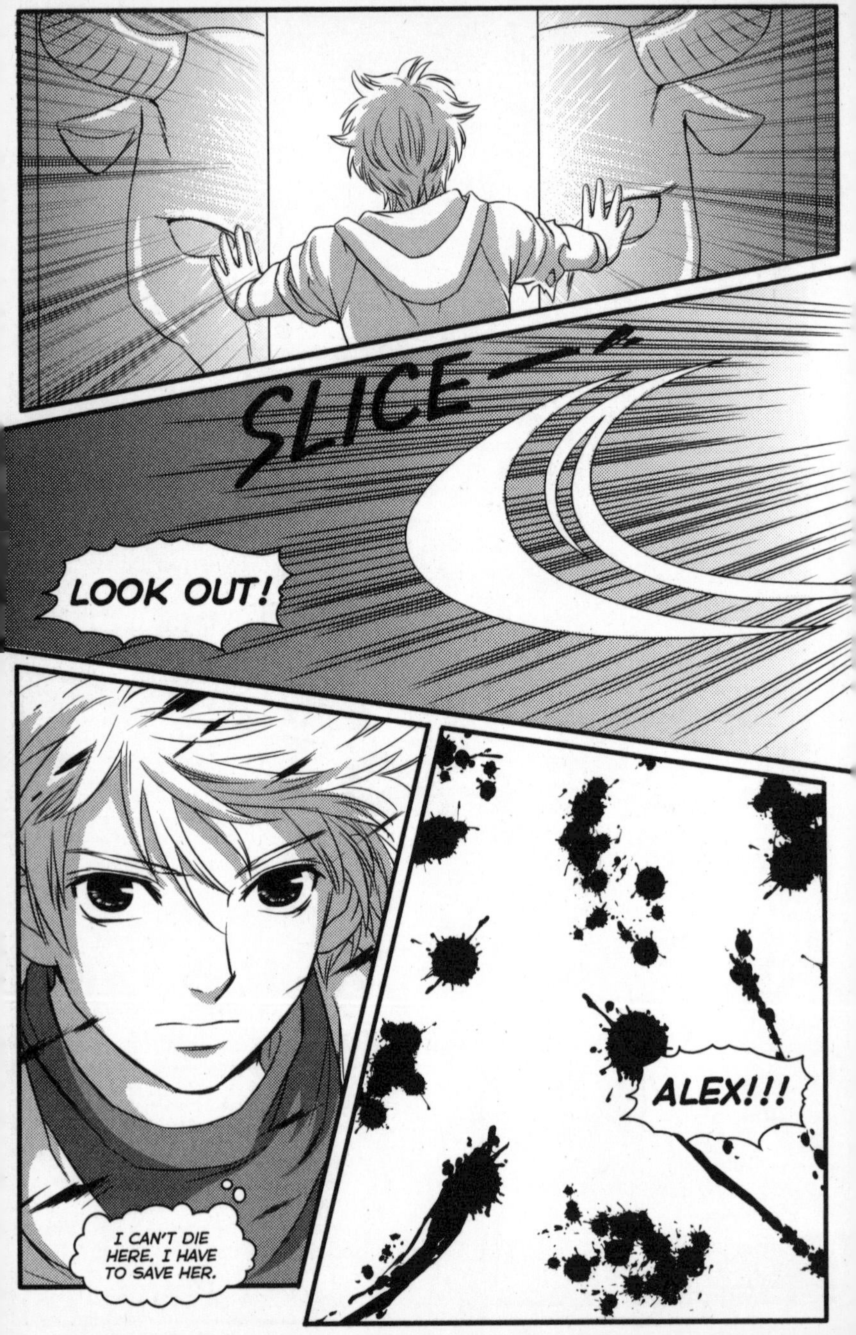
SLICE
LOOK OUT!
I CAN'T DIE HERE. I HAVE TO SAVE HER.
ALEX!!!

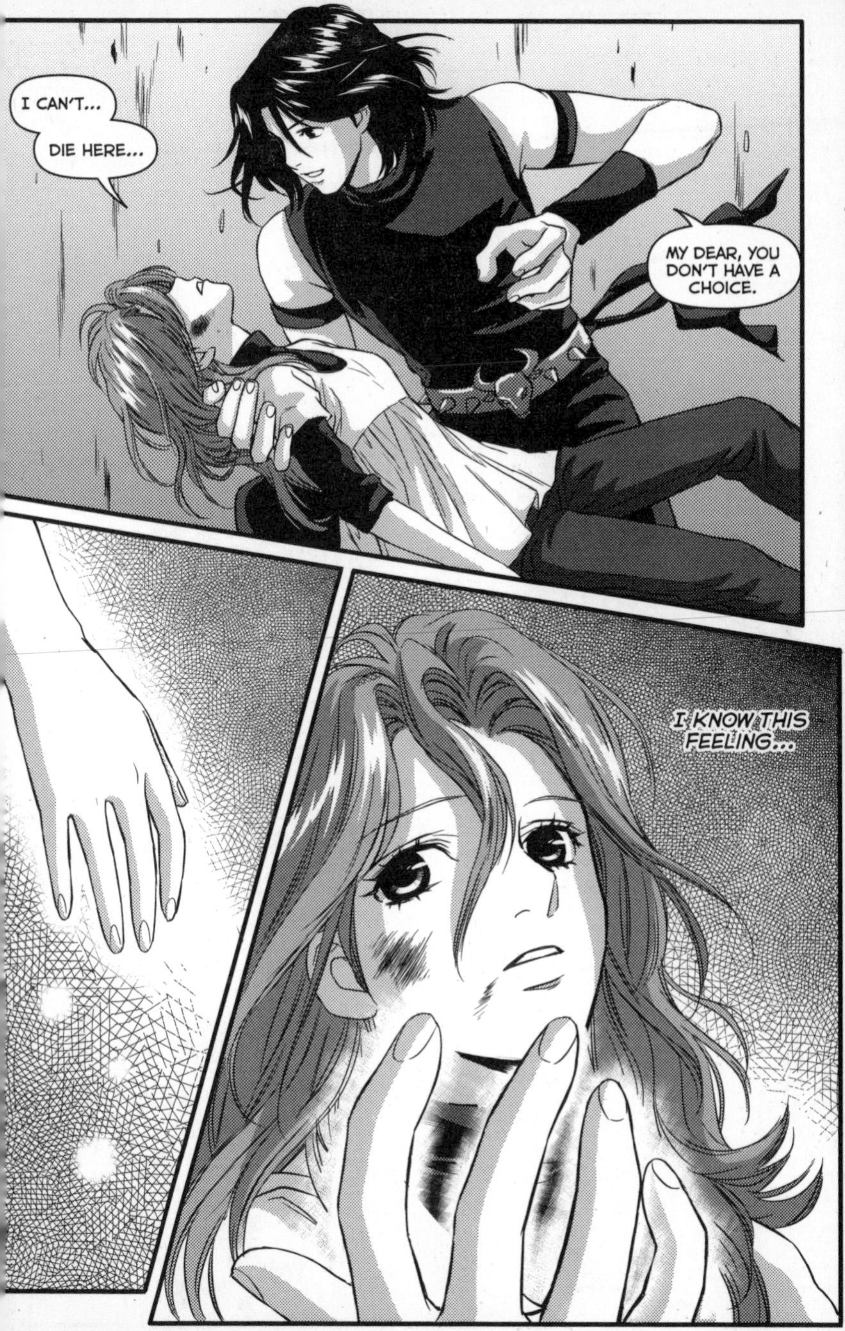
I CAN'T...
DIE HERE...
MY DEAR, YOU DON'T HAVE A CHOICE.
I KNOW THIS FEELING...

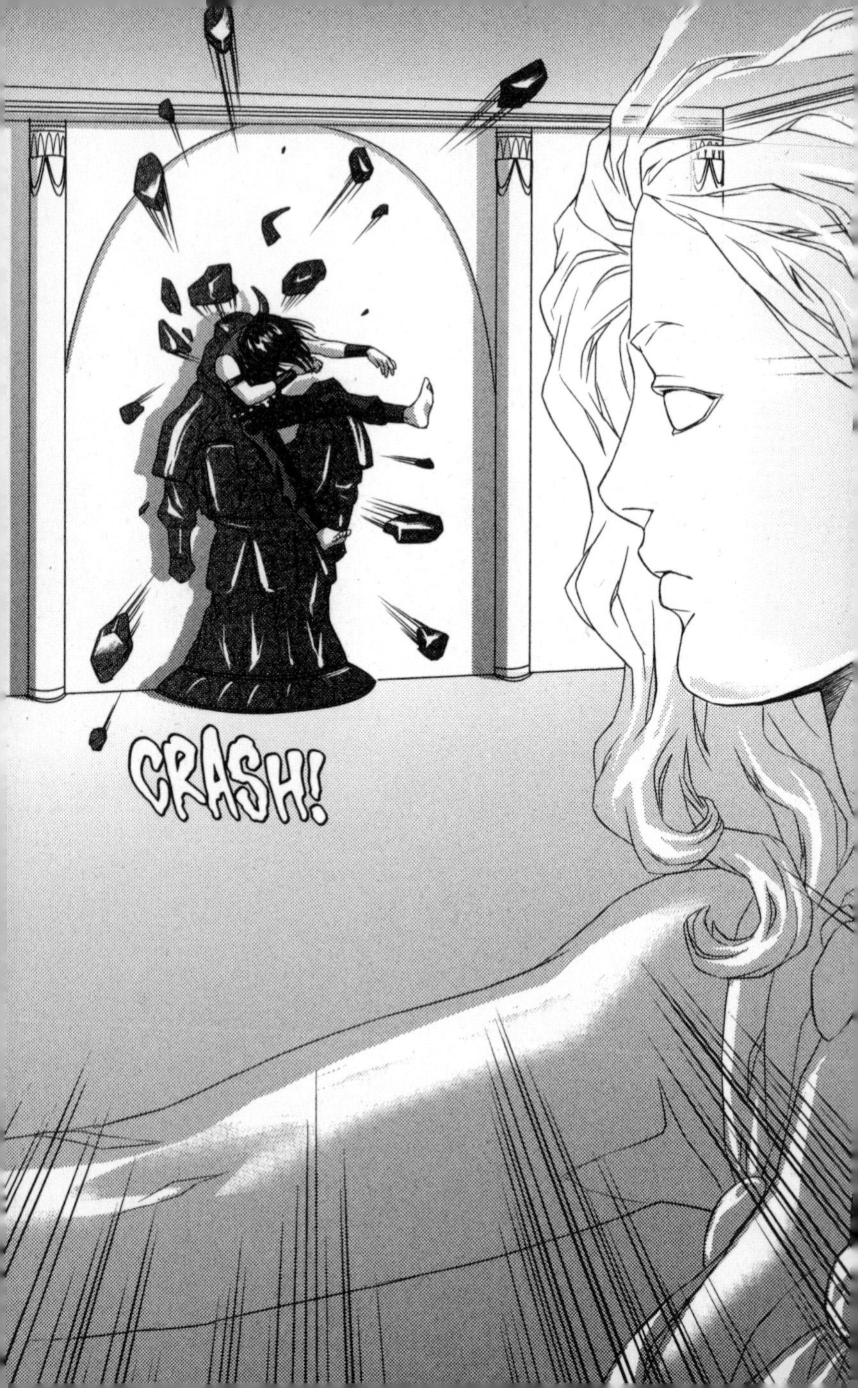
CRASH!

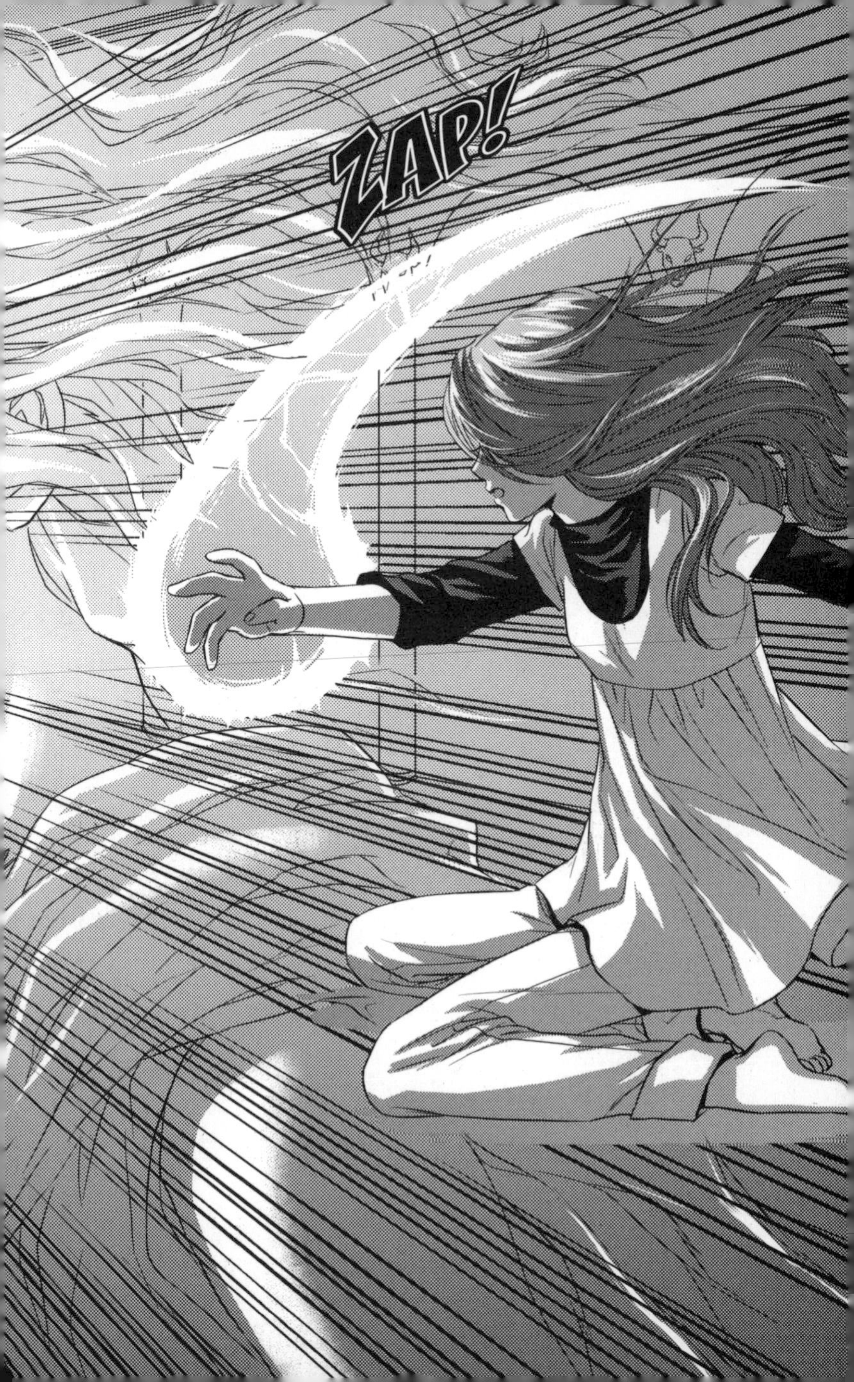
ZAP!

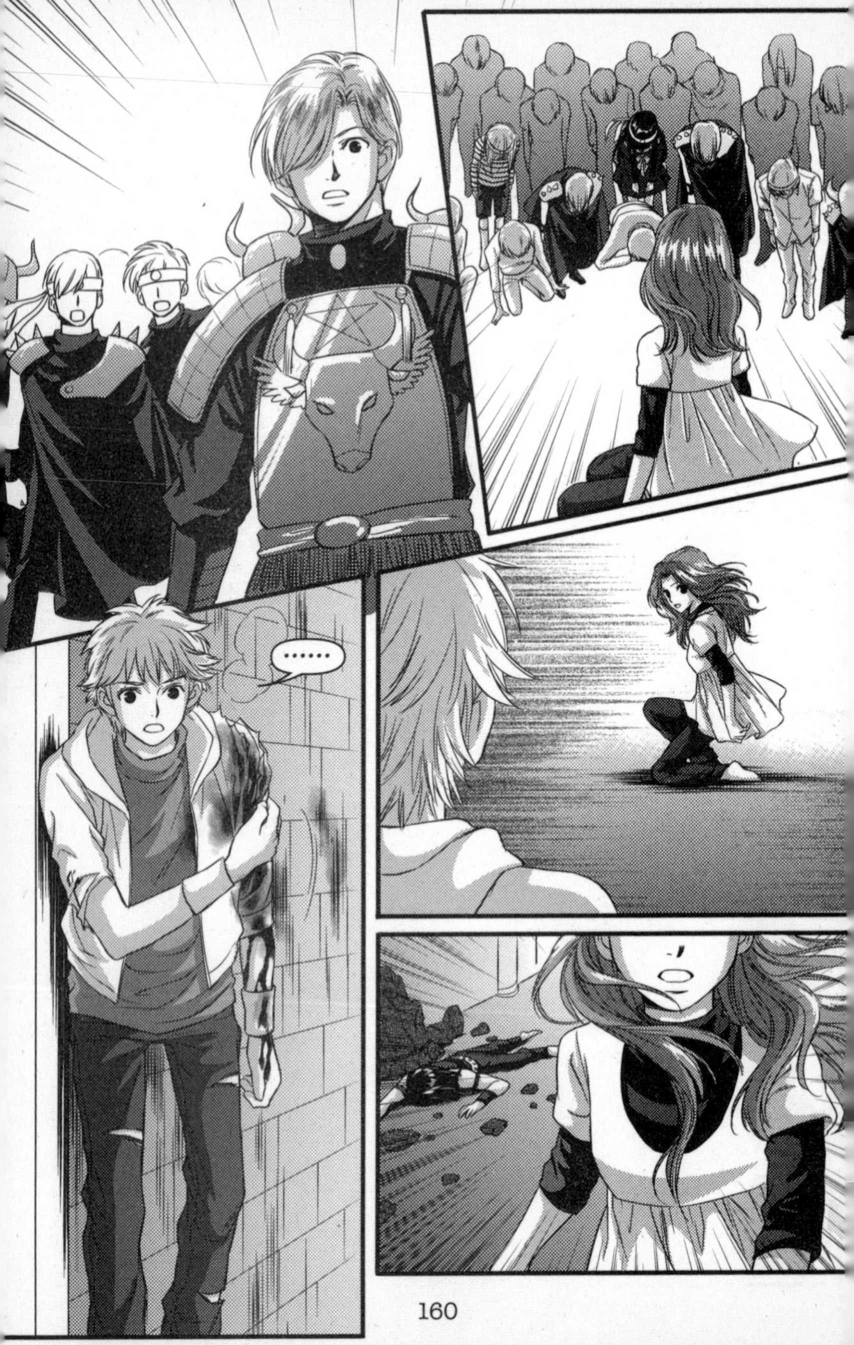
......

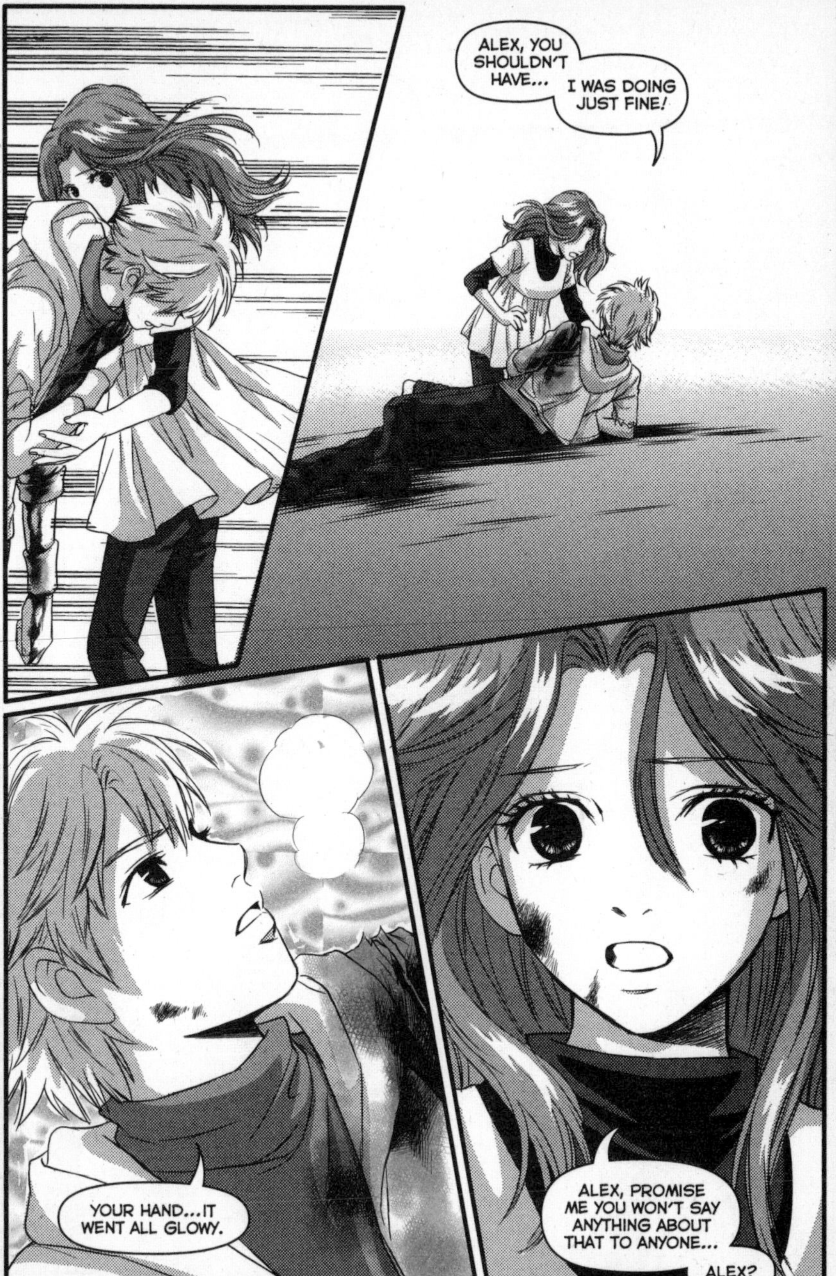
ALEX, YOU SHOULDN'T HAVE...
I WAS DOING JUST FINE!
YOUR HAND...IT WENT ALL GLOWY.
ALEX, PROMISE ME YOU WON'T SAY ANYTHING ABOUT THAT TO ANYONE...
ALEX?

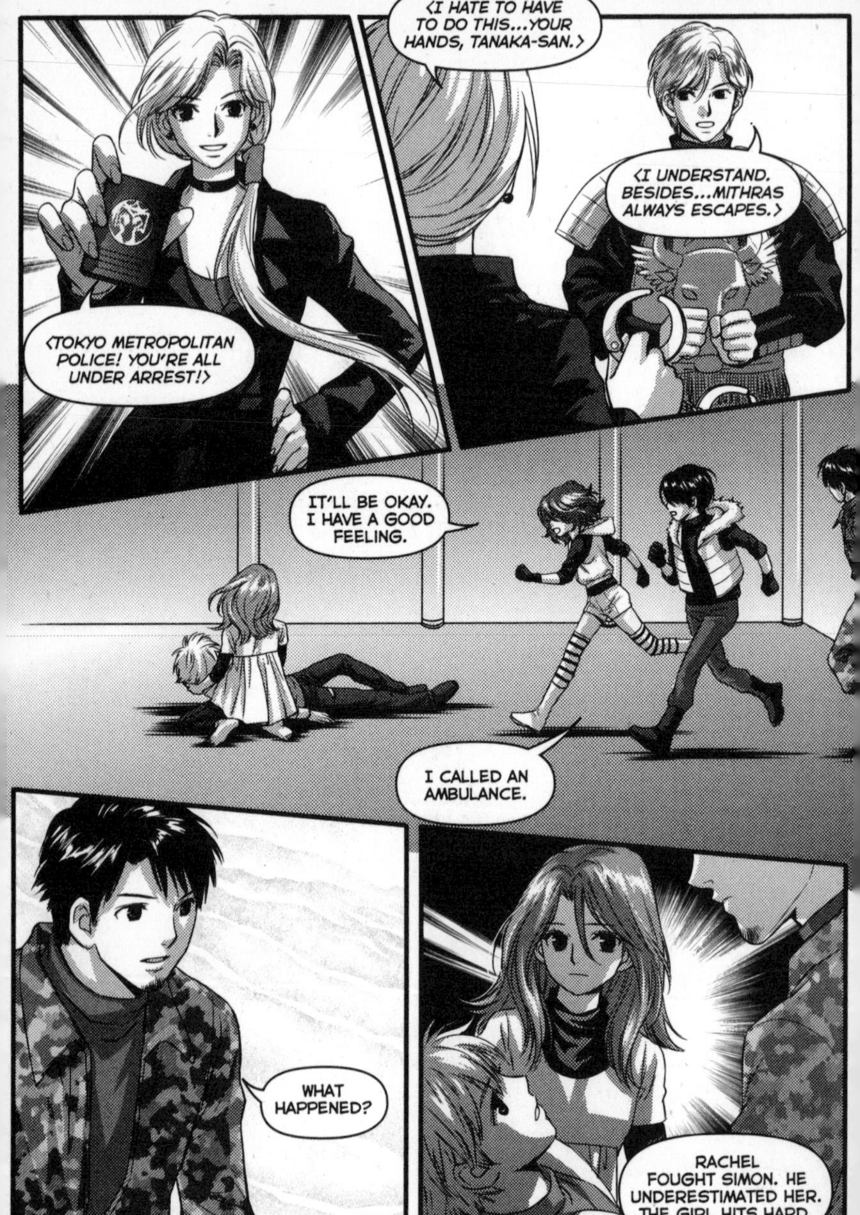
<TOKYO METROPOLITAN POLICE! YOU'RE ALL UNDER ARREST!>
<I HATE TO HAVE TO DO THIS...YOUR HANDS, TANAKA-SAN.>
<I UNDERSTAND. BESIDES...MITHRAS ALWAYS ESCAPES.>
IT'LL BE OKAY. I HAVE A GOOD FEELING.
I CALLED AN AMBULANCE.
WHAT HAPPENED?
RACHEL FOUGHT SIMON. HE UNDERESTIMATED HER. THE GIRL HITS HARD.

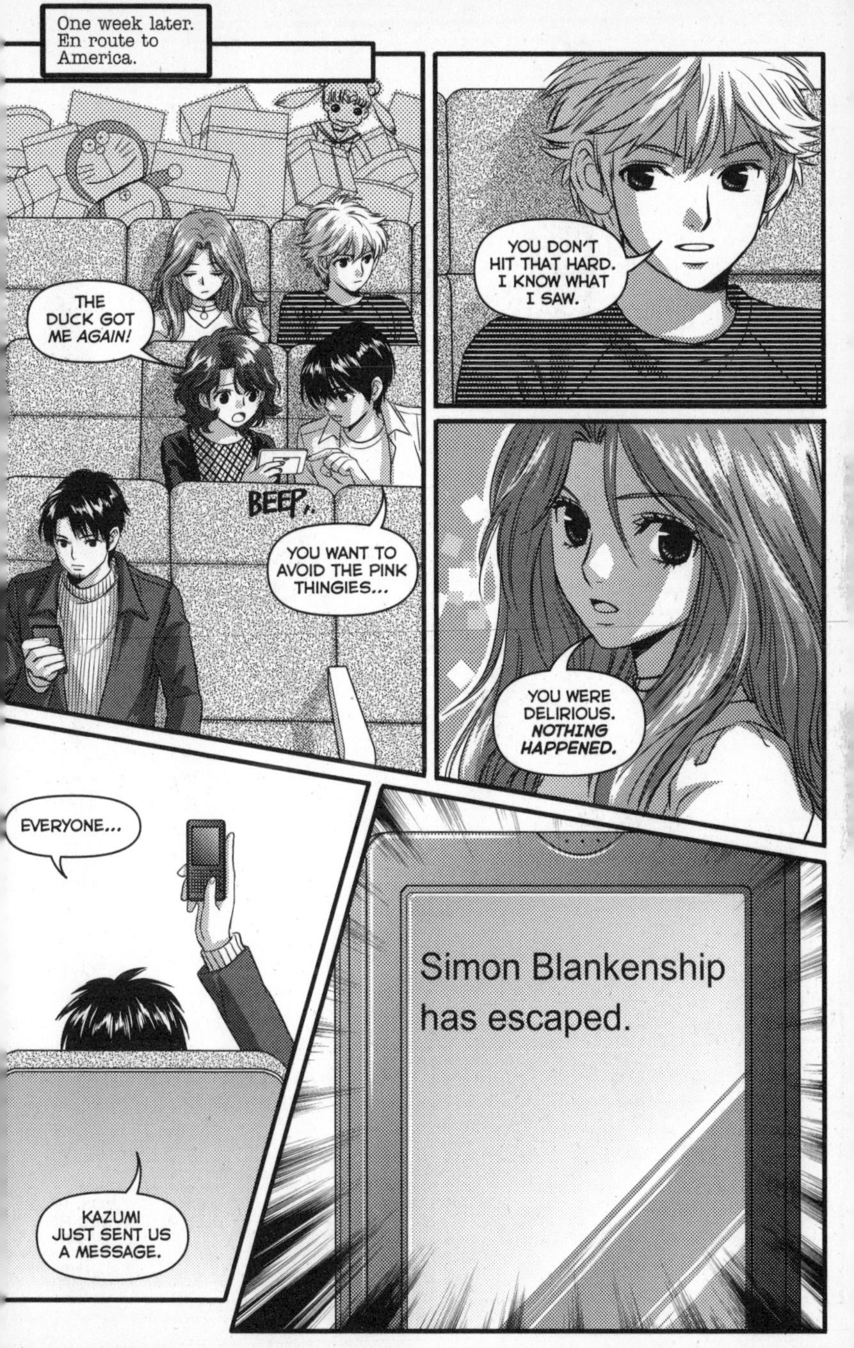
One week later. En route to America.
THE DUCK GOT ME AGAIN!
BEEP
YOU WANT TO AVOID THE PINK THINGIES...
YOU DON'T HIT THAT HARD. I KNOW WHAT I SAW.
YOU WERE DELIRIOUS. NOTHING HAPPENED.
EVERYONE...
KAZUMI JUST SENT US A MESSAGE.
Simon Blankenship has escaped.

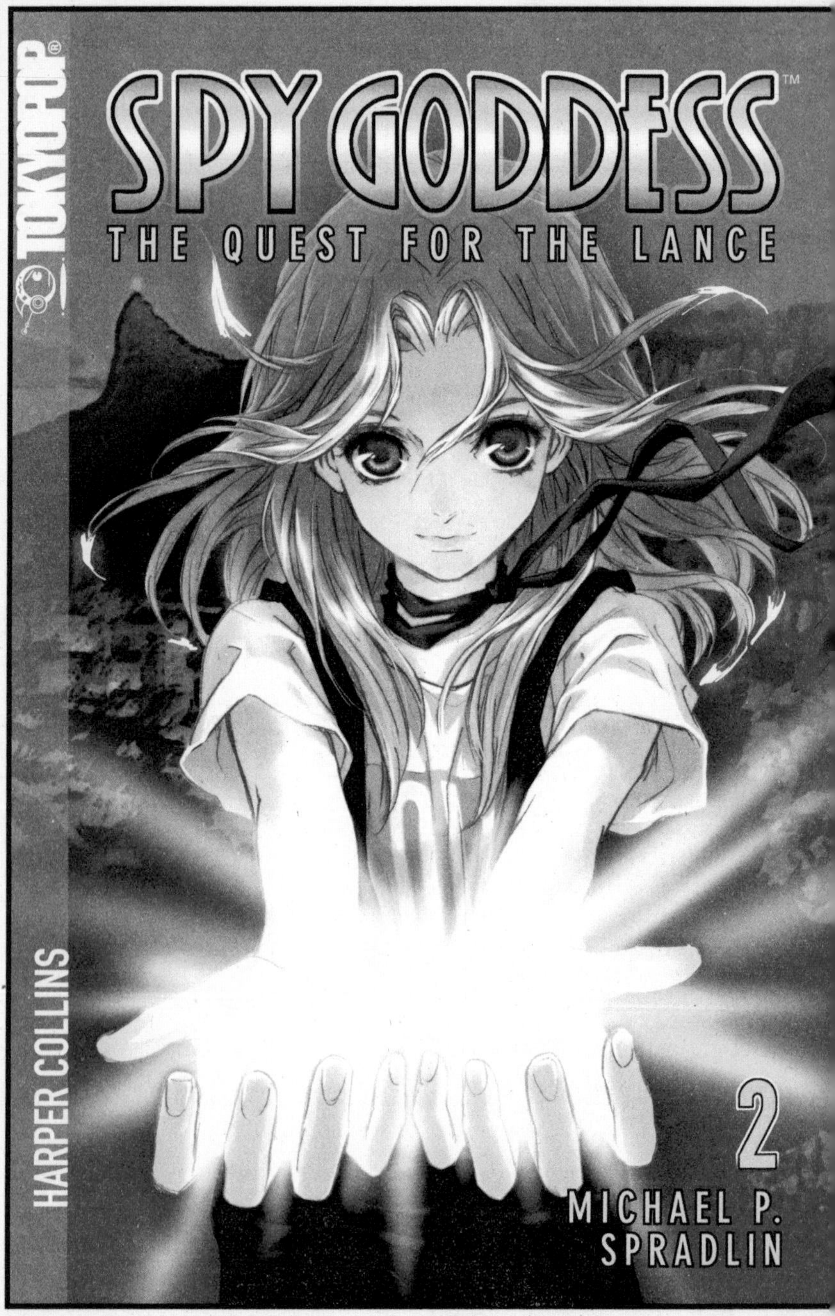
TOKYOPOP
SPY GODDESS™
THE QUEST FOR THE LANCE
HARPER COLLINS
2
MICHAEL P.
SPRADLIN

In the next volume of

SPY GODDESS

Fresh from pounding the streets of Tokyo in her designer boots, spy goddess Rachel Buchanan is called to yet another corner of the world.

When a Mithrian artifact is pinpointed deep in the thick, sticky, dark, and endangered Brazilian rain forest, Rachel packs a bikini and heads for Latin America.

Of course, it being the season of Carnival in Rio, the rest of the team might have a tough time dragging her away from the greatest party ever...at least long enough to beat her archrival, Simon Blankenship, to the prize.

SPY GODDESS

Michael P. Spradlin is the captivating author of all the novels and manga volumes of the Spy Goddess series. He lives in Michigan with his family, but his not-so-secret mission is to entertain readers across the globe with his high-action, thrill-packed Spy Goddess adventures. You can visit him online at www.michaelspradlin.com.

Rachel Manija Brown writes manga, TV, books, and a livejournal. Her first book, *All the Fishes Come Home to Roost: An American Misfit in India*, has been published in the USA, Canada, the UK, New Zealand, Australia, South Africa, and India. It's the true story of how her post-hippie parents raised her on a bizarre ashram in India. *USA Today* called it "hilarious."

Rachel and artist Ayudya "Bayou" Riadini created the fantasy manga *The Nine-Lives* for TOKYOPOP. Rachel and artist Stephanie Folse created the manga *Project Blue Rose*, about gay secret agents in Texas, and *Spindrift*, about gay martial artists in Tibet.

Rachel and novelist Sherwood Smith created the TV series *Game World* for the Jim Henson Company.

CLASSIFIED INFORMATION

Name: Yifan Ling
Known Aliases: Ivy,
    Rainbow Buddy
Gender: Female
Date of Birth: Jan. 8, 1983

Location: Beijing, China
Blood type: A
Family members: Parents
Pet: Shiu-Shiu (Shetland
    sheepdog)

Yifan Ling was born in Beijing, China, and started learning to draw at the age of four. In middle school, she fell in love with manga and started trying to draw it. After four years of learning Industrial Design at a university, Yifan followed her manga dream to the UK and enrolled in the M.A. course of Visual Communication (Illustration) at the Birmingham Institute of Art and Design.

After graduation, Yifan moved to London and her work soon began appearing in UK publications. While in London, Yifan made a connection with TOKYOPOP and one of the results is in your hands now.

Yifan's many manga influences include *Tokyo Babylon*, *Love Hina*, *Ranma 1/2*, *Mars*, and *Full Metal Alchemist*.

Read the Spy Goddess novel that started it all!
An excerpt from

LIVE AND LET SHOP

After what seemed like an hour walk, Blackthorn's headmaster, Mr. Kim, and I finally got to a corridor that led to the girls' wing of the academy. Most of the doors in the corridor were closed, but as we walked past I could hear voices and music. So this place wasn't totally dead. About halfway down the hall, Mr. Kim knocked on a door and swung it open when a voice said to come in.

"Hello, Pilar," said Mr. Kim. "I'd like you to meet your new roommate, Rachel Buchanan." Pilar was tall and slender. She had dark brown curly hair, shoulder length, and beautiful dark brown eyes. She had been sitting at her desk, staring at the door, like she was waiting for us to show up. Okay, not too creepy. She waved to me from where she sat.

"Hi," she said. "Welcome to Blackthorn."

I really didn't know what else to do, so I mumbled a hello and stood there shifting my weight from my left side to my right and back. I looked around the room. It was a two-room suite: a bedroom with two beds and closets in one room, and a study/ sitting room with desks and a couple of chairs in the other. Over Pilar's desk was a Blink 182 poster. Okay, that was a good sign. Each of the two rooms had a window, and you could look out of the window and see the athletic fields and the woods beyond. But overall it was small. Very small, compared to home.

Mr. Kim was talking to Pilar about something, so I just kept looking around the room. I saw my suitcase and duffel bag in the bedroom, stacked by one of the closets. At least they hadn't lost my luggage.

"Well, I'll leave you two to get to know each other," Mr. Kim finally said. "We will meet in the *do jang* in thirty minutes. Rachel, your *do bak* is in your closet. Pilar can help you with the belt. See you there."

With that he turned and left. I didn't know what to do. I felt like crying. Pilar looked at me and smiled.

"Don't worry," she said, "I remember how I felt my first day here. It's a little overwhelming. You'll get used to it. The time goes by fast."

"What are you in for?" I asked.

"In for?" she asked.

"Yeah, you know—drugs, stealing, stuff like that?" I said.

She looked puzzled. "I don't understand," she said.

"Didn't the judge in your case send you here?"

A look of understanding came over her face.

"Oh, no—no drugs, no judge. I'm an orphan. My aunt was raising me, but she got sick and couldn't take care of me anymore. A neighbor of ours was a friend of Mr. Kim and knew about Blackthorn, so she arranged for me to get a scholarship. I've been here three years. My aunt passed away last year, so Blackthorn is now my home." She turned around and sat back down at her desk. She had a really sad look on her face, and it made me feel about two inches tall.

So to top off the great day I was having, I had just managed to act like a total jerk to my new roommate. *Someone kill me now.*

"Sorry. I thought . . . never mind. Just . . . I'm sorry," I stammered.

Pilar nodded slightly and returned to reading her book. I took that opportunity to exit stage left and went into the bedroom to unpack my stuff. It took all of ten minutes to stuff all my clothes into the closet and the built-in drawers in the wall. The last thing I pulled out was my laptop, an IBM ThinkPad that my parents, Charles and Cynthia, had given me for my birthday three months before. Actually, they hadn't really given it to me. They'd given me the money and told me to buy it for myself. They were too busy to shop for my birthday. I loved that laptop—it was probably my most prized possession. But so far I hadn't seen a phone in the room, which probably meant no Internet access. That would cause me to wither and die quicker than anything. I would have to find a way around that somehow.

Pilar came in and opened her closet door. "We don't have phones in our rooms," she said. "You can make calls to your parents from the conference room next to Mr. Kim's office, but you have to reserve a time with Mrs. Marquardt."

"What?" I said.

She pointed to the laptop I held in my hand.

"You were probably wondering where the phone was, and I was just saying we don't have them in our rooms." She stood there watching me with this bizarrely intense expression.

"Is there a problem?" I snapped.

She kind of jumped, like I'd caught her going through my underwear drawer. "No. Uh, sorry. It's just . . . it's nothing really."

"What?" I said. I was still a little cranky from dealing with Mr. Kim, and I needed to get things straight with this chick right away. We had to be roommates, but I didn't have to like it, so she could just step off and give me my space.

"I just feel like I've seen you before. Have you ever been to Detroit, by any chance?"

"No. Ever been to Beverly Hills?" I said it with a rather snotty tone.

"Gosh, no. Is that where you're from?" Gosh? Who the heck says gosh?

"Yeah."

"Cool. Beverly Hills must be awesome. Still, it's weird," she said. "I just have this feeling like I've seen you somewhere."

She began putting on a white martial arts uniform, which fit her like a glove. She pulled a blue belt from a hook inside the closet and fastened it around her waist.

"We better get going. It's a ten-minute walk to the *do jang*, and tardiness means fifty push-ups on your knuckles," she said.

I managed to get the uniform on okay, but the white belt that went with it was hopeless. Pilar stepped over and showed me how to tie it. It looked complicated. It was really bugging me that I had to do this Tae Kwon Do thing. But it couldn't be that hard, could it?

"Come on," she said, and we headed out the door.

DON'T MISS ALL THE BOOKS IN THE ACTION-PACKED TEEN SERIES SPY GODDESS!

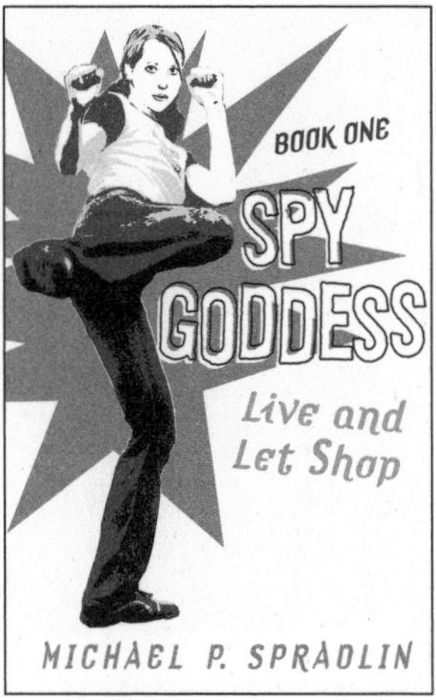

BOOK ONE
SPY GODDESS
Live and Let Shop
MICHAEL P. SPRADLIN

SPY GODDESS, BOOK ONE: LIVE AND LET SHOP

Beverly Hills princess Rachel Buchanan has been in trouble one too many times. So she's shipped off to freaky Blackthorn Academy, a mysterious school for delinquents where the classes include Intro to Code Theory and Microelectronics. Then an ancient artifact is stolen, her headmaster disappears...and Rachel decides to find out once and for all exactly what Blackthorn Academy is hiding.

SPY GODDESS, BOOK TWO: TO HAWAII, WITH LOVE

So fourteen-year-old Rachel Buchanan is a reincarnated goddess. But, apparently, being a goddess doesn't come with any neat-o superpowers. Nope. The only thing Rachel gets is one stark-raving mad nemesis—Simon Blankenship. And the only thing standing between him and total world domination? Oh, right: Rachel. But Rachel is in luck because the next Talisman on her list is in Hawaii. Think she'll be able to fit some surfing in around saving the world?

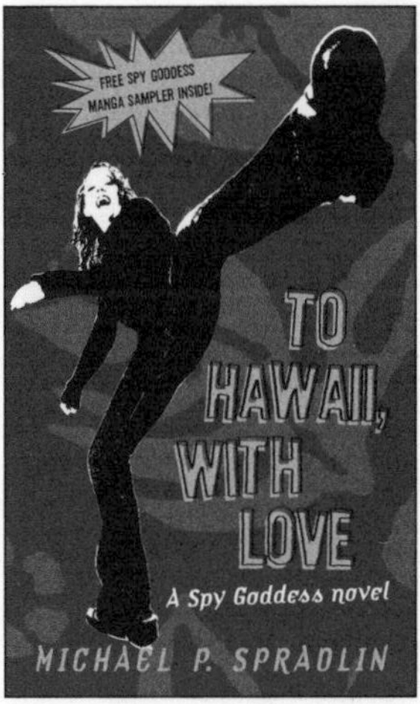

FREE SPY GODDESS MANGA SAMPLER INSIDE!
TO HAWAII, WITH LOVE
A Spy Goddess novel
MICHAEL P. SPRADLIN

HARPER TEEN
An Imprint of HarperCollinsPublishers

WWW.HARPERTEEN.COM